FIGHTING SONGS AND WARRING WORDS

FIGHTING SONGS AND WARRING WORDS

Popular lyrics of two world wars

BRIAN MURDOCH

ROUTLEDGE
London and New York

First published 1990
by Routledge
11 New Fetter Lane, London EC4P 4EE
29 West 35th Street, New York, NY 10001

Typeset in 10/12pt Baskerville by Columns of Reading

Printed in Great Britain by T.J. Press (Padstow) Ltd.,
Padstow, Cornwall

British Library Cataloguing in Publication Data

Fighting songs and warring words:
popular lyrics of two world wars.
1. Songs in German. Special subjects. War
2. Songs in English. Special subjects. War
3. Poetry in German 1900–1945.
Special subjects. War
4. Poetry in English 1900–1945. Special subjects. War
I. Murdoch, Brian O.
784.6′835502′0931

ISBN 0–415–03184–2

Library of Congress Cataloging in Publication Data

available on request

'Trumpeter, what are you sounding now?
(Is it the call I'm seeking?)'
'Can't mistake the call', said the Trumpeter tall,
'When my trumpet goes a-speakin'.
I'm urgin' 'em on, they're scamperin' on,
There's a drummin' of hoofs like thunder.
There's a mad'nin' shout as the sabres flash out,
For I'm sounding the "Charge" – no wonder!

And it's *Hell*', said the Trumpeter tall.

J. Francis Barron
The Trumpeter (1904)

CONTENTS

PREFACE

The two world wars are the major historical events of the present century. They were new in that they were wars of machinery and of killing on an unprecedented scale; they were wars fought by soldiers who were mostly civilians in uniform; and as world wars they involved directly and on a massive scale people who were not soldiers at all. But they gave rise to an enormous amount of poetry, they used the lyric in a variety of ways and, beyond that, they affected the idea of poetry. The starting point for this book was the question of how to define war poetry in this century and, beyond that, how a good war poem is to be recognized. The view that war poetry in the twentieth century actually means anti-war poetry appears inadequate given the enormous amount of poetry produced, and an aesthetic approach to poetry seems limited. With these – doubtless naive – questions came a series of others. How useful in the context of the lyrics of the world wars was an aesthetic division between 'poetry' and 'verse', and what was the place of song? Could aesthetic and moral judgements be mixed? Are war poems only those produced by soldiers who fought (and, so some interpretations seem to imply, actually fell) in the wars, or is a broader view of all lyrics associated with the events of the two world wars possible? How can we distinguish between the reception of war poems in their own time and their reception now?

Some points seem fairly clear. Since wars are fought between nations, the study of modern war poetry ought surely to be comparative, even though there are enormous contrasts within and between national literatures. The greatness of – say – the English poets of the First World War who showed its horror is undeniable, but other attitudes to the wars in the lyric need not be neglected. It is of historical and sociological interest to consider the reception of a patriotic and pro-war poem in its contemporary context, however difficult it may sometimes be to appreciate literary effect in a work the morality of which is questionable. For the present-day reader with historical hindsight, however, the reading of and moral response to that same poem will be different, the very overtness of the patriotism causing the modern reader precisely to reject its implications. Poetry does not need to be expressly anti-war to make the point that wars, especially on the scale of those in the twentieth century, are bad.

To suggest that pro-war poetry can be an object of literary study in this way does not, incidentally, imply any revisionism, nor does it justify militarism as such. No one denies the catastrophic nature of the wars. This study intends only to suggest with some examples that the range of what is now normally understood as war poetry might be extended, with particular reference to the popular lyrics occasioned by the world wars. 'Popular' is a humpty dumpty word, it is true. However, some of the war poetry now accepted as canonical in English, for example, has become widely read only relatively recently, and then in limited contexts, while a great range of relevant material had (and sometimes still has) a popularity of a different and in some cases far wider kind. The word 'popular' can mean 'read and appreciated by a large number of people' (in its own time or since), 'made available to a wide audience', or 'produced by or for the ordinary soldier'.

Several different examples may illustrate the kind of neglected war lyrics involved. The work of the Salamander Oasis Trust has recently made available a great deal of soldier poetry of the Second World War. There has been considerable scholarly interest in Germany in the Fascist lyrics of the period from 1933, lyrics which draw on a view of one war to prepare for another. War poetry of specific groups (such as women writers, for example) is now being collected and examined, but there is still scope for study of the establishment poets, so widely read in book and newspaper form in Britain during the Second World War. The poetry of some of the partisan groups in Europe (popular in a different way, and with a hatred of war overriden completely by the need to survive and win) merits attention. Only rarely, too, is proper attention paid either to commercially produced or orally evolved song lyrics, though the fact that they are used by some anthologists as crisp section headings bespeaks a clear poetic value. By casting the net as widely as possible (and involving not only songs but jingles, postcard verse, rhymed slogans on medals or even on the walls of military latrines and cited in contemporary writings) it is possible to examine not only the reflection and rejection of war as such, but the ways in which lyric – poetry and song – contributed on the one hand to the war efforts, and on the other helped the soldier and the civilian to cope. The lyric of aggression and of solace are of interest in historical-social, and also in aesthetic terms. This best known lyrics of the two world wars – in their own time or now – are not necessarily those found customarily in the anthologies.

All comparative studies require an initial apology which is not just a modesty formula. The constraints of linguistic competence, the availability of translations and the obtainability of material always apply, and there are also limitations in what can be achieved in a study the potential range of which is very large. The availability of material (especially in the less well-known languages, but also in the case of material that is on the side neither of the moral nor the literary angels) is another. Here English and German materials predominate – this is probably inevitable – and the former is, without any pretensions to completeness, more fully represented than other languages. Translations are necessary, but once again a preliminary apology is needed. Patriotic poetry may always contain allusions not clear in translation, and even when rendering what seem to be the simplest of words, difficulties arise: the German *Volk* might be rendered as 'People', 'Folk', 'Nation' or 'Race', while its collocations *Reich* and *Führer* are probably best left untranslated.

Much of the material included here has been presented in classes or as lectures: in the English departments at the Universities of Katowice in Poland and Trier in Germany, and in the departments of German and of Music at Stirling. I have always profited from the discussions at these sessions. For providing me with material, translations, and comments I have to express my gratitude to a large number of people, including Dr L. Archibald, Miss H. Beale, Mr A. Blyth, Dr L. Jillings, Dr W. Kidd, Mr R. Kilborn, Mr R. Melville, Mr M. Mitchell, Mr A.P. Murdoch, Mr and Mrs C. Murdoch, Mr W. Pertaub, Dr M. Read, Mr I. Ruxton, Mr P. Schulze, Mr R. Riffer, Mr C. Rowe, Mrs H. Valencia, Mr A. Walker, Mr M. Ward, Mrs A. Young, and many others. As ever I am indebted to my wife for support. Errors remain, of course, my responsibility. Other debts of gratitude include those to the Imperial War Museum, Collet's International Bookshop, the Interlibrary Loans department at Stirling University library, and the editorial staff at Routledge. Those who have granted permission for text quotation are thanked separately.

Brian Murdoch
Stirling University/
Trinity Hall, Cambridge
1989

Acknowledgements

The author and publisher wish to thank the following for permission to quote from copyright material. While every effort has been made to trace holders of copyrights, it was not always possible. Some enquiries went unanswered, and in other cases, even with valuable assistance from many different publishers – to whom thanks are offered even if they are not named – current copyright holders could not be traced. Although much of the material is by now public, or was always part of an oral tradition not subject to formalities of copyright, sincere apologies are offered for any missed.

I am particularly grateful to R. G. Auckland, The Auckland Collection and David Elliott and the Museum of Modern Art, Oxford, for material from *The Falling Leaf* exhibition; to Lady Felicity Longmore, Lady Pamela Humphrys, and Lady Joan Robertson for permission to quote material by their father, Lord Wavell (and also to Jonathan Cape, publisher of *Other Men's Flowers*); to Mr H. C. E. Noyes and the family of the late Alfred Noyes for permission to quote from *Shadows on the Down*; to Mr Victor Selwyn and the Salamander Oasis Trust – quotations from J. E. Brookes's 'Tobruk 1941' and 'Thermopylae '41', Elsie Cawser's 'Salvage Song', Kevin McHale's 'Com-bloody-parisons', Dennis McHarrie's 'Luck', and E. Storey's 'The Northumberland Fusiliers' appear by kind permission of the Salamander Oasis Trust and the poets.

I should also like to record my gratitude to the following for use of copyright material. Laurence Binyon's 'For the Fallen (September 1914)' is cited by permission of Mrs Nicolete Gray and the Society of Authors on behalf of the Laurence Binyon Estate; thanks are due to the Bodley Head and Jonathan Cape for the poetry of Brian Brooke and of Saggitarius; Boosey & Hawkes Ltd for 'The Trumpeter' and 'Won't You Join the Army'; Warner Chappell Music Ltd and their subsidiary, Ascherberg, Hopwood and Crew Ltd for 'Keep the Home Fires Burning'; Chappell Music Ltd and the Noel Coward Estate for the words of 'London Pride' © 1941 and 'Don't Let's be Beastly to the Germans' © 1943; the Estate of Clemence Dane for 'Trafalgar Day 1940'; EMI for 'Ten Days Leave', 'Taffy's Got His Jenny', 'The One Man Band', 'Pack up Your Troubles', 'Goodbyee', 'Upward, Trusty Brothers', 'The Civilians', 'My England', and the English text of 'Lilli Marlene' (© Apollo Verlag, Germany, by permission of Peter Maurice Co. Ltd, London); the editor and publishers of *Country Life* for Violet Jacob's 'The Twa Weelums'; Curtis Brown and John Farquharson for John Wain's 'Major Eatherly'; the editor and publishers of *Gairm* for Iain Crichton Smith's 'A' dol dhachaidh'; Victor Gollancz for Iain Crichton Smith's 'Your Brother Clanked his Sword'; William Heinemann Ltd., London for poems by Sir George Rostrevor Hamilton; David Higham Associates for John Pudney's poetry and in particular for 'For Johnny', for Francis Brett Young's *The Island*, and for Dorothy L. Sayers's 'An English War'; Ernst Kabel Verlag for Hans Leip's 'Lili Marleen'; Luchterhand Literaturverlag for Ernst Jandl's 'Fragment'; John Murray (Publishers) Ltd. for Lord Gorell's poems from *Wings of the Morning*, for R. A. Hopwood's 'The Auxiliary' and for Joseph Lee's 'The Bullet', 'Tommy and Fritz' and 'I Cannae See the Sergeant'; the editor and publishers of the *Observer* newspaper for Robin Henderson's 'Hiro Shima'; Oxford University Press for Peter Porter's 'Your Attention Please'; quotations from Roger McGough's 'Why Patriots are a Bit Nuts in the Head' and 'A Square Dance' are reprinted by permission of the Peters Fraser and Dunlop Group Ltd.; thanks are due to the Society of Authors for Cecil Roberts's '*A Man Arose*'; Sidgwick and Jackson Ltd. for the lyrics of Richard Spender; Charles Skilton Ltd/Fortune Press for poems from the collection *Poets in Battledress*; Suhrkamp Verlag for 'Der Schatten von Hiroshima' by Günter Eich; A. P. Watt on behalf of Timothy d'Arch Smith for Gilbert Frankau's *The City of Fear* and on behalf of Crystal Hale and Jocelyn Lawrence for the poems of A. P. Herbert.

1

Good War Poetry?

Damn your writing,
Mind your fighting.
Anon., cited by Field Marshal Wavell[1]

The present century is dominated by two world wars, from both of which arose a massive amount of poetry, the extent of which is only gradually becoming clear. 'War poetry' and 'war poet' have become everyday literary terms, and they figure in the titles of an increasingly large number of anthologies. Indeed, although the terms could be and were applied before the twentieth century, they are encountered for the most part in discussions of poetry connected with the world wars of 1914–18 and 1939–45.

The terms are far less straightforward than they might seem, and from an early stage some of the poets directly involved made a point of avoiding them.[2] Poetry itself has been affected by the experience of the wars, so that many earlier yardsticks have lost their meaning; most clear of all the changes is the loss of any stress on the heroic aspects of war. In a simplified, but widely accepted view, an awareness of a grimmer reality displaced the heroics after the Somme, although it may already have done so at Mafeking or perhaps at Bull Run (or even at Balaclava). Other poetic standards, too, were called into question. Poetry delights and instructs, but delight is no longer possible with the reality of a modern war, here seen by Isaac Rosenberg in a much anthologized poem:

> A man's brains spattered on
> A stretcher-bearer's face . . .[3]

Nor can Coleridge's dictum of the best words in the best order apply to this by August Stramm:

> Die Steine feinden
> Fenster grinst Verrat
> Äste würgen

1

Berge Sträucher blättern raschlig
gellen
Tod.[4]

[The stones enemy/ window grins treachery/ branches strangle/
mountains bushes leaf rustling/ yell/ death]

The sole function of war poetry is seen to be that of reflecting the
events of the wars in order to convey to the audience that war is
unacceptable. War poetry is generally taken to mean poetry
written during the wars against the war, so that war poetry in
effect means contemporary anti-war poetry.[5] Some critics, indeed,
have limited war poetry even more, to that written by those who
had actually fought, and refer to 'soldier poets', 'fighter poets', or –
for the First World War – 'trench poets', although Edgell Rickword
gave the term a different twist in a poem of that name.[6] In spite of
this, soldier poets did write militaristic verse, just as W.B. Yeats,
who was not a fighter poet, displayed a broader understanding of
the term 'war poem' when he responded negatively to a request for
one.[7]

A distinction between poetry and verse is sometimes used as a
value judgement, with verse effectively meaning inferior poetry.
This can make 'good poetry' a tautology, and 'good verse' difficult
to define. Equally, however, verse can be a self-conscious form with
aims that are different from those of poetry. The two will overlap in
matters of form (verse may indeed be more rigid than poetry), but
verse will not aspire to the tag *quod semper, quod ubique, quod ab
omnibus*. . . Nevertheless, it may still be original, witty, memorable,
and above all effective in conveying its point. There is a usefully
neutral alternative in the word 'lyric', (although we may meet the
occasional epic) even if in popular speech this has come to mean
the words of a song. In the present century the song has probably
played a more extensive role than most other lyric forms, given
wide dissemination through the media, but songs are frequently
ignored by critics of poetry.

Holger M. Klein addresses the difficulty of defining 'war poetry'
and the perils of the adjective 'good' in a broad study of English-
language anthologies which considers collections by Sir John
Squire and A.P. Herbert in the Second World War beside
Tambimuttu and others,[8] and he stresses the value of an historical
and social approach. Once this is accepted, some of the value

judgements encountered in criticism of war poetry become questionable. 'Brooke is a bad poet and he was a bad influence'[9] demands the response that he was an enormously important influence. Dismissal of Kipling as a purveyor of 'loud-mouthed imperialism'[10] is at best one-sided, and needs to be balanced against the exaggerations of Nazi poetry, some of it written during Kipling's lifetime. The question of reception is also vital in the assessment of war poetry. The two world wars involved more soldiers than ever before, most of them effectively civilians in uniform. They also drew in more civilians than ever, by placing them in the front line of bombing or invasion. It is in this context that the lyric reached larger numbers of people than ever before, and it very often had a public function.

What, then, is a good war poem? A poem, perhaps, that shows clearly that war is a bad thing? This is fairly limited; there are few who would deny as a general principle that wars mean large-scale killing in a modern world, and that this is unacceptable. 'Good' can mean a number of things, of course, and particularly so in collocation with war poetry: does it mean moral, or just effective, aesthetically satisfying, well-made, original, memorable? Taken at face value, of course, a good war poem might imply one the sentiments of which encourage the war effort of a particular side, which may or may not be good morally or aesthetically. Equally, it may discourage war as a whole, comfort the contemporary reader, warn others, or act as a catharsis for those involved. A propaganda piece which is designed to discourage the other side may be seen as a good war poem – effective in the objective sense, and morally good if produced on what is perceived as the side of the angels, so long as the reader is clear about which side that is.

To examine war poetry in the twentieth century is to set up a series of contrasts and juxtapositions to avoid narrowness. Wars, plainly enough, are fought by two sides, and all nationalities in both world wars produced and used the lyric. It implies neither a misplaced liberal intellectualism, nor indeed a covert revisionism to demand that the lyrics of all sides be taken into consideration, but this has only gradually been seen in anthologies. In the First World War the angels – in spite of their celebrated but fictional intervention at Mons – were not really on either side. In the Second World War the position is far clearer, but there is a different justification for the study of war poetry in, say, Nazi

Germany. The Nazi regime was all too aware of the power of the lyric to justify and to encourage war. This is a particular kind of war poetry, and its evil exposes itself so that it can serve as a memorial and a warning.

Michael Hamburger proposes casting the net very wide:

> A comprehensive survey of twentieth-century war poetry would have to embrace the political poetry of the twenties and thirties, both militant and pacifist, and especially the poetry occasioned by the Spanish Civil War. For the same reason it would have to embrace the German and Russian 'war poetry' and anti-war poetry written after the Second World War as well as poems occasioned by the wars in Korea and Vietnam; and it would have to consider poems about war written before the event. . . Much of the most durable war poetry of the Second World War was written by non-combatants or by men of the Resistance. . . In the era of total politics, in fact, war poetry has become continuous, ubiquitous and hardly distinguishable from any other kind of poetry.[11]

The demand that the poetry should incorporate first-hand experience is hard to justify. Pursued to its conclusion (as some critics did), it requires that Erich Maria Remarque should have fallen in 1918 to be able to write *Im Westen nichts Neues* [All Quiet on the Western Front]. War poetry must be extended to cover poems about the world wars written after the event, or by those who fought in neither. Hamburger might have referred, too, to the patriotic verse of the years before the First World War. The scope is patently very wide indeed, and all that a study of this kind can hope for is to indicate some areas which might be pursued with profit, whilst remaining aware of the difficulties of all the separate elements in the concept of 'good war poetry'.

Just how much material is actually available in English-language poetry in Britain alone may be gauged from the two large bibliographies produced by Catherine Reilly. They include poetry in all forms, from the anthology to the postcard. Both contain a prodigious amount of material, and neither is complete.[12] Songs are not included – the Imperial War Museum is to produce a bibliography of its own very large collection of sheet-music of the First World War – and beyond the postcard lie more ephemeral uses of verse. Medallions, for example, sometimes carry comments in lyric form, while public utterances in verse exhorted the readers of a children's comic to defeat Hitler by collecting scrap paper, and the Wehrmacht dropped aerial leaflets in verse to warn French troops of the perfidy of their British allies.

War lyrics can be anti-war or can be in favour of war. Moreover, the latter category can be acceptable for various reasons. It may be functional in combatting evil (as with Yiddish partisan poems from Poland encouraging the fight against Hitler). Even patriotically pro-war lyrics may from an historical point of view stand as a memorial to the events and to the way in which poetry may be perverted. War poetry can be written from within, or with hindsight, by soldiers or civilians, men or women. Nor can attitudes always be pinned down or predicted: many of the establishment poets of the Second World War had served in the First.

Given the clear need for an international approach, too, not only may Owen stand beside Trakl or Ungaretti or Bernard, but Lissauer's 'Hymn of Hate' bears comparison with British exhortations against the Hun, and both with the poetic justifications of their own war aims by the Nazis. Against that, in its turn, may be set the poetry of the partisans, which is not specifically anti-war, but sees the combating of a greater and a specific evil as a necessity. It is not easy even for the student of comparative literature to locate Japanese war poetry, but that connected with the events that ended the war, the exploding of the bomb over Hiroshima is also war poetry.

Soldiers' lyrics are themselves varied. The term can imply lyrics written by soldiers about the war and published individually by soldiers as poets. It may imply official poetry or songs intended – commercially or ideologically – *for* soldiers, or popular lyrics, sung or otherwise, of the unofficial variety. Songs, too, can range from the national anthems, which take on a new life and occasionally new lyrics in wartime, to popular songs designed to reassure the civilian that there will be bluebirds over the white cliffs of Dover, or the soldier that he and his love will meet again. Soldiers' own songs may readily be classed as war poetry even within the most narrow constraints. They reflect upon the immediate situation or upon war as an idea, depict the horrors of war and criticize either the enemy or their own superior officers. They may simply look forward to a time when it is over. All categories, though, may contribute to the war effort, either as a catharsis or as a direct encouragement to fight.

War lyrics may be found anywhere from poetry books to regimental magazines to lavatory walls. Theodor Plievier's novel about the German naval mutiny of 1917, *Des Kaisers Kulis* [The Kaiser's Coolies] reports the verses scrawled in latrines in a naval dockyard:

> Wir kämpfen nicht für Vaterland
> und nicht für deutsche Ehre!
> Wir sterben für den Unverstand
> und für die Millionäre

[We are not fighting for the Fatherland, nor for German honour. We are dying for ignorance and for the millionaires]

and an all-embracing comment on war is made by the soldiers on Remarque's Western Front:

> Gleiche Lohnung, gleiches Fressen
> und der Krieg wär längst vergessen.

[Equal pay and equal grub and the war would soon be forgotten][13]

Anthologies of war poetry are, however, a useful starting point, even though they do feed upon themselves. Randall Jarrell, indeed, has spoken of anthologists a little acidly as 'cultural entrepreneurs', but acknowledges that 'the average reader knows poetry mainly from anthologies'.[14] Anthologies vary in their view of what constitutes war poetry, depending partly on whether they were compiled during or after one or both wars. Post-1945 retrospective anthologies sometimes apply aesthetic criteria which are not always clear. Jon Silkin's Penguin anthology of the poetry of the First World War even stigmatizes with an asterisk poems which 'a great many people have liked, even loved, as they responded to the horror and pity of war', when he as an editor 'dissented from the implied judgements of taste'.[15] Silkin does, on the other hand, include some poems in translation, even some German poems, but the distinction approvingly interpreted by one reviewer as between poems with 'literary merit' and 'sub-standard' work remains questionable.[16] Most recent anthologies follow an assumed literary canon of English poetry only.[17] That by Dominic Hibberd and

John Onions is of particular interest in that it does contain patriotic lyrics, but 'Poetry of the Great War' means 'English Poetry', and that written for the most part during the 1914–18 war. Sometimes, of course, representation is specifically restricted to those who fell in the war, as in Tim Cross's recent (and admirably international) collection.[18] Poetry of the Second World War has a less firmly fixed canon of 'good' poems, although anthologies do overlap to an extent. A recent anthology by Anne Harvey makes use of popular song and of verse designed for the dissemination of information, as well as of children's rhymes alongside an imaginative selection of poetry in English, offering a broader view than is usual.[19] Larger-scale anthologies, such as the *Oxford Book of War Poetry*, remain canonical in their approach; the works included are almost all printed poems (though Exodus, Homer, and some Chinese material are present) and nearly all are in English, although two French poems are included for the First World War, one of them an Apollinaire Calligram. Philip Larkin's *Oxford Book of Twentieth Century English Verse* does include, on the other hand, some (few) satirical wartime pieces by A.P. Herbert and by Olga Katzin ('Saggitarius').[20]

Of the expressly comparative anthologies, the excellent trilingual *Ohne Hass und Fahne* [No Hatred and No Flag], with all the poems included in English, French, and German, is specifically anti-war.[21] Some recent anthologies have concentrated on aspects felt to have been neglected in the major anthologies. Catherine Reilly has produced for each world war an anthology of women's poetry, for example, whilst Brian Page has published two extremely interesting collections of soldiers' songs and poems, including material that is obscene as well as witty and poetically striking. A German equivalent was provided by Rudolf Walter Leonhardt, who includes some English and French material too.[22] The Salamander Oasis Trust has published two volumes of poetry by serving soldiers which include anonymous pieces. Its express intent is to broaden the range of Second World War poetry once again.[23] War poetry from different ideological standpoints has been included in modern anthologies of German political lyrics, although Nazi anthologies themselves, such as Herbert Böhme's *Rufe in das Reich* have a clear message of their own. Similar comments may be made about the poetry of Italian Fascism, although the lyrics of Vichy France are difficult to find. Modern French and German specialist anthologies have been compiled of the war seen from the concentration camps, or by German prisoners of war – Hans Werner Richter's *Deine Söhne, Europa* first appeared in 1947.[24]

Collections of war poems date from the beginnings in 1914, but it is appropriate to take into account some of the anthologies published in the years before the First World War. These include schoolbooks such as the Clarendon *Lyra Historica*, the collection by Arthur Burrell in the early stages of the popular Everyman's Library, *A Book of Heroic and Patriotic Verse*, which underlines an express emphasis on individual heroism, or general anthologies such as Christopher Stone's *War Songs*, published in 1908, with an introduction by Sir Ian Hamilton which quotes Japanese patriotic poetry of the Russo-Japanese War and a few barrack-room songs. He also notes the attraction (for officers and privates, we are assured) of sentimental songs in a general sense. The collection itself includes (with an historical irony that would not be apparent for some years) a poem about the capture of Mons in 1691 called 'The Couragious English Boys', and such pieces as Sir Francis Doyle's 'Private of the Buffs', the rough but proud English lad who dies bravely, while 'dusky Indians whine and kneel'. Doyle's poem was very well known at least up to the First World War, and has been discussed in the context of patriotic literature in general.[25] The motif is more tenacious still.

The poem was included in V.H. Collins' *Poems of War and Battle*, of 1914, a collection which ranges from Drayton on Agincourt to Alfred Noyes, and includes not only Kipling's 'Hymn Before Battle' but also Chesterton's 'Last Charge at Ethandune', a good example of a particular type of patriotic poem. Ostensibly in praise of an heroic deed from the remote past in which an English king fought off a Germanic invader (for all that the Saxons were Germanic, too), the Anglo-Saxons fight side by side with the Celts, and are supported somewhat improbably by 'the ghastly war-pipes of the Gael'. The Black Watch fight beside the Buffs beneath this thin historical guise, and Guthrum is duly defeated.[26]

Anthology titles from the beginning of the First World War (though the patriotic strain lasted throughout the war and beyond it) include *Songs and Sonnets for England in War Time* and indeed, the start of the Second World War saw titles like *The British Empire at War*. German anthologies of the same period carry titles like *Gedichte zum Heiligen Krieg* [Poems of the Holy War].[27] Throughout the war, too, various associations[28] published anthologies for fundraising purposes. The Queen Mary Needlework Guild, for example, gave its anthology a title from Kipling's 'Recessional' which would later be found on a thousand war-memorials. *Lest We Forget*, with a foreword by the romantic novelist Baroness Orczy, contained a few poems apparently by soldiers (which saw the war in terms of 'playing the game') as well as Flecker's version of 'God save the King'. There is poetry and prose in *King Albert's Book*, published as a tribute to what Hall Caine in the preface (dated Christmas 1914) terms the 'martyr nation of the war'. *The Blinded Soldiers and Sailors Gift Book* has a clear and worthy aim, but what poetry it includes is pro-war:

> England, my country, speak to each of your sons today!
> Trampled and desecrate now are the foreign woodlands and
>   meadows
> God give us grace to face the shells and the gas, the guns!

Those lines are from the somewhat unlikely hand of Edith Nesbit, who is, however, also represented in Reilly's modern anthology with a similar poem which once more invokes the God of Battles.[29]

During the war, too, many anthologies appeared of soldiers' own writing. Galloway Kyle of the *Poetry Review* published through Erskine Macdonald two collections of *Songs of the Fighting Men*, in trench editions, containing poems which used Latin tags like 'Dulce et decorum est pro patria mori' without irony. The second volume appeared in December 1917 and sold well in the last year of the war. Lyrics appeared in and were collected from trench magazines on both sides, usually cheerful and ironic, bolstering up morale with mockery of the enemy or of the officers, though without the savage irony of Sassoon.[30] At home and on the establishment side the proprietors of *Punch* produced in 1919 a history of the war which contains many of the war verses printed in that magazine.[31]

At the very end of the war – in July 1918 – Bertram Lloyd edited an anthology that commands some interest in that it printed poems for and against war, claiming a

> hatred of the cant and idealization and false glamour wherewith
> the conception of war is still so thickly overlaid in the minds of
> numbers of otherwise reasonable people,[32]

and after the First World War a different assessment of some of the war poets could be undertaken. At the very end of the war J. Bruce Glasier brought out an anthology called *The Minstrelsy of Peace*, while nevertheless making clear that the poets represented were not all 'uncompromisingly opposed to war under all circumstances'.[33] The memorial function that was already apparent throughout in the individual volumes produced during the war became stronger as regimental and individual volumes appeared, both kinds sometimes very large indeed, such as Pamela Glenconner's tribute to her son, Edward Wyndham Tennant. St John Adcock published a study with photographs of most of the well-known English poets who had fallen in the war (almost all of them officers), and this line was taken up by Frederick Ziv in 1936.[34] A collection by an American, G.H. Clarke, of British and American poetry from 1914 to 1919 includes both militant and pacifist poetry, as well as poetry by and about women. Owen is not yet represented, Sassoon by only two poems, but there is a full representation of those who would become establishment poets of the Second World War – like Lord Gorell and Alfred Noyes, or those who already were established, like Newbolt or Hardy.[35] For much of the period between the wars, some of the names now best known as war poets are rare. Yeats's distaste for Owen is well known and well documented, but it is interesting that a poet of the Second World War, Vernon Scannell, does not entirely disagree with some of the ideas behind Yeats's familiar but perhaps gratuitously offensive statement.[36] While Owen and Sassoon did appear in the anthologies between the wars, so did Brooke, whose influence, bad or not, should at least not be underestimated. It is no accident that he continued to be the standard (and occasionally the frontispiece) for the war poets. It is only since the Second World War, too, that Newbolt's star has fallen, or that of Noyes.

Patriotism is now generally taken negatively, and patriotism of any sort is perceived as dangerous. Potentially this is true (as Dr Johnson recognized), and certainly when inflated to the level of blood-and-soil nationalism it can manifestly lead to aggression. In evaluation of the patriotic poetry of both wars, however, its precise nature requires consideration. The confusion with imperialism, of a cultural, linguistic, or territorial kind must be looked at with care.[37]

In 1914 Edward Thomas called for a distinction between poetry

and verse, and he commented, perhaps with unconscious ambiguity, that it was 'not always the greatest songs that have sent men
to victory'.[38] Songs, in fact, show a rather clearer acceptance of the
war, either through patriotism or just through resignation to the
inescapable. During the war, R. Nettleingham produced *Tommy's
Tunes*, and in 1930 John Brophy and Eric Partridge brought out
(perhaps primarily for linguistic interest) the first edition of their
collection of soldiers' songs, necessarily somewhat bowdlerized.
Commercial publishers collected 'songs that won the war' during
the 1930s at a time when Nazi Germany was producing song
material to inspire militarism, and war poetry even of a jingoistic
kind was still being republished in Britain. A volume of airmen's
songs grew gradually to a final version at the end of the Second
World War. All these contain lyric reflections of the war,[39] many of
which can be regarded even on aesthetic grounds as good war
poetry.

The outbreak of the Second World War saw a certain revival in
patriotic material, but its anthologies tend to convey what
Tambimuttu, one of its most celebrated anthologists, called a
'strain of sadness'. Tambimuttu's *Poetry in Wartime* is famous and
much discussed, but the war also saw Harold Nicolson's *England*,
and an anonymous act of comfort produced by the Readers Union
and Cambridge University Press in *Fear No More*, the title of which
explains its aim, and every poem of which is presented as
anonymous.[40] Anthologies were produced at home and by soldiers
from different theatres of war or branches of the service, but two
anthologies, by Julian Symons and by Field Marshall Wavell,
merit attention.

Symons' anthology appeared in 1942 in the Pelican series, aimed
therefore at a wide audience (including soldiers). It is historical,
though it concentrates on poetry contemporary with the wars
treated. Thus there is a soldier's view of Culloden from an English-
patriotic standpoint, though that battle is mourned by the Scots
and glossed over somewhat by the English now. It reminds us that
wars always have victors and vanquished, and that loyalties can
be problematic. Symons includes some more recent soldiers' songs,
and even if these are relatively few it is nonetheless of interest to
have some of the safety-valve grumbling of these songs of 1914–18
beside Brooke's 'Soldier' and poems by Owen and Sassoon.[41]

Wavell's anthology is not one of war poetry alone, but it was a best seller, was reprinted twice before the war was out and has been much reissued. Three sections of *Other Men's Flowers* are of interest, quite apart from the fact of its production by a serving officer of such high rank. One is entitled 'Good Fighting', and places Kipling, Newbolt, and Macaulay's 'Lays of Ancient Rome' together. More interesting still, it juxtaposes two poems as 'Leaders, old and new', the first being an extract from Scott's *Marmion* and the second Sassoon's bitter piece 'The General', though it is significant that Wavell sees the piece as a poem about a general, rather than about the men.

Wavell comments from time to time on the poems he selects, which are sometimes unusual. He includes a piece 'found in an Egyptian newspaper' in 1941, which declares London's defiance under bombardment in not very striking lines:

> . . . my people's faith and courage are lights of London
>   Town
> which still would shine in legend though my last broad
>   bridge were down.[42]

London Bridge is falling down, when the lights go on again in London. The fortuitous finding of Greta Briggs's poem may have outweighed questions of poetic value for Wavell, but its inclusion makes an interesting comment on poetic reception, and other poems have their own similar fates and mystiques. One such is the 'Prayer' poem included in the anthology *Poems from the Desert*, and John Pudney's 'For Johnny' is another.[43]

Wavell's own comments on war poetry are down to earth. He sees war as a 'grim but dull business' which 'does not tend to inspire poetry in those who practise it'. He makes implicit distinctions between types of war poetry ('battle poems are seldom written by those who have been in battle'),[44] and he distinguishes between a war poet and a poetic warrior. All this springs from an awareness of the paradox of war poetry. He was fond of citing the lines of an Indian Army general used at the head of this chapter, and it is an irony that the lines have form and rhyme, and that they are so very memorable. But Wavell is also aware of the dullness of war, and is at pains to show how it can be seen in poetry. Although the anthology does not include songs formally, it refers to them, and Wavell comments on the necessity for such songs, again as safety valves.

His second section of war-related material is called 'Hymns of Hate', and he cites an English version of the famous poem by Ernst Lissauer. It is the sole translated poem in the collection. In English it has the ritual effect of a curse, but Wavell is again interested in its reception, this time in the English trenches, from whence it was sometimes chanted back at the 'pardonably bewildered' Germans with a heavy stress on the word 'England'. The third relevant section is concerned with death, and ends with a poem of his own that again is not often anthologized. His Shakespearian sonnet was written in 1943, and if its rhymes are a little predictable, it balances the soldiers' resigned tones with the point of view of a senior officer in the Second World War. 'Long years of battle, bitterness and waste' are set against the adversary: 'greed for power and hate and lies'. And the soldier 'goes back to fight'; an ending for a mid-war anthology as fitting as the conclusion of post-war anthologies with poems concerned with the atomic bomb. Wavell was not yet able to take in that aspect.[45]

Some anthologies of a rather different kind may be mentioned briefly. Between the wars Guy Chapman's *Vain Glory*, which was mostly prose but had some verse, included English and German material, and after the Second, Peter Vansittart's *Voices from the Great War* provides a wealth of material – uncommented – about the First World War from all kinds of sources, and includes poetry and popular song. More limited were Second World War anthologies in English of comments from Nazi sources, again frequently presented without comment.[46] Popular songs of the First World War formed the basis for the Theatre Workshop's *Oh What a Lovely War* and thus remained in the public ear, while contributions to popular social history such as Susan Briggs's valuable *Keep Smiling Through* use songs of the Second World War as markers throughout. Studies in French and German have been rather more systematic regarding the songs.[47]

Secondary literature on war poetry is also subject to changes in taste. The Marquess of Crewe gave a lecture to the English Association in September 1917 which approached the theme from an historical point of view only, mentioning only Newbolt and Kipling of the living poets. In the same year, C.F.E. Spurgeon saw in his paper on 'Poetry in the Light of War' that the possibility of death might lead to an intensification of the life force. Although he recognized the worth of C.H. Sorley, however, he ends with

Brooke, and sees war poetry as an individual catharsis. In 1944, Alfred Noyes was still defending Kipling as a 'genuine patriot', though aware that the dead of the First World war should not be pushed out of sight or covered up by the prettiness of Flanders poppies.[48] Kipling has tended, not always justifiably, to be dismissed in spite of sustained interest in his work well after his death and the fact that there is a great deal of value in some of his war poetry not found elsewhere.[49] The same applies to other establishment poets whose work is of social and historical value. Here, though, is I.A. Richards on several relevant poets:

> there is a time in most lives when, rightly enough, Mr Masefield, Mr Kipling, Mr Drinkwater or even Mr Noyes or Mr Studdert Kennedy may profitably affect the wakening mind. . .[50]

So long as it grows out of them. All, however, are significant in the broader context of war poetry, a context advocated in English by Catherine Reilly, by Martin van Wyk Smith in an important study of the Boer War, and by critics like Paul Fussell in one of the most interesting of all books on the literature of the First World War.[51] Such a broad base seems to be the most satisfactory approach to the lyrics of war in the twentieth century. Against (often unacknowledged) snobbery must be set the point that however important a message may be, it is worthless if no one hears it. Poetry has been functional in the two world wars, and this is its most significant feature. The trumpeter sounds different tunes in the Edwardian song of that name which stands at the beginning of this study: the attack, the retreat, the last post. But throughout that song is the implicit idea of reception. War poetry can be a personal statement that is capable of generalization, but it can also – and perhaps more often – shape, direct, even command.

Modern warfare involving large-scale and mechanized killing in front of a world audience dates probably from the American Civil War. Edmund Wilson's *Patriotic Gore* considers the poems of that war in detail, and looks at a few of the songs, most notably the 'Battle Hymn of the Republic'. Other studies have treated those songs alone,[52] some of which survived into the First World War. Martin van Wyk Smith's *Drummer Hodge* takes the popular and music hall songs of the Boer War into account, and several of these, too, survived to 1914 and beyond. The two world wars, however, may be seen as a continuum, the poetry of the Nazis forming a bridge between them. It is even difficult to know where to place the beginnings of the Second World War – anywhere from the invasion of the Sudetenland to Pearl Harbor could serve, although the poets of the Third Reich considered Versailles the beginning. The Spanish Civil War has been seen as a rehearsal, and its songs and poems are of importance (though they lie beyond the scope of the present study), from the work of John Cornford or Roy Campbell to songs like that set to the tune of the 'Red River Valley' after the battle of Jarama, which reassured the defeated that the war could still be won.[53] Some studies have taken into account popular material in English, but few have compared Spanish and foreign material or looked at songs to any extent.

Moving onwards, Korea produced some poetry, and since it threatened to develop into a larger-scale war, some of the poetry of the atomic bomb is associated with Korea as much as with the end of the Second World War. Vietnam produced, and continues to produce, popular material as well as poetry with a smaller audience. Steve Mason is billed on the cover of the English edition of *Johnny's Song* as 'the Vietnam veteran' and writes movingly of his experience.[54] Vietnam is still present in popular music, however: 'Nineteen' kept up the tradition of the anti-Vietnam protest song (of which 'Saigon Bride' was probably one of the best examples), although the mythologization born out of the need to come to terms with a lost war is also found in popular song lyrics ('Camouflage').[55] But Vietnam war poetry (especially outside America) expresses confusion. The view is also necessarily from the West.[56]

The involvement of British troops in Cyprus gave rise to a small amount of poetry, and the problems in Ireland have produced poetry and song. Loyalties here are complex, and what one side at least would consider war poetry could elsewhere be seen as incitement to terrorism: eulogies of the Armalite rifle, for example, are one kind of lyric, though a type with a long tradition. There is also a serious and reflective poetry. On the other hand, the conflict in the Falklands was perhaps too brief to give rise to much poetry. A letter to *The Times* on 21 June 1982 contained a parody by Rear-Admiral John Hervey of Kipling's 'The Dutch in the Medway' with reference to facts known by 'the Argies' and commenting on the lack of military equipment, but in spite of the well-documented patriotic fervour, it is an odd comment on history that the British task force left to the tune of 'Don't Cry for Me, Argentina', which is (apart from the title) singularly inappropriate, given that Andrew Lloyd Webber and Tim Rice place it in the mouth of the eponymous Evita Perón as a declaration of love to that country; it is unsurprising that the lyrics were not quoted. Occasionally, negative references to the Falklands incident have cropped up in popular songs: Elvis Costello's 'Peace in Our Time' has as a throwaway line in an ironic context a reference to 'just another tiny island invaded'.[57]

Even with a concentration upon the two world wars, much material has to be excluded. The theme of the atomic bomb takes the study of the lyric well beyond 1945, but the bombing of Hiroshima and Nagasaki was the final act of the war as such. What of the other name that preoccupies post-war thought, however: Auschwitz? In spite of the celebrated denial of the possibility of any poetry after Auschwitz it has been demonstrated in a number of major studies that there was not only a poetry of Auschwitz after the event, but that the camps even produced their own poetry – an amazing testimony to the strength of the human spirit. There is a poetry, too, from the survivors, and images of the Holocaust are found in contexts far removed from the camps themselves.[58] Although it is clearly of the Second World War, and an element of what was being fought against, the memorial poetry for the victims – in English, French, German, Yiddish, Russian or Hebrew – is too broad a topic on the one hand, and in a sense too straightforward, to be treated here.

The definition of popularity is as difficult as that of poetry itself, and the concept of popular war lyrics especially so. The avoidance of value judgements and the acceptance of a broad basis leads us to define popular war poetry in the first instance as any texts in poetic form to do with the two world wars, which were widely read or listened to by large numbers, whether or not this was because these lyrics were genuinely well liked and therefore known, or because they were placed before the public by means of a media dissemination unprecedented in other wars. Popular songs, music hall monologues, the vast amount of now neglected establishment poetry, propaganda, and patriotic verse – all these come into play. Equally, however, the word may imply lyrics emanating from the people, the oral tradition of anonymous lyrics to do with the war, and in particular the great mass of poetry produced in the two wars by those fighting, work which is not fully exploited or even known, and is certainly not invariably anti-war.

The question of poetic evaluation is made more problematic when it involves moral judgements, and different viewpoints need to be adopted in different cases. The view that any poetry which advocates fighting is morally unacceptable is, as indicated, less clear when we are faced with a partisan poem of the Second World War. So too, a purely poetic judgement may refer to the presentation of the chosen content or to poetic language and style, taken without prejudice. Although Ernst Lissauer's 'Hassgesang gegen England' [Hymn of Hate] has been dismissed as worthless in poetic terms, though interesting as a document,[59] it may be seen as poetically skilful, structured to lead to a climax (as Wavell recognized). On the other hand, lines like the following, from a song of 1915, are demonstrably worthless on poetic grounds:

> You have left the girl behind you,
> And we know you love her true,
> But she'll keep you in her heart, lad
> Yes, and in her prayers too.
> She's a woman like the mother
> Of the King you serve today,
> And will be the last to whimper
> For the price you have to pay.[60]

Compared to Lissauer's piling up of images, this is limp in the extreme. Metrically propped up by insertions like 'lad' or 'yes', it still falls down unless 'prayers' is exaggerated to a full disyllable. It is not particularly enlightening to be told that the girl left behind is a woman, and the idea of 'mother' is uncomfortably linked with that of serving the King (both Victoria and Mary would have been better models as mothers of the country, but short of 'granny' or 'missus', 'mother' is required metrically). Given the implications of the last line, 'whimper' is ridiculous. In fact that song was not popularly known, but it serves as a demonstration. Neither is morally acceptable: one poem is about hatred, the other about war as a game. Yet both merit study as war lyrics. The English song is of interest as document, the German as a poem as well.

What are the best-known lyrics of the world wars? While some responders to the question might name Owen or Sassoon (but no one from the later war) a realistic list might include 'Hymn of

Hate', 'When This Bleeding War is Over' (and probably a few more songs by soldiers, as well as the commercial 'Keep the Home Fires Burning' and later on, 'We'll Meet Again'), 'Lili Marleen', 'Hitler Has Only Got One Ball', 'Bless 'em All', and a few poems: 'The Soldier', some snatches of 'For the Fallen' or 'the one about poppies in Flanders Field. . .' Rupert Brooke will be named, but probably neither Binyon nor McCrae. Some Kipling might be recalled, though probably with some confusion as to which war is at issue. For the Second World War, probably the only poem to come to mind will be 'For Johnny', if that. If prompted, there might be a reference to 'Deutschland über alles' or the 'Horst Wessel Song' or 'the one about Germany today and tomorrow the world'. The song most likely to come to mind – 'Tipperary' – has in its text nothing to do with war at all. All of these are important as documents, and many have poetic value too, yet they are usually excluded from anthologies.

In the pursuit of the elusive term 'war poetry', poetry itself has on occasion run itself into a logical impasse. War poetry as such is impossible and therefore the only possible theme for the war poet is the statement of that impossibility. Many examples may be cited from Yeats onwards. War poets may or may not have been directly involved, and when historical distance is great, complications arise once more. How are we to tackle poetry concerned with the world wars but written from a strictly historical point of view? McCrae in the First World War demanded that later men should not break faith with those who lie in Flanders Field. Roger McGough has a pragmatic rejection of Brooke, though, commenting on the undesirability of being 'spread over some corner of a foreign field' simply as fertilizer. The poem, called 'Why Patriots Are a Bit Nuts in the Head', offers a fairly limited reading of a text which claims enrichment of the foreign soil,[61] and other poets have made clear that in an age which is post-Passchendaele, post-Auschwitz, and post-Hiroshima the image of men going over the top can still haunt us, not as a memorial to war only but to human stupidity, or perhaps to the whole idea of mortality. McGough is specifically historic, however, in his poem 'A Square Dance', which turns the First World War into a modern dance of death set in Flanders Field. The awful jollity of the poem's form contrasts with the historical realities mentioned in it – bayonets, mustard gas, going over the top, khaki, and so on. It even utilizes the kind of rhymes (and ideas) found in the worst kind of militaristic lyrics of 1914: it is still fun to kill a Hun.[62] This is not gratuitous cynicism, but historical reflection:

> It is rather fun making these entanglements and imagining the Germans coming along in the dark and falling over these things and starting to shout; whereupon you immediately send up a flare . . . and turn a machine gun on them as they struggle in the wire. It sounds cruel but it is War.[63]

That was the eighteen-year-old Edward Wyndham Tennant writing to his mother in 1915. His later letters reflect a crueller reality, and he fell almost exactly a year later.

In considering the term 'war poet', James Simmons returns to Wavell's old general and to the theme of the impossibility of war poetry:

> 'Pack up your troubles and go home and write
> or get back on the parapet and fight'.[64]

The choice of words is clearly an echo of the First World War, however. Possibly the Second World War is still too close for such a reflection, although it occasionally crops up in song lyrics: a rock song from 1985, for example, uses the concept and situation of a Second World War dog-fight with emphasis on the glory of flying ('fly to live, live to fly') – Yeats's Irish Airman or St-Exupéry rather than John Pudney. Nevertheless, the historicity is there, and the title, 'Aces High', is interestingly polysemic, the second word implying not only the actual height of flying, but also the idea of emotional high spirits (provided now by drugs, then by air battles).[65]

Some of the light verse of the Second World War is fixed in its time because it addressed itself to contemporary issues that are sometimes no longer recognized. Hitler is not forgotten, and neither is Mussolini, but who was Ciano, or Graziani? Even in accepted poetry, however, such questions may arise. What does the title of Ewart's often anthologized poem 'When a Beau Goes In' mean? So too we may always ask where Bapaume is, or Vlamertinghe, or Langemarck, for all that some names have survived (John Pudney originally entitled one of his poems 'Graves, Tobruk' and changed it to 'Graves, El Alamein' later). In Owen's 'Strange Meeting' the name 'Passchendaele' adds an evocative element that is historical, but the poem could survive without it. With a poem like Sassoon's

19

'Blighters', however, the question may arise of how readily the title alone is now understood. The image of a tank coming through the stalls at a music hall is striking, although music hall is a dated concept now. The climax remains difficult: but in spite of the poetic play on jokes and riddles upon which some critics have commented, the last line:

> to mock the riddled corpses round Bapaume

requires historical knowledge for an understanding, if the poem itself is not strong enough to keep the name alive.

The attitude to war in the lyric may be divided into categories. The first concentrates in a global or in a fragmented manner on the war itself and can (but need not) reflect the reality and horror; it can use vivid and modern language or it can utilize an earlier and probably inadequate language of drums and trumpets, and this attitude can vary from rejection of the futility of war to an acceptance of its necessity and, indeed, a patriotic encouragement to fight, with a later insistence on the glory and the idea that those who died did not do so in vain. A second type attacks those behind the war: this can be the profiteers and those who make money from munitions, or the war lords, usually those of the enemy, although in the First World War it is unclear whether the Kaiser serves as an embodiment of the enemy or is criticized as the sole begetter of the war; and in this category we may include the high-ranking officers, the donkeys who led the lions. The third category is that of coping with the war: this might imply attacks on the fact of army life, and include comments not on the generals but on the immediate superiors, the sergeants and corporals and W.O.1s, and also the simple and unreflective self-assurance that peace would come and the war would be over. A final category is social: will the soldier get a job, and will his children be fed?

The canonical anti-war poetry of the first category is of undeniable value, but it represents just one response to the mechanized wars. This poetry evokes pity in the modern reader for the individual soldier. Other lyrics, however, which at the time may have had a clearer function, can still make valid points. Kipling's pre-war 'Absent Minded Beggar', which was much recited in the First World War, some pieces by Studdert Kennedy, a song by Billy Rose, and later on John Pudney's 'For Johnny' are all linked by a social awareness not in the war-centred poems.

Patriotism, mockery, sentiment and resignation – in lyrics of all kinds – can also tell us a great deal. The aim of this study is a modest one: to extend the view of war poetry into areas sometimes dismissed as not worthy of consideration, such as the song, even though these have a far wider currency than some of the poetry; and to look at poetry that is not anti-war. Sometimes the perspective of that poetry makes it acceptable in moral terms; at others, the standpoint of historical hindsight permits us to see intrinsically unacceptable attitudes for what they are, and therefore precisely to take from such poetry an anti-war message, to feel pity for those who suffered under what it represents.

We Hate As One
Poems of the First World War

We must say au revoir *for a time, dear heart,*
While I'm doing my bit for the state;
For men must work when nations war
And you must patiently wait
Till we've trodden the Teuton beneath our heel
And silenced his hymn of hate.

E.M.K. (Postcard)[1]

Throughout the First World War, the enormous amount of poetry that was written concerned itself regularly with heroes, deeds, lands, glory, honour, and all that Wilfred Owen and others rejected.[2] The war was reflected in verse in every imaginable sphere. A postcard dated 1915 shows a somewhat unconvincing dove wearing a tricolour ribbon and carrying an envelope full of flowers. Above this patriotic bird is the verse

Je suis le messager fidèle
À tous j'apporte des nouvelles.

[I am the faithful messenger, bringing news to all]

but below it a group of poilus are going into battle. The incongruity of the bird which is a symbol of peace (though messenger pigeons were used in the war) and the scene depicted is striking. In fact, this particular card does carry a message – albeit in English, though with a Field Post Office stamp and a censor's triangle – to the effect that the writer is 'very much alive'.

Another verse on a German medallion bears witness to the sacrifices made at home during the war:

Gold gab ich zur Wehr
Eisen nahm ich zur Ehr

[I gave gold for defence; I took iron for honour]

On the face of the medal is a woman on her knees offering what is apparently a necklace, with the legend 'In eiserner Zeit 1916' [In a time of iron, 1916]. The iron medallion was given in return for contributions of gold or jewellery to support the war. Even small children were exhorted in verse to help the war effort: Mary Cadogan and Patricia Craig note how in *Little Folks* Mary Quite Contrary abandons silver bells and cockleshells for more useful gardening to assist the war.[3]

These are slight forms of popular war poetry. Beyond them come poems printed in newspapers and magazines at home or in the trenches, on postcards or broadsheets, in volumes of poetry printed privately or by large publishers, in anthologies and collections, sometimes of poems by serving soldiers. Prose works frequently began with a poem, even sober military analyses.[4] Beside printed material there were recitations in theatres and music halls that were sometimes published, but not always; and at the fronts there was an oral tradition even harder to pin down, though referred to sometimes in contemporary and later writing.

Nor does the poetry of the First World War end in 1918. Volumes of poetry designed as memorials to fallen soldiers appeared throughout the war, usually with a photograph or drawing of the poet, most often a young officer, as frontispiece to a collection of letters, juvenilia, and poems. Many more appeared after the armistice, and war poetry continued to appear in the anthologies in spite of new movements and rejections by individuals. Retrospective poetry appeared, some on an epic scale, well into the 1920s.

In Germany, of course, the position was somewhat different. With the fall of the Weimar Republic the Nazi regime revived with programmatic uniformity that poetry of the First World War which stressed the heroism, the love for and the willing death for the homeland. In Britain some of the heroic poets survived to write about a new war, while Brooke, Newbolt, and Kipling were still imitated. Patriotic poetry was also widely read, and now-forgotten poets like John Oxenham, whose little volumes of verse sold in large numbers in the First World War, were reprinted and sold as well in the Second. The war was reflected first of all in the writing of established poets, like Newbolt or Kipling, or Thomas Hardy, and in Germany war poems appeared at the beginning by celebrated and indeed unlikely poets such as Rilke, George, and

Hauptmann. During the war and for a long time afterwards, the non-combatants had a loud and influential voice. At the fronts, too, there were soldier-poets of all ranks, and in all areas of the services – including the Red Cross, the Ambulance Corps, and the chaplaincy – as well as all three services.

Different responses to the war may be picked out, but there is no linear development. War as a great game or adventure in the spirit of Sir Henry Newbolt's 'Vitai Lampada' remained a common theme during the First World War. Kipling is linked with the imperial belligerence of the God of Battles, although blanket dismissals of his work ignore his feeling for the ordinary soldier and the fact that he makes social points not always found elsewhere. Brooke is known best for the acceptance of a patriotic death. All of these contrast with the presentation of the pity of war by Owen, and the anger against it by Sassoon, but there was no sudden change, and poems about heroes and about dying gloriously continued to be written. In a war in which so many people lost their young men, it is as understandable a response to see the dead as glorious as it is to see them all on the same side in a futile war.

Some elements of war poetry might be expected to be constant, such as longing for home and for those left behind, putting up with the business of being a soldier, and simply getting the job done. But in spite of the changing realities of the war itself, a straightforward patriotism is equally constant: insistence on the flag, on the rightness of the cause and of the love of that *patria* that is at the root of patriotism, plus the use of essentially outdated military images, such as the call of the trumpet. Kipling had already invoked the God of Battles; Robert Bridges, the Poet Laureate, echoed Blake in demanding that England should awake.[5] A few typical examples representing a great many more must serve to illustrate the patriotic poetry that was written throughout the war by soldiers and non-combatants alike. Consideration of a range of lyric of this sort provides a useful test for moral and nationalist as well as aesthetic judgements.

Poets like Rupert Brooke welcomed the war as some of the Expressionists did in Germany, as a proving of their youth. In the main, however, patriotic poetry is less specific, but it is not necessarily, on the other hand, overtly jingoistic. In English poetry the mood of much of it was a rigid acceptance of the idea of honour. Thus a public poet, Sir Owen Seaman, wrote in his 'Pro Patria' in August 1914:

> England, in this great fight to which you go
> Because, where Honours calls you, go you must,
> Be glad, whatever comes, at least to know
> You have your quarrel just.[6]

The editor of *Punch* goes on to refer to the sending of 'your warrior sons', which has an effect almost like: 'Now God be thanked, who matched *you* with this hour', but others were more military:

> Our blades shall not be sheathed, our banners furled,
> Till Honours utmost task be trebly done;
> Till, bright across the devastated world,
> New-risen and blood-cleansed, Freedom's sun
> Dawns for God's vengeance on the shattered Hun![7]

God was called upon to defend the right, and the poets were clear where the right lay. The religious fervour was sometimes even greater:

> Trumpeter, sound for the last crusade!
> Sound for the fire of the red-cross kings,
> Sound for the passion, the splendour, the pity. . .[8]

Alfred Noyes's poem from 1915 is a sustained battle-call in the name of Christ, with a crescendo effect that is by no means without skill. Lesser versifiers, too, sounded the same notes:

> Shall Britain fail and Caesar rule by might?[9]

The question was put by the author of a book of poems printed in West Hartlepool in 1917, who acknowledges in his efforts to strike a classically heroic tone the identity of Caesar and Kaiser as words, presumably forgetting that Rome did conquer Britain.

Patriotism in the strictest sense appears in poetry throughout the war, reinforcing the notion that the war was just on the side of the writer's own country. The poem 'My Country' appeared in a collection published at the end of the war:

> 'Twere joy to those who bear the flag unfurl'd
> In ruthless strife, to keep thine acres free;

> To dip the hand in blood, the face to scare
> With sword of death, that thou unconquered may
> For freedom stand, the vanquisher of war,
> Chaste guardian of the unprotected way
> To peace and right.[10]

This is not by a home-based poem, but by Captain John Mason, who served in the Royal Scots.

In German poems the same trumpets called the soldiers to defend the same freedom:

> Was hallen die Trompeten?
> Gilt's neuen Siegesritt? –
> Sie rufen es für jeden:
> Du, Deutscher, ziehe mit!
> Zieh' mit, die Freiheit schaffen.
> Ein Ziel gar wunderbar –
> Wie einst die stolzen Waffen
> Vor einmal hundert Jahr.[11]

[What are the trumpets sounding? Is it for a new ride out to victory? They are calling everyone – O German, go with them, go with them to bring freedom, a most wonderful goal, as our proud weapons did a hundred years ago.]

The call to arms is in support of the abstract of freedom once again, which, like honour, remains undefined. The allusion to the fight against Napoleon is of course entirely appropriate, and English poems tend also to list victories against various invaders, including Napoleon. In a poem which links Germany and Austria-Hungary, too, another poet makes the same plea to God for defence of the cause:

> Was können wir gemeinsam nicht vollbringen!
> Rings um uns beide steht die Welt in Brand,
> Wir aber halten aneinander Hand
> Und niemand wird uns Einige bezwingen.
>
> Wir haben Hand in Hand in hoher Stunde
> Herr Gott, gelegt und rufen Dich zum Zeugen,
> Dein ist das Reich, die Kraft, die Herrlichkeit!

Giess aus den heiligen Geist ob unserm Bunde!
Mit reinen Klingen knien wir hier und beugen
Das Haupt vor Dir, der die Gekreuzten weiht.[12]

[What can we not achieve united! All around us the world is in
flames, but we stand hand in hand, and no-one can force us in
our unity. We have placed hand in hand at this great hour, o
Lord, and call upon Thee as a witness, for Thine is the kingdom,
the power and the glory. Pour out Thy holy spirit on our bond.
We kneel before Thee with pure swords and bow our heads to
Thee, who blesses the crusaders.]

Both God, and indeed St George, are invoked by both sides, and
Brooke's welcome of the hour has a precise parallel in lyrics like
those by Richard Dehmel, which appeared in the *Frankfurter Zeitung*
on 4 August 1914. His welcoming of the war appears to be because
it offers unity first of all:

Sei gesegnet, ernste Stunde,
Die uns endlich stählern eint;

but the war is honourable:

Jetzt kommt der Krieg
Der ehrliche Krieg![13]

[Bless you, solemn hour, which unites us all with a bond of iron
. . .now comes war, honourable war!]

The poem, however, is addressed 'an alle' ('to everyone'), and the
view of death that the later part of the poem offers seems
applicable to Brooke and those like him as well:

Feurig wird nun Klarheit schweben
Über Staub und Pulverdampf;
Nicht ums Leben, nicht ums Leben
Führt der Mensch den Lebenskampf –
Stets kommt der Tod,
Der göttliche Tod!

[Clarity will now hover like fire over dust and gunpowder; it is
not for life, not for life that man goes through life's struggle.
There is always death – divine death!]

One patriotic and, indeed, aggressive poem was delivered in public in a well-documented context. The poem was written in England by a civilian, but in this case by a Belgian poet, Emile Cammaerts, and it was included in the volume of statements, poems, music, and paintings issued in support of the Belgian people in 1914, *King Albert's Book*. If aggressive war poetry is now dismissed, the question of a moral response is less clear when we are faced with a belligerent poem from a Belgian, whose country had been invaded. 'Carillon' was recited at the Queen's Hall in London in December 1914 to the accompaniment of music by Elgar. Thomas Dunhill, writing in 1938, recollects the triumphant reception of the event and describes the work as 'an almost frenzied appeal to the Belgians to rejoice in their cause, to sing of the pride of their defeats, and to push on wildly until at last they shall enter the enemy's capital'[14], although he goes on to say that the poem is very firmly fixed in its time. It is impossible, of course, to reconstruct this piece in its musical context, but the text alone may be considered.

The defiance in spite of defeat is sustained. The last strophe has a *maestoso* accompaniment for the final bars:

> Chantons, Belges, chantons,
> Même si les blessures saignent et si la voix se brise,
> Plus haut que la tourmente, plus fort que les canons,
> Même si les blessures saignent, même si le coeur se brise,
> Chantons l'espoir et la haine implacable,
> Par ce beau soleil d'automne,
> Et la fierté de rester charitables
> Quand la Vengeance nous serait si bonne![15]

[Let us sing, Belgians, sing, even though our wounds bleed and the voice cracks, above the turmoil, stronger than the guns, even if our wounds bleed, even if our hearts break, let us sing our hope and our implacable hate in this fine August sun, and the pride of keeping charity when vengeance smiles so sweetly on us!]

Cammaerts envisages the entry in triumph into Berlin as a response to the loss of Brussels, Malines, Namur, Liege, and Louvain – the catalogue of names evoking, perhaps, a different response from a Belgian national than for others. Cammaerts, who had settled in England before the war, also published a number of volumes in the Belgian cause (*Belgian Poems, À ma patrie enchaînée,* and others).

The reflection of the enemy in poetry of the First World War differs frequently from Owen's 'I am the enemy you killed, my friend' or Sorley's address 'To Germany', beginning 'You are blind like us'. [16] Sometimes the attitude from the point of view of the trenches is ambiguous. Heinrich Lersch's 'Im Schützengraben' [In the Trench] addresses the Frenchman he has shot as 'Mein Kamerad Franzos' ('comrade Frenchy'), but assures him that it was necessary; the Frenchman has, he says, died for 'deines Reiches Herrlichkeit', the glory of your land, whilst the poet fights for 'unseres Tuns Gerechtigkeit', ('the justness of our deeds').[17] Poets on both sides, however, adopted a more clearly hostile approach: 'war hath no fury like a non-combatant', noted C.E. Montague.[18] One of the poems in the 1915 *Lest We Forget* anthology, however, is by a soldier, though many changed their attitude as the war progressed. A.E. Whiting-Baker, a Second Lieutenant, contributed the following:

> Zip! — Zing! —
> A bullet sped!
> The grim Hun chuckled;
> A poor heart bled.
>
> Then the lilt of a boyish voice
> Rang out through the murky night:
> 'Say, Dad – I'm hurt – and, why, here's Joyce:
> Play – up – old school – Good-night!'
>
> And wan and dreary crept up the day
> On a lonely outpost place;
> For the light of life had stolen away
> From a dear brown smiling face.
>
> Then pray to your gods for the life, grit and power,
> To tear with your hands, sword and gun –
> O! English sons, avenge that hour! –
> And CHOKE that chuckling Hun.[19]

This is expressly functional, conjuring up a situation to which the response was recruitment. It is easy to point out the flaws: the adjectives are well-worn, and the poet has tried too hard for his rhyme and metre. In the third strophe, 'place' is unnecessary except for the rhyme, and it is unclear why the face is brown. Finally it is hard to imagine how to choke anybody with a gun and a sword. Yet that verb makes the attack more personal, and there are elements in the piece that are striking. It is hard to forget the chuckling Hun, who apparently enjoys killing the unfortunate schoolboy, who was so bravely playing the game.

Three years later, and not long before the Armistice, Robert Bridges looked forward to a fate worse than choking for the treatment by the 'foe inhuman' of British prisoners-of-war:

> Their reek floats round the world on all lands 'neath the
>   sun:
> Tho' in craven Germany was no man found, not one
> With spirit enough to cry Shame! – Nay, but on such sin
> Follows Perdition eternal. . .[20]

German lyrics can adopt similar views of the enemy, French, British, or Russian. Gerhard Hauptmann visualizes three villains attacking Germany – a Frenchman, a Russian, and an Englishman. Each attacks Germany's honour and is repulsed, and the final strophe links the three:

> Es kamen drei Räuber auf einmal daher. . .
> . . .
> Und wärt ihr nicht drei, sondern wäret ihr neun
> Meine Ehr' und mein Land blieben ewig mein:
> Nimmer nimmt sie uns irgendwer,
> Dafür sorgt Gott, Kaiser und deutsches Heer.
> Nimmermehr![21]

[Three robbers came upon us together. . . 'And even if there were not three but nine of you, my honour and country would stay my own for ever: no one will ever take them from us – God, the Kaiser and the German army will see to that. Nevermore!]

English lyrics regularly use the term 'Hun', with its inevitable rhymes of 'gun' and 'fun', but much anti-German poetry centres rather upon the Kaiser. German verse of the equivalent type tends to be more general; the contrast, for example, between form and content is striking in this structurally competent sonnet in which the Belgians, French, and Russians are the aggressors:

Ihr Hunde − nein, ich darf das Tier nicht schänden,
Den guten, treuen Freund, dem wir vertrauen, −
Ihr Satansbrut, die mit Hyänenklauen,
Mit Geiersfangen, nicht mit Menschenhanden,

Mit Mordgewehren und mit Feuerbränden
Vergreifen sich an wehrlos schwachen Frauen,
Die Greise, Kinder, Kranke niederhauen,
Da sie zur Heimat still zuruck sich wenden.

Ihr rohen, niederträchtigen Barbaren,
Die deutsches Glut in toller Wut zerstören,
Sollt unser Strafgericht gar bald erfahren.

Euch Schurken soll vergehen Seh'n und Hören.
Zwar werden uns're Ehre streng wir wahren,
Doch euer Winseln soll uns nicht betören.[22]

[You dogs − no, I must not insult the animal, the good, true
friend we can trust − you brood of Satan, who, with hyaena's
claws and vulture's talons, not with human hands, with weapons
of death and with fire have attacked weak and defenceless
women, have struck down the old, children, the sick as they
turned in silence towards their homeland. You coarse and
vicious barbarians, who destroy German warmth in mad frenzy,
you will soon experience our court and judgement. You
wretches, you will lose your sight and hearing. We shall preserve
our honour, and will not be deceived by your whimperings.]

The text needs no special comment, save that a poetic form is used
in a violent piece of propaganda, and one which utilized the
various myths of the war: the woman and the old are the
equivalent of the Belgian babies.[23]

As many poems attack Belgium in German as declare support
for her in English, and attacks on other countries could be as
extreme. The fall of Tsingtau gave rise to:

Sie standen einer gegen zehn
Standen gegen Japaner und Inder
Und gegen die britischen Bastardkinder,
Die uns die Brut auf den Leib gehetzt
Und die ganzen Welt in Brand gesetzt.[24]

[They were one against ten, standing against Japanese and

31

Indians and the bastards of the British, who egged the whole
rabble on against us, and plunged the world into flames.]

Special fury was reserved for Italy. Contemporary lyrics at the time
of Italy's joining the war in 1915 refer to Luther's defiance of Rome
and to the victory of Hermann over the Legions. On the other
hand, German poems attempted to invoke Nordic solidarity,
largely against Russia, whilst English material sought American
intervention, and it is an interesting historical aside that poetry on
all sides praised the Polish legions, whose position in a partitioned
country was complex.[25]

The poetry of functional hostility was used on all fronts. A
typical trench-magazine parody (from Salonika in 1917) refers to
Johnny (Turk, *Bulgar*):

> Gin a Tommy meet a johnny
> Comin' thro' the rye,
> He must always throw a Mills bomb
> Make poor johnny die;
> Every Tommy has a rifle
> And a wary eye.[26]

The typography is as cited, and the enemy is not given the honour
of a capital letter. The same enemy is referred to as Abdul in
another poem, the irony of which is missed in a modern study,
which presents it as a contrast to home newspaper reports
portraying the Turk as an inhuman barbarian. The poem seems to
reject such views but in fact it accepts them, adding only that the
Turk can die like a gentleman. The poem does not contradict the
fact that Abdul's name is

> black as ink
> For murder and rapine
> Carried out in happy concert
> With your Christians from the Rhine.[27]

English poetry portrayed Germany as a land which had betrayed
its past, and the translator William Archer pictured Luther, Kant,
and Bach dismissing their barbarian descendants as a 'breed
reversive-bred'. On the other side, Hermann von Frankenberg
depicted a wounded soldier who responds precisely to this charge:

Von Kugeln war er jüngst umbraust. . . .
Er lächelt: 'Bringt mir Goethes Faust!'
. . .
So sind wir, wir 'Barbaren!'[28]

[Not long ago he was in a hail of bullets. . . . He smiles: 'Bring me Goethe's *Faust!*' . . . That is the way we are, we 'barbarians!']

One poem directed against England had a particularly powerful effect, and was one of the most significant poems of the First World War, although it rarely appears in anthologies. Ernst Lissauer's 'Hassgesang gegen England' [Hymn of Hate Against England] quickly became known on a massive scale from its publication at the beginning of the war. Unlike other poems of a similar nature it was not revived under the Nazis, because Lissauer (who by then regretted the work, and who died in 1937) was a Jew, but it was recalled with some frequency on the Allied side in the Second World War.

The poem became a focus for attacks on the supposed blind hatred motivating the Germans. *Punch* cartoons showed soldiers being driven into battle by a recording (there were such) as well as a Prussian family 'at their morning Hate'.[29] Hall Caine cited in 1915 in his *The Drama of 365 Days* the opening of Lissauer's poem, with the comment that it embodied 'a form of hatred not unfamiliar in asylums for the insane'. The American ambassador to Berlin, James W. Gerard, devotes a whole chapter of his memoirs to 'Hate', noting with amazement the award of 'the Order of the Red Eagle of the Second Class as a reward for having composed this extraordinary document'. Gerard reproduces a propaganda pamphlet of 1914 in which the poem figured. Parallels to it in Germany included a religious poem of hate by Will Vesper, later a leading poet of the Third Reich, in which the speaker argues against Christ that hate for the enemy is acceptable because it is the fruit of the deepest love possible, that for the country.[30] On the other hand, Lissauer's poem led the montage-artist Helmut Herzfeld to change his name to John Heartfield.

Outside Germany, allusions to the poem were very frequent, and it was not forgotten. *Punch* reminded its readers of it in 1918 rather neatly:

A Fatherland Poet was busy of late
In making the Kaiser a new Hymn of Hate;
Perhaps, ere its echoes have time to grow dim,
The Huns may be learning a new Hate of Him.[31]

Part of the fame of Lissauer's poem rests very simply upon its effectiveness. It builds up the single idea of hatred for the enemy into an incantatory and self-conscious crescendo, calling within itself for a response:

Vernehmt das Wort, sagt nach das Wort
Es wälze sich durch ganz Deutschland fort:
Wir wollen nicht lassen von unserem Hass
Wir haben alle nur einen Hass,
Wir lieben vereint, wir hassen vereint
Wir haben alle nur einen Feind:
England!

[Hear the word, repeat the word, may it run through all Germany: we shall never abandon our hate, we have only one hate, we love as one, we hate as one, we all have only one enemy: England!]

The repetitions, especially the anaphoric personal pronoun, hammer the point home. The religious overtones of the idea of a logos of hatred are also apparent. Internal rhymes and internal repetitions, with a paratactic build-up of ideas and a rhythm based on stressed syllables recall early Germanic poetry, and the sixth and final strophe shows even more clearly the incoherent, but at the same time, cumulatively effective piling up of ideas:

Und schliessen Frieden irgend einmal,
Dich werden wir hassen mit langem Hass,
Wir werden nicht lassen von unserm Hass,
Hass zu Wasser und Hass zu Land,
Hass der Hammer und Hass der Kronen,
Drosselnder Hass von siebzig Millionen,
Sie lieben vereint, sie hassen vereint,
Sie haben alle nur einen Feind:
England!

[And if one day there is a peace, we shall still hate you with enduring hate, we shall not give up our hate, hate on the water,

hate on land, hate of the hammers and of the crowns, choking
hate of seventy millions, they love as one, they hate as one, they
all have only one enemy: England!]

Verb and noun are repeated nine times and echoed acoustically.
The sentiment is hardly admirable, but as a war poem it manifests
a sustained attitude, albeit an hysterical one, in an undeniably
functional way. Its reception as a war poem on both sides in its
own time, and by a modern reader merit consideration. It remains
one of the most important pieces of the First World War.

Of the many responses to Lissauer's poem in English, some were
predictable:

> A song of hate is a song of Hell;
> Some there be that sing it well.
> Let them sing it loud and long,
> We lift our hearts in a loftier song:
> We lift our hearts to Heaven above,
> Singing the glory of her we love –
> England![32]

Helen Gray Cone went on to list a series of historical glories, but
the technique is Lissauer's throughout, and the poem builds up to
an identical climax, recalling uncomfortably Will Vesper's casuistic
identification of hate with love. Other responses were more
eccentric, as in the two-penny pamphlet published in 1915 with an
invitation to the press to reprint it. R.A. Kennedy's *New Benedicite*
describes itself as 'the true answer to the Hymn of Hate', and a
'Paean whose tune is within the soul', calling for love between the
nations in the name of God. In doing so it 'presents an ethnological
survey of the world's human life', which even includes

> Ye deep-thinking modern Germans of many teutonic
> parts.[33]

A war poem? It is anti-war in its spiritual internationalism, but it
derives directly from the 'Hymn of Hate'.

The chief target for popular war poetry in English for much of
the war was Wilhelm II, whose untranslated title of Kaiser became
part of the language. Early in the war the tone was forthright:

> megalomania impious, whose cant
> Proclaims: 'God is the Highest, but of all,

The Highest is the Kaiser.' Miscreant! –
Daring the Hosts of Heaven to battle call;
Sealed is thy doom, and, e'en as Lucifer, thou, too, shall
    fall.[34]

Later on, the whole war was seen as the Kaiser's:

Thousands are lyin' stiff an' stark,
An' in the trenches deein',
Gae look upon your deevil's wark,
An' greet at what you're seein'.[35]

Soldier-poets used the same tone. Hamish Mann, who fell in 1917, placed into the Kaiser's mouth in 1915 a parody of Lovelace which concluded

I could not love mein Gott so much
Loved I not bloodshed more!

In 1916 he, like many others, warned the Kaiser of an impending day of reckoning, and blamed him for the same atrocities already noted in a German poem. His 'To the Kaiser' is startling, if somewhat confused:

You violate the rich red blood of pregnant motherhood,
Or hunt the weary maid who flies as from a beast of prey;
You put to ling'ring death the aged ones. . .
Frail little children writhe beneath your heels. . .[36]

This is the poetic equivalent of the Partridge cartoon (reproduced in *Lest We Forget*) in which the Kaiser stands gun in hand, his foot resting on a dead woman with her child. Another soldier-poet, Joseph Lee, a Lance-Corporal in the Black Watch, whose *Ballads of Battle* appeared in 1916, links the Crucifixion with the Kaiser's deeds:

Proud Kaiser, who has drowned the world in tears,
And deluged all the earth with reddest rain –
Christ's brow is torn
With crown of thorn –
Thine bears the brand of Cain![37]

Paul Fussell has commented on the Crucifixion as a poetic motif, and also on the myth of the crucified Canadian, though variations were perhaps more widely used in verse than he implies. John Oxenham included in his widely sold collection *The Vision Splendid* of 1917 a ballad of the 'rough-diamond-turned-hero' type, in which 'Jim Baxter' (Oxenham states that he made up the name) is nailed to a cross by 'a mob of jeering Huns':

> Just like the Christs you find out there
> On every country road.[38]

Jim is taken to heaven, and vengeance is promised in the poem on the perpetrators. The lateness of the work and the popularity of the collection in which it appeared – one which also had pieces on Edith Cavell and on Jack Cornwell, the sixteen-year-old VC – are significant.

The German emperor had for some long time been a target for satire (as Owen Seaman pointed out in his 'Dies Irae', which was reprinted in anthologies), and the war quickly became the Kaiser's own. Individual poems and whole books were devoted to this theme and special attention may be drawn to parodies. Three favourite bases were *Alice in Wonderland*, *Omar Khayyam*, and *Hiawatha*, though 'Holy Willy's Prayer' was another. Alice, indeed, would be pressed into service again against Hitler, but Horace Wyatt's *Malice in Kulturland* reminds us of the ironic approach to German 'Kultur', 'civilization' throughout the war. It features instead of Jabberwocky the Kaiserhog:

> 'Twas dertag, and the slithy Huns
> Did sturm and sturgel through the sludge;
> All bulgous were the blunderguns
> And the bosch bombs outbludge.
> . . .
> And as in uffish thought he stood
> The Kaiserhog, with eyes of flame
> Came prumpling through the tulgey wood
> And blasphied as it came. . .

Tweedledum and Tweedledee become a divided Austrian emperor, Francis and Joseph, figments of the Kaiser's dream, and 'You Are Old, Father William' gives good scope for mockery both of the Crown Prince and his father. Other parodies are similar: *Allies in Wilhelmsland* appeared at Christmas 1915 and included the final injunction to 'Speak roughly to this Bully Hun'. In the trenches, the *BEF Times* placed a 'Rubaiyat of William Hohenzollern' into the Kaiser's mouth in 1917:

> Should any doubt my will, or us dispute
> Man, woman, child, don't hesitate to shoot;
> We'll play the policeman, and for Kultur's sake
> My son, young Bill, will pick up all the loot.[39]

A final recurrent motif was the setting of a single British soldier against the Kaiser himself. Violet Jacob, writing in Scots, set a sergeant of the Black Watch against his namesake in a poem which appeared in *Country Life*:

> Fegs-aye! Yon Weelum that's in Gairmanie,
> He hadna reckoned
> Wi' Sairgeant Weelum Henderson, an' wi'
> The Forty-Second!
> . . .
> But me an' Weelum's got to get to grips
> Afore we're deid;
> An' gin he thinks he hasn't met his match
> He'll sune be wiser.
> Here's to mysel'! Here's to the auld Black Watch
> An' damn the Kaiser![40]

In Germany, of course, the attitudes were rather different:

> In Ost und West vom Feind umstellt,
> Braust Deutschlands Kampfgeschwur durch die Welt
> Gott hör's: Es lebe der Kaiser!
> In Not und Tod – noch sind wir da!
> Kaiser – hurra![41]

[Surrounded east and west by the enemy, Germany's battle-vow echoes round the world. May God himself hear it: long live the Kaiser! In peril and in death – we are still at hand – hurrah for the Kaiser!]

Rudolf Herzog was a much read public poet, whose history of Prussia sold as well as his verse. The 1914 collection from which that poem is taken includes (beside a prophetically titled piece on the Kaiser's birthday called 'Führer und Volk') a description of a nationalistically ecumenical church parade, as the soldiers wait with

Nicht Papst, nicht Luther, Gott nur im Gefühle,
Den deutschen Gott. . .

[Neither the Pope nor Luther in mind, just God, the German
God,]
. . .

until the arrival of the Kaiser:

Wie Eisen grau das Haar, und Stahl die Mienen,
Im hellen Aug' ein heisses Schwertgefunkel. . .

[Hair grey as iron, features of steel, and the flash of a sword in
his bright eye. . .]

At the beginning of the war the Kaiser was even seen as
'Wilhelm der Eroberer' ('William the Conqueror').[42] German
militaristic poetry also attacked the enemy rulers, and the following
verses depend upon the tune *O Tannenbaum*. Tsar Nicholas II,
Poincaré, and George V are all promised a lesson from the German
fist:

Zar Nikolaus, Zar Nikolaus,
Der spielt den harmlos Frommen;
Posaunt den Frieden in die Welt
Indessen er uns überfällt. . .

Poincaré, Poincaré,
Der liebt die Renommage:
Prahlt noch mit seiner 'Grande' Nation,
Dieweil wir sie verdreschen schon. . .

Der King George, der King George,
Versteht das Profitieren!
Hat stets die andern gern 'beschützt',
Und – sich dabei nur selbst genützt. . .[43]

[Tsar Nicholas . . . plays the harmless man of God, trumpets
peace all round the world and meanwhile attacks us. . . Poincaré
. . . loves fame, still boasts about his 'grande nation', and at the
same time we are thrashing them. . . King George . . . knows all
about profiteering! He always likes to 'protect' others, and all he
does is line his own pockets. . .]

Possibly the most functional lyrics of the beginning of the First
World War are those concerned with recruiting. The poetic

techniques employed are straightforward: the emotional solidarity implied in the first person plural pronoun ('Come and Join Us', 'We Are Coming Father Abraham') and the direct address to the target (what will you have done in the war, Daddy?). Amongst the most widely distributed is Harold Begbie's 'Fall In' of August 1914:

> Where will you look, sonny, where will you look
> When your children yet to be
> Clamour to learn of the part you took
> In the War that kept men free?[44]

The address as 'sonny' is a patronizing reminder of the old men who sent the young to die, a motif taken up negatively by Owen and Sassoon. Join up, the poem demands, because if you don't you will be unable to attract a girl, and people will 'know you funked'. That notice was taken of this kind of material is clear in the lyrics of those who had joined. Charles John Beech Masefield, who was killed in 1917 and whose poems are represented in the second volume of *Soldier Poets*, states in 'Enlisted, or The Recruits'

> Humbly, O England, we offer what is of little worth,
> Just our bodies and souls and everything else we have;
> But thou with thy holy cause wilt hallow our common earth,
> Giving us strength in the battle — and peace, if need, in the grave.[45]

Recruiting poems were thought (by their poets, at least) worth reprinting *after* the war. George Guthrie included in what looks admittedly like a privately printed collection from 1928 a whole series castigating the 'slackers and shirkers' or the 'Kings of Cockaigne' and invoking Belgium, the Empire, and the flag. In a presumably early poem, the gallant volunteers are set explicitly against 'the conscript foe', a nice affirmation of the spirit of amateurism that would be overtaken by events. Also published after the war, however, was a piece which shows at least that recruiting verse could be humorous. C.J. Dennis's Australian call to the colours leaves gaps for an appropriate adjective. The 'Austral—Aise' includes the verse:

> Fellers of Australier
> Cobbers, chaps an' mates,

Hear the ———— enemy
Kickin' at the gates!
Blow the ———— bugle,
Beat the ———— drum,
Upper-cut and out the cow
To kingdom ———— come![46]

Usually, however, poems were more serious. In German a sixth-former turned soldier, Friedrich Meissel, sounds very like Charles Masefield:

Der Kaiser rief,
Wir zogen hinaus –
Liessen Sport und Spiel
Liessen Freunde und Haus. . .

Wir klagen nicht,
Dein sind wir, Vaterland![47]

[The Kaiser called, we enlisted – left sport and games, left friends and home . . . we do not complain, we are yours, o Fatherland!]

Later in the war, non-combatants felt the need to justify themselves in verse. William Dunbar Birrell, a Dundonian whose portrait in his *War and Patriotic Poems* of 1918 shows him as middle-aged, distinguished between 'Shirkers and Workers' and stressed that it was acceptable to do one's bit at home. He acknowledges the soldier, of course, but the following verses would hardly have commended themselves to those who had fought:

We who toil at desks and benches
Here at home are all secure.
Those within the distant trenches,
What long sufferings they endure!
Theirs is not a soft existence,
Guarding there with bated breath
Fighting with a stern resistance
'Mid flying bullets dealing death.

When the guns have ceased their rattle
When the victory has been won,
For the brave who come from battle
There shall be the loud Well Done!

41

> Who shall dare to underrate them?
> What they've done — go, think of it,
> All the Empire shall await them
> Hearts aglow and eyes alit
> Our soldiers who have done their bit![48]

Especially worrying is the faintness of the praise in the bad verse. The clichés (toiling at desks, bated breath, stern resistance, flying bullets dealing death, guns that rattle) make it quite clear that Birrell has no idea, however loud his 'Well Done', of the fighting. Yet this is a public poem included in a collection of avowedly patriotic poems which even warranted a second edition. To a modern audience, the pallidity of this attitude is chilling.

As a motif, the viewing of war as a game owes much in English to Newbolt's 'Vitai lampada', in which the conclusion of a cricket match is precisely similar to a situation in which the Gatling is jammed and the colonel is dead. Some examples were produced, however, by soldiers, though primarily officers. Ralph Vernède's 'The Call' is often quoted:

> Here is the game of games to play

and another of the poets who died in the war, Eric Wilkinson, echoed Newbolt directly:

> There are many who fight, and many who fall
> Where the big guns play at the Kaiser's ball,
> But hark! – can you hear it? Over all –
> Now, School! Now, School! Play up!

So did others. C.E.C.H. Burton's 'The Game', which appeared in the *Daily Mail* in 1916, was based on a genuine incident in which soldiers dribbled footballs into the enemy trenches:

> A deathless place they claim
> In England's splendid story,
> The men who played the game![49]

In contrast to poets like Owen, many wrote precisely about individual heroism, developing the idea that the war could give meaning to an otherwise useless existence.[50] The universality of the war gave prominence to the *unlikely* hero, the rough diamond, of a lower social class, often presented in (rarely authentic) dialect. The immediate ancestor of this type of poetry in English at least is Kipling's *Barrack-Room Ballads* ('Gunga Din'), and Boer War imitators like 'Coldstreamer' with his *Ballads of the Boer War* 'selected from the haversack of Sergeant J. Smith', or, indeed, the 'ranked and ready' rhymes of Robert W. Service.[51] Nevertheless, individual heroes are a subject for both sides. Herzog's collection also has poems celebrating NCOs:

> Um Reims schlang der blutige Reigen den Kreis –
> Ich weiss einen Tag, und der Tag war heiss,
> Und ich weiss eine Tat in Blei und Blut,
> Die den Tod bezwingt, weil ein Tapfrer sie tut.
> Kameraden, für euch ging er drauf und dran.
> Fünfte Kompagnie, wie heisst euer Mann?
> Feldwebel Bachmann.[52]

[The bloody dance of death wound around Rheims. I remember a day, a hot one, and I remember a deed with bullets and blood, a deed that defeats death when a brave man does it. Pals, he went at it for your sakes. Company Five, who is your man? Sergeant Bachmann.]

The poem concludes that every company has a Bachmann somewhere. In Scots, Joseph Lee adapted the soldiers' song 'We Haven't Seen the Sergeant' to a more positive view; the sergeant is not visible because of gunsmoke:

> Now we can see him nearer –
> Upon the topmost parapet
> He's foremost o' us a'[53]

But rough diamonds in English-language war poems tend to be of even lower rank. Another soldier, R.W. Campbell, published the tale of 'The Making of Micky McGhee', in which the eponymous hero, a 'nomad from smelling slums', spends much of his time on a charge until a another stereotype, a public-school captain who is much loved by his men, persuades him to 'play the game'. At Mons, however, he and the captain are both killed. The final strophe adds an extra type of sentiment as we hear of McGhee's bequest (including his medal) to a woman who had shown him some charity:

> she, like the Fairies of Joyland, has her dreams of the past
> as well
>
> . . .
>
> And her pride in a silver medal. . .[54]

The Fairies of Joyland are hard to take, and the poem as a whole
seems to claim that military life has been the making of the rough
McGhee, although it had to kill him to prove it. The paradox (and
also the fact that the pride of the woman apparently outweighs any
pain she might have felt) is not considered. The rough diamonds
are regularly Scots, Cockneys, or Australians, and they nearly
always fall. Brian Brooke's grumbling 'O'Mara, P., a Jock of the
Ninety-Two' gains interest from the fact that its author later died
in an attack on an enemy trench, but at home the music hall
reciters were fond of the theme. ''Erbert, A.B.' dies saving a
German, 'Pincher, DCM' abandons looted goods to save a
comrade, and the ''Oxton 'Ero' does in fact survive, as does an
Australian equivalent in ballad-narrative in the style of Kipling.
C.J. Dennis creates an outback drover with the nickname 'Got-a-
Fag', an individualistic fighter who dismissively rounds up enemy
soldiers as he had rounded up cattle. He, however, is an
entertaining survivor (Stanley Holloway's Sam Small took things
further), and for that reason the poem is more effective than those
which embody the paradox of a war philosophy which gives
meaning to life only to bring it to an abrupt end.[55] The use of
dialect for realism is very frequent in war-poems of all kinds,
incidentally, although few poets sustain it as well as Kipling did.
Its function is simply to remind us of the role of the ordinary man,
however.[56]

Recruiting verses play on the idea of cowardice, and often an
initial description of a coward turns into a poem of the unlikely
hero category. Brian Brooke's collected poems, however, include
amongst the heroic deeds a genuine attack on 'Cowards' – the title
of the poem – which contains the lines:

> If you who fear to go and fight and fear to risk your lives
> Should marry, as perhaps you might, if you could get the
>   wives;
> And if you're men enough to breed, which God forbid you
>   are,

> Then, Lord have mercy on your seed and spread it not too
> far!
> By God, I'd rather lie and bleed and die with shrieks and
> cries
> Than live to let a woman read the coward in my eyes.[57]

It has to be remembered that this carefully built-up pattern of
concessive clauses was not written by a home poet, but by a poet
who died at the front. The posthumous collection, first published in
1918, was reprinted. Brian Brooke's poetry is now unacceptable in
its entirely unreflective oversimplification; however, it was read,
and it represented an attitude which did exist. Montague's dictum
about the fury of a non-combatant requires some modification in
the light of Brian Brooke.

Beside realistic depictions of the military life, soldier verse, often
in trench magazines, treated aspects of the war with considerable
humour. Walter Dorias wrote for the *Champagne-Kamerad* a witty
piece about one hazard, 'Ein friedlich Lied an die Ratten meines
Unterstandes' [A Brotherly Song to the Rats in My Dug-Out], in
which he comments first on how much he has provided for them:

> Was ich an Zwieback und an Marmelade
> Besass, ward eure nachste Beute dann,
> Ich sah Filet in Remoulade schwinden
> Und Lachs in Öl – ich trug es wie ein Mann.

[What biscuit I had, and all my jam became your booty. I
watched filet en remoulade vanish, also salmon in olive oil – and
I bore it like a man.]

Even his cap is eaten by the rats, but the last straw is when they
eat his candle, after which he pleads:

> Ihr seht, ich bin kein Unmensch, gab euch alles,
> Was ich besass, als meiner Freundschaft Pfand.
> Lasst mir dafür, zum Lesen und zum Schreiben,
> Ein wenig Helle nur im Unterstand.

[You've seen, I am no monster; I gave you all I had in token of
my love. For that, do leave me – so that I can read and write –
a little light here in my dugout.]

Other German soldier poetry is ironic, and one small piece that
appears in a collection drawn from the field newspaper of the 54th

Infantry Division, published at Christmas 1916 with the title *Im Schützengraben* [In the Trench], is worth considering. Much of the collection deals as expected with mothers and sweethearts, or with fighting in general. Some even of the 'humorous pieces' grouped together are somewhat grim, including a poem about a machine gun which feeds on metal and spews it over the French. A Private, M. Steffen, wrote in 1916 a series of questioning verses, and one is addressed to the 'Bierbankstrategen' [Saloon Bar Tacticians]. It makes a serious point, though the context is comic-ironic:

Im Posemukler Tagblatt steht geschrieben
Es müsse schneller gehen mit den Hieben. . .
Nur vorwärts und den Feind zu Tod gehetzt.
Was aber, wenn der Feind zur Wehr sich setzt?[58]

[In the Puddleton Advertiser it says that things have to move a little faster. . . Just get on with it and hound the enemy to their death. But what if they resist?]

In English, the cartoonist Bruce Bairnsfather has his characters express themselves in sanguine fashion on the subject of their general situation:

Where is it that I try to sleep
Betwixt alarms when up I leap
And dash through water four feet deep?
My dug-out.[59]

So, too, the following resigned advice from the *BEF Times* in 1918:

What matter though the wily Hun
With bomb, and gas and many a gun
In futile fury, lashes out,
Don't wonder what it's all about –
Stick it![60]

In Britain after the war, privately printed sets of verses appeared recalling details of the war almost with affection. One such volume by a member of a drivers' unit, an unidentified 'Rochan', with the title *Verses of Section 2*, appeared in 1919 and is for the most part scarcely understandable now. A 'Chauffeur's Hymn of Love' mocks not only the 'Hymn of Hate' but also the soldier parodies of the hymn 'We are but little children meek' in which 'children' was replaced, here by 'chauffeurs'. Rochan protests how much they have suffered in noble silence, and ends not with 'amen' but with 'ahem'. From the modern point of view these are the most remote of First World War lyrics, although even in the anthologized poetry, names and incidents need glossing.[61] The same applies to works such as Captain Owen Rutter's sustained *Hiawatha* parody from the Dardanelles. *The Song of Tiadatha* appeared in instalments in the *Orient Weekly* in Salonika, and then in a full edition as 'a most happy blend of descriptive realism, humour and sentiment'. It repays study. 'Tired Arthur's' progress through the entire war is pursued in Longfellow's metre, and beside the jokes stand realistic passages. The mixture is of interest in itself:

> Into No Man's Land they sallied,
> Through the din of bursting shrapnel
> Through the bursting high explosives.
> Down the steep Patte d'Oie he led them,
> Down that steep and rocky gully,
> Rocky as a Cornish headland,
> Steeper than a traveller's story:
> There the dread trench mortar barrage
> Swept upon them like a hailstorm. . .[62]

The central figure is wounded, and many are killed; but the next stage is treated lightly:

> Soon my wounded Tiadatha
> Carefully labelled like a parcel
> Started on his jouney Baseward. . .

Rutter does not clean up the battles, although some soldier poetry did do so. A Private in the Royal Warwicks, H. Spurrier, described 'The Charge at Neuve-Chapelle' (in the first *Soldier Poets* volume) presumably from experience, but in a style that is as unskilled as the intent is clear. It is difficult to find an appropriate response to the verse:

> Some furlongs four we had to run
> And Hell did intervene;
> A death that rode invisible,
> In agony unseen.
> At every step a comrade fell,
> Nor face of foe we saw.

> Fell young Lieutenant Anderson
> And gallant Captain Shaw.[63]

Yet there is reality in the poem:

> Our bayonets glinting in the sun,
> Our faces fierce and white,
> With sobbing breath and staring eye,
> Yet bright with battle-light.

The exultation in victory and lack of reflection represent a genuine response from an ordinary soldier:

> Then shouted Sergeant-Major Jones –
> 'On, lads, and follow me!'
> We gave a hoarse and broken cheer
> And swept to VICTORY.
> Right through that belch of roaring death,
> Amidst the fiery drench,
> Hacked through their wire-entanglements,
> And leaped and took the trench.

A bad poem? A morally unacceptable poem, since it exults in a victory? At all events it is a detailed picture of reality (wire-entanglements, hacking, fire, sobbing breath) represented as best the poet could.

Naval officers produced English verse with a strong historical bias. Captain Ronald A. Hopwood published 'The Old Way' in the London *Times* in 1916, a poem in which galleons, brigs, and pinnances of the past wonder if the new ships fight in the way they did, and are reassured that they do. The poem became the title-piece of Hopwood's collected verses in the same year and they were reprinted in 1917. Hopwood included an effectively done conversation with an auxiliary trawler in which he plays with the rhyme as he gives a picture of an unusual aspect of the war. The rhyme-words are avoided to underline the secrecy with which the auxiliary trawler is operating:

> 'Little trawler, little trawler, have you truly told me all?
> That's a wicked-looking Hotchkiss, is it used to shoot the
>   trawl?'
> 'Now I wonder,' said the trawler, 'where I got the beggar
>   from?

Or the thing that you are kicking, that's the newest kind
 of. . .

football, and

We use it when we play for Merrie England;
But it's delicate, and liable to fits,
So we're careful where we stow it, till we get a chance

to throw it
At a certain fish below it, name of Fritz.

Oh, Gott strafe England!
How it would have tickled Drake and Captain Hawkins!
For it's risky when it isn't full of fun.
Oh I've got a job of work to do for England,
And I'll not be back at Grimsby till it's done.[64]

It must be added that the trawler, though successful, loses its
skipper, who joins Drake and Hawkins in 'a harbour shining
brighter than the sun'.

In German, too, heroic naval deeds were eulogized. The exploits
of the Emden, for example, were celebrated:

Wie viele eiserne Kiele jagte England auf deine Spur?
Und wie oft entkamst du der Meute, die klaffend hinter dir
 her?
. . .
Emden, du Heldenschiff, wir werden dich nie vergessen.[65]

[How many ironclads has England sent out on your tracks! And
how many times did you escape the pack that were snapping
after you. . . ? Emden, heroic ship, we shall never forget you.]

It was in the First World War, too, that Hermann Löns, who fell in
September 1914, wrote a 'Deutsches Matrosenlied' [German
Sailor's Song] that was to become very well known in the Second
World War as 'Denn wir fahren gegen Engelland' [We Are Off
Against England].

The war in the air, too, was treated very frequently in heroic
terms:

Sekunde ist Leben, Sekunde ist Tod;
Ich fliege kampftlustdurchloht.

> Der Feind braust an,
> Mann gegen Mann!
> Über dem Feinde ist Sonne und Sieg!
> Adler empor! Adler, flieg![66]

[A second for life, a second for death; I fly transfigured with battle-lust; the enemy roars towards me, man against man! Sun and victory over the enemy! Up eagle, fly, eagle!]

or, on reconnaissance aircraft:

> Line – target – short or over –
> Come, plain as clock hands run,
> Words from the birds that hover,
> Unblinded, tail to sun;
> Words out of air to range them fair,
> From hawks that guide the guns.[67]

Sentimental verse was produced by all. Postcard verses were an extremely widespread form of war poetry, and if the verse is banal, they are often interesting as documents. A typical format in Britain had an insert photograph of a girl above a picture of a soldier or soldiers, with a trite verse beneath that. Thus the unremarkable:

> I'm thinking many times a day
> Of you at home so far away
> In fancy dear your face I see
> And know your thoughts are all with me.

These appear on a card which depicts soldiers apparently going into action (though the photograph was probably taken in training). Other verses provide reminders of the 'homeland far away'. Sometimes full poems appear. That cited at the head of this chapter reads initially like a recruiting poem (apart from the 'dear heart'), but its real aim is to ensure that Britain's daughters encourage the troops:

> And a letter the job will do;
> So send one along to Witley Camp
> By the very next post. Adieu![68]

Sweethearts and mothers both play dominant roles. A German woman, Hedda von Schmid, depicts a mother urging her son on to victory; she hears *his* voice in the night calling to her, and she prays

50

that God should protect her only son.[69] Joseph Lee's 'The Mother' depicts with even greater sentimental effect the ghost of the soldier's mother coming to him in a dream, so that when he is found shot there is a smile on his face. But Lee also reflects in an earlier poem on the nature of war, extrapolating from the thoughts of mother:

> Every bullet has its billet;
> Many bullets more than one:
> God! Perhaps I killed a mother
> When I killed a mother's son.

Another piece by Lee shows a broader reflectiveness, and an awareness of a question to which he has no answer. In 'Tommy and Fritz' he describes in naive terms and once more in a self-conscious and inconsistent demotic the reaction of soldier to enemy:

> Sometimes he whistles his 'Ymn of 'Ate,
> Or opens his mug to sing.
> And when he gives us 'Die Wacht am Rhein'
> I give 'im 'God Save the King';
> And then – we 'get up the wind' again
> And the bullets begin to ping –
> (If we're in luck our machine gun nips
> A working squad on the wing.)[70]

The tone is studiedly ironic, referring to 'paying visits' with a bayonet, and 'returning the compliment'. However, the final strophes make a more serious impression. Sometimes there is genuine antagonism, though reduced, significantly, to tag words (and we do not see what the German is thinking):

> For sometimes I mutters 'Belgium',
> Or 'Lusitani – a',
> And I slackens my bay'net in its sheath,
> And stiffens my lower jaw,
> And 'An eye for an eye; a tooth for a tooth',
> Is all I know of the Law.

But this attitude (and it is not the same as an insistence on abstract glory) is at once contrasted with a different mood:

> But sometimes when things is quiet,
> And the old kindly stars come out,
> I stand up behind my sand-bag,
> And think, 'What's it all about?'
> And – tho I'm a damned sight better nor him,
> Yet sometimes I have a doubt,
> That if you got under his hide you would see
> A bloke with a heart just the same's you or me.

This is a stage before that certainty of evil that Owen came to know.

Religious responses to the war were often simple, as in the 'De profundis' of Jean-Marc Bernard, already an established poet, who was killed in 1915. He expresses a simple prayer:

> Du plus profond de la tranchée,
> Nous élevons les main vers vous,
> Seigneur! ayez pitié de nous
> Et de notre âme desséchée!
> . . .
> Nous sommes si privés d'espoir,
> La paix est toujours si lointaine,
> Que parfois vous savons à peine
> Où se trouve notre devoir.[71]

[From the depths of the trenches we raise our hands to Thee, O Lord! Have mercy on us and on our drained souls . . .We are so robbed of hope and peace is always so distant that sometimes we hardly know where our duty lies.]

Yet what is being asked for is encouragement to carry on:

> Ah! rendez-nous l'enthousiasme!

[Oh, give us back our eagerness!]

and the sacrifice of the dead is seen as worthy of God's grace:

> Donnez le repos ineffable,
> Seigneur! ils l'ont bien mérité!

[Give them ineffable peace, O Lord, they have deserved it!]

In English poetry, two names stand out as popular religious poets, though they are rarely included in anthologies in spite of having sold well during and after the war, and into the next. John

Oxenham and Studdert Kennedy were both household names. Oxenham was an enormously prolific and now quite unread author, whose 'Hymn For the Men at the Front' sold several million copies during the war in postcard form (a khaki postcard with music sold at one shilling for a dozen, and in ordinary form without music was advertised at half-a-crown per thousand). His books are octavos for pocket or haversack, and selections of his First World War poetry were reprinted during the Second World War in a matching format. Oxenham visited the trenches in 1917 and wrote about the experience in *High Altars*, in which he reflected that one is unable to 'prevail pacifically with a mad dog or a maniac'. The picture which emerges, however, is of men determined 'to see the business through'.[72] Oxenham's poems underline the idea that fighting the war was doing the will of God. 'In Church 1916' asks (as would be asked in a different context later) where all the young men have gone, and concludes that in following their duty, 'they are making history'.[73]

Oxenham's religion provides little more of an answer than the complete submission to God's will. The massive scale of death becomes the image of a gardener pruning hard to make the rose grow better, but it is not a happy one. The death of young men is compared with Christ, but Oxenham could also in 1915 present as a blessing the opportunity to die in a valid cause:

> He died as few men get the chance to die, –
> Fighting to save a world's morality.
> He died the noblest death a man may die,
> Fighting for God, and Right, and Liberty; –
> And such a death is immortality.

That poem was reprinted in 1940 together with a poem from 1938 which quickly became ironic, beginning 'Peace in our time, O Lord'.[74]

The printing history of Studdert Kennedy's *Rough Rhymes of a Padre* is rather similar. Kennedy, known as 'Woodbine Willie', served as a padre in the trenches throughout the war, and his poems were very well known indeed. A memorial volume was published on his death in 1929, and reprinted virtually every year until late in the 1930s. Some interest is now shown in him, and as Hibberd and Onions (in whose anthology he is represented) point out, his verse shows both the real horror and the heroism of the war. At his starkest he is neither patriotic nor partisan: the poem 'Waste' has the anaphoric force of the 'Hymn of Hate':

> Waste of Blood, and waste of Tears,
> Waste of Youth's most precious years,
> Waste of ways the Saints have trod,
> Waste of Glory, waste of God –
> War![75]

However, other poems imply that the task faced by the British soldiers is God's attack on Satan, and a new Britain is to be built to the honour of the dead. Kennedy produced poems in working-class demotic, and if these are a distancing from his own voice, many are clear in their patriotism. 'What's the Good?' is aware that war has turned men into butchers, but still the cause is accepted:

> But the kids will some day bless us
> When they grows up British men,
> 'Cause we tamed the Prussian tyrant,
> And brought peace to earth again.

Kennedy's very popular verse can ask questions of social importance that others avoid. He attacks not the enemy army, but other targets in 'No Retaliations', which condemns the strikers who are preventing sufficient munitions arriving, but ends

> All them dudes what's profiteerin
> Oughter be out 'ere – in 'ell.

In 'Worry' his speaker, a blinded soldier, does not voice the anger of the wounded man in Sassoon's 'Does it Matter', but is more practical in his fear:

> There'll be thousands same as me, sir,
> Out to do what work they can. . .
> That's the only thing as worries
> When I sits me down to think,
> Will I get my charnce of 'ome, sir,
> And enough to eat and drink?

Kennedy's closeness to the soldiers is apparent in some of his writing. In 'Missing – Believed Killed' Kennedy (a strong personal note that permits us to identify speaker with poet) refers to a letter from a mother, and exclaims almost with bitterness:

> God has not even let her know
> Where his dead body lies.

The last strophe cries out against the Pauline 'Death, where is thy sting', reminding us that a version of this was sung as an ironic song by the soldiers in the face of death. For the mother, and for the poet trying to come to terms, the answer is not ironic mockery, however, but bitter:

> Thy victory is ev'rywhere
> Thy sting's in ev'rything.

Elsewhere, Kennedy's verse plays with his own role as 'Woodbine Willie'. It is not religion, or drill, or bravery that will win the war, but Woodbines – and tanks. Close to the soldiers, his rhymes (he did not call them poems) end with a very familiar injunction:

> When the world is red and reeking,
> And the shrapnel shells are shrieking,
> And your blood is slowly leaking,
> Carry on!

Much of Studdert Kennedy's verse bears re-reading: it tries with some honesty to come to terms with problems, even within its patriotism, and it condemns war, whilst accepting the necessity to fight in this one. Kennedy is even able to distance himself from Oxenham's too facile insistence on the will of God. Most of all, though, he expresses not only despair, but genuine worry for the soldier after the conflict.

The reference by Kennedy to the strikers is not uncommon, and it is found in propaganda pieces. In an American piece by Edgar Guest sent out by a steel corporation, for example, the workman declares to the sailor in 1917:

> While you're over there for freedom, you can safely bank on
>   me!
> I'll be just as brave as you are, in a safer sort of way,
> And I'll keep production going every minute of the day.[76]

In other political contexts, however, different attitudes could arise. In 1916 Nikolai Gumilev envisaged in his poem 'Rabochii' [Worker] a soldier imagining a worker making the bullet that will kill him.[77] With the Revolution, too, attitudes to the war were turned around, and A. Bogdanov, in some verses added to Pottier's 'Internationale', comments first that

> Tsari nas porokhom kormili
>
> [The Tsars fed us with gunpowder]

and then commands the soldiers away:

> Soldati! S fronta – po stankam![78]
>
> [Soldiers – from the front to the workbench!]

War means death, and to this axiom several attitudes are possible: that the death of the soldier is wasteful and futile, or a wicked effect of other men's stupidity; that death for a cause is glorious; or – a soldier's view – that death is likely and must be accepted as a possibility and perhaps even mocked. Above all else there is the memorial element. Brooke's 'Soldier' is the best known of the dead, his corpse making the earth forever England and therefore richer. That the soldiers died for their country's honour is, of course, regularly emphasized, and with this emphasis comes the notion that they are somehow not dead at all, an understandable and comforting message. Many poems adopt, too, the motif of the army of the dead. In German it was used after the war and into the Nazi period as an image for keeping faith with those who fell. On the other side of the trenches, however, W.D. Cocker describes in Scots 'The Phantom Platoon', and there are several variations on the theme: Wilfrid Wilson Gibson envisaged a soldier from the days of Waterloo marching beside a soldier in Flanders, and John Squire, in 'The March' in 1915, depicted the army of the dead, a hundred thousand of them, passing endlessly, but he is horrified by a look from one of them:

> And in the Face that turned I saw two eyes that burned,
> Never-forgotten eyes, and they had things to say.[79]

The primary assertion, however, remains that the individual death was not in vain. Some poets, indeed, wrote verse *for* war memorials, although Kipling's 'Recessional' and Binyon's 'For the Fallen' are the main sources. John Drinkwater provided such an 'Inscription for a War Memorial Fountain' in 1917:

They nothing feared whose names I celebrate.
Greater than death they died; and their estate
Is here on Cotswold comradely to live
Upon your lips in every draught I give[80]

The war memorial itself became an image after the war, and J.B. Salmond has a poem in Scots representing the thoughts of an ex-soldier at Ypres in 1928 ('Pilgrimage') at the Menin Gate memorial. His child wants to know if he killed any Germans, his wife is proud of his medals as he stands at the ceremony, but he himself thinks of the small details of the war:

The sangs, an' the mud, an' the claes,
An' my buits, an' yon glint through the haze
O' anither lad's bayonet, an' lichts
Makin' day o' the darkest o' nichts. . [81]

and most of all his lost friend, so that the poem reduces his very existence from a family, to man and wife, to himself aware only of loss.

In English poetry and elsewhere, books of collected verse became war memorials. Sometimes they contained very little in the way of war poetry – Robert W. Stirling's *Poems* include only eight lines 'written in the trenches'. It went into a second impression in 1916, however. Other memorial volumes sold well: the poetry and prose of William Noel Hodgson went into three editions and was reprinted in 1920. Two books may be examined as war memorials in their own right, however. Rupert Brooke's *1914 and Other Poems* first appeared in May 1915, reached its eighth impression by September, and was reprinted many times. The five 1914 poems are still well known, but the fact of the book, with its soft-tone pencil drawing of Brooke in profile (not in uniform, as so many of the others) furthered a sentimental image that maintained his position as the war poet. 'The Soldier', further, became the most familiar war poem for many. On the memorials as such, though, and at Remembrance Day services, the words of Laurence Binyon are usually read, and in 1917 Hodder & Stoughton produced a kind of bibliographic war memorial of his verse, just as it appeared on postcards. The question of reception (here in a literal sense too) is impossible to elucidate. The book has the title 'For the Fallen', is large octavo, hard-bound with a purple cover decorated in gold.[82]

It contains only twenty-eight unnumbered leaves of thick paper, with small colour illustrations tipped in. It contains the texts of three poems – 'For the Fallen', 'The Fourth of August', and 'To Women', on one side of the leaves only, in large lettering; a strophe per leaf. Binyon's most famous lines are there:

> They shall not grow old, as we that are left grow old:
> Age shall not weary them, nor the years condemn.
> At the going down of the sun and in the morning
> We will remember them.

But the last of the three poems is as significant: a war memorial, or a memorial volume such as this might well belong to a bereaved woman, and the last piece, after the reassurance that the dead will not be forgotten, and another that they were fighting for a just cause, is directed to women themselves, and the last lines in this large book of few words refer to their hearts, which are

> to bleed,
> To bear, to break, but not to fail!

When the war ended, a poem which appeared anonymously in *The Times* in November 1918 was scathing about the arrival of the German fleet at the Forth, and summed up the years of war in terms of this surrender:

> They'll rage like bulls sans reason or rhyme,
> And next day, as if 'twere a pantomime,
> They'll walk in like cows at milking time,
> On a grey November morning.
> We're four year's sick of the pestilent mob;
> – You've heard of our biblical *Battle in Gob?* –
> At times it was hardly a gentleman's job
> Of a grey November morning.[83]

The poet was Bridges, the Laureate. Elsewhere, a rather less well-known poet, one Antoni Lange, (a Pole with a Germanic name) writing in French dedicated a long piece to the victory and to France ('À La France'). Echoing the 'Marseillaise' he notes that

> il est arrivé enfin, le jour de gloire

but goes on to make the point that the victory in 1918 paid for the defeats at German hands, and renewed the lost glory of Napoleonic battles, before the shame of 1871:

> Le barbare Teuton
> Provoqua par son feu ta résurrection.
> C'est dans son bois sacré que Némesis farouche
> Décréta: à bas tout ce qui est faux et louche!
> De nouveau, au tocsin triomphal, éclata
> l'astre d'Ulm, d'Austerlitz, de Wagram, de Iéna.[84]

[the day of glory has come. . . The barbarous Teuton provoked your resurrection with his guns. Fierce Nemesis in the sacred wood decreed: down with all that is false or dubious. Once more, with the bells of victory shone out again the star of Ulm, of Austerlitz, of Wagram or of Jena.]

The attitude is of some interest, given that Nazi Germany would interpret the events of 1918 as the provocation for a reborn thousand-year Reich. In Germany and Austria in 1918–9, however, poets were now able to express their horror at the years of war,[85] and to look for new political paths:

> Vier Jahre hat die Welt der Knechte
> ihr Blut verspritzt fürs Kapital
> Jetzt steht sie auf zum ersten mal
> für eigne Freiheit, eigne Rechte.
> Germane, Römer, Jud' und Russ'
> in einem Bund zusammen –
> der Völker brüderlicher Kuss
> löscht alle Kriegesflammen.
> Jetzt gilts, die Freiheit aufzustellen.
> Die rote Fahne hoch, Rebellen![86]

[For four years the world of the underdogs has been shedding their blood for profit. Now that world is rising for the first time for her own freedom and rights. Germans, Romans, Jews, and Russians in one group – the brotherly kiss of the peoples puts out all the flames of war. Now it is time to put up freedom. Raise the red flag, rebels!]

Elsewhere, too, there were allusions to the profiteers. In 1919 Tom Clare performed his own and Greatrex Newman's 'What did you do in the Great War, Daddy', which runs through a series of people and their exploits in the recent war. Apart from the land-girl, the people involved all stayed civilians, either ladies who knitted useless garments, or who sang to wounded soldiers 'without an anaesthetic', or men who profited from munitions. They had not done their bit, but they had made their bit in the war, and fell to sighing and sobbing 'now that it was over'. Other monologues in the same tradition did, however, as early as 1919–20, indulge in a certain nostalgia for the soldiering (and sometimes for French girls).[87]

It was not until ten years after the war that the literary presentations of it came to appear: 1928, 1929, 1930, midway between two wars, saw the publication of novels by Remarque, Arnold Zweig, Richard Aldington, and the autobiographical works of Graves, Blunden and others, as well as, in 1931, the Blunden collection of Owen's poetry – although it was Brooke's portrait that decorated the modern anthologies more often as the poet of the war. There also appeared in that period, however, a series of epic pieces on the war in English, war poetry on the largest scale, and rarely considered because it is too large for the anthology form. Some of it is heroic. Sir Shane Leslie published in 1930 his *Jutland*, subtitled 'a fragment of an epic', a minute-by-minute poetic account of the battle of Jutland in rhymed verse in the style of Pope, a *tour de force* which is by no means unsuccesful:

> Upon the bridge of the *Invincible*
> Stood ship-compelling Hood, impassible
> Of tumult; calmly gleaning in his glass
> The shells that splash or shorten. . .[88]

Jutland, however, occupies a singular position in the history of the war, and Leslie's poem as a whole is not heroic, but fatalistic. It concludes:

> By Destiny is mockery made of Cause,
> And Man's events sink shattered with his Laws.

Other works have more limited themes. Horace Horsnell's autobiographical poem of around four thousand lines includes material from the war:

> The Yorks pour out the roses of their blood;
> The earth receives, and turns their red to mud.

The long day, loud with various alarms,
Crowns not with Victory their valiant arms:
And he who, fighting not, stands to the fray
May live to lose his life another day. . .[89]

The prize for sheer endurance must surely be held, however, by Angus Mills's *The Gamble of War*, a rhymed chronicle of the entire war, published in 1929 in Forfar. Mills's stated aim is to record the 'singular and plural' heroism of the war years in the manner of the romances. While not quite in the tradition of McGonagall, the rhyming is relentless and all-embracing, the text enormously detailed. Two small samples must suffice:

The Cathedrals of Old Senlis and Soisson,
Suffered amid the carnage of each town;
But Rheims, 'twas sadder still to look upon;
Contemptuous of her fabric's fair renown;
The vandal foe, his fiery deluge sent
On civil dwelling, tower, and monument.

and at the end of the war:

Great Allemagne was down, the terms she signed
Contained surrender of her high seas fleet;
Her naval bulwarks, numbers all defined,
In battleships, cruisers and destroyers complete.[90]

The work is almost 350 pages long, and is very much a local production, and the photographs which illustrate it show scenes from all the theatres of war, and also of the cenotaph in Whitehall and the war memorial in Forfar. This juxtaposition may cause a smile, but there is a justification in considering this work. The war touched every part of Britain as everywhere else. The importance of it was clear even to this poet, and the desire to record its events in verse form readily understood. However much the heroism is stressed, too, the last words consider whether the whole war was worth while. The question is not answered, but is left to God's judgement, while the poem concludes with a prayer for the League of Nations.

It is appropriate to leave the last comments on the war to the soldiers. In the final edition of *The Better Times* in December 1918, was a small anonymous poem called 'At Last', which deliberately avoids glorying in victory:

> No blatant music-hall refrain
> Or ill-timed boast of what we'd do
> To smash the Kaiser and his train,
> And then to 'Wind a Watch Up' too.
> Yet words which bridge four years of gloom
> Which made us doubt the sun could shine,
> Throughout the World the message boom: –
> Our Cavalry have crossed the Rhine.[91]

The same issue began with a quotation from the soldier's song that ended: 'no more soldiering for me'.

3

When This Bleeding War is Over
Songs of the First World War

Soldat allemand très bon coucher
Avec Madame français

Après la guerre fini
Anglais soldat parti
Mademoiselle in the family way
Après la guerre fini
[German and British, Western Front][1]

The songs of the First World War made as great an impact on as many people, at home and serving, as the poetry. Patriotism in any of its forms (aggressive or mocking), as well as sentimental declarations of love for country, sweetheart, or mother predominate in the commercial songs of all the combatant countries. The songs of the soldiers themselves were simple, memorable (and often still familiar) cathartic expressions of dissatisfaction with soldiering and the war. Lyrics grumbled about the system or the officers, or lack of comforts, drink, and women. There is some overlap between the commercial and the soldiers' songs in an age of emerging mechanical recording, but the songs all reflect the war, and supported the war effort by encouragement. In terms of poetic effect, clarity, memorability, and even in durability, many of the pieces involved have a greater claim to represent the war lyric than other texts. The music hall was alive, and concert-parties were popular and emotionally received even at the front. The Theatre Workshop's *Oh What a Lovely War*, especially in its film version, underscores the way in which many of the songs have become historical, however. We now hear a tragic irony in the patriotic songs and the others are left with their own irony and realism.[2]

It is appropriate to begin with the national anthems, although most predate the war. Their use, together with other patriotic songs established from the time of the Boer War, the Franco-Prussian War, or even earlier, was on an enormous scale, and they

were occasionally updated. James Elroy Flecker, writing patriotic
verse at the very end of his life in the first months of the war added
to 'God Save the King' the words:

> Grant him good Peace Divine,
> But if his Wars be Thine
> Flash on his Fighting Line
> Victory's Wing![3]

The German national anthem was sung at that time to the same
melody, although the nineteenth century verse 'Deutschland über
alles' (meaning 'Above all, a united Germany' and set to the
Haydn tune which became the national anthem after 1922) was
known. Indeed, one of the leaders of the 1916 Irish rising, Eamonn
Ceannt, adapted it with some fidelity to the original conception, as
'Ireland Over All', and it reminds us that there was a body of
lyrics in Ireland between 1914 and 1918 against England's war.[4]
The only official addition to the Austrian anthem itself during the
war was a verse referring to the new Emperor Karl and Empress
Zita in 1916, just as an addition to 'God Save the King' included
the Prince of Wales after the coronation of King George V.[5] The
point of Flecker's reworking is presumably that the first and only
well-known verse is insufficiently militaristic, especially compared
with the then German anthem, which does not invoke divine
assistance, but greets the monarch as *already* victorious:

> Heil Dir im Siegeskranz
> Herrscher des Vaterlands
> Heil, Kaiser, dir![6]

[Hail to thee in victory-wreath, lord of the Fatherland, hail, O
emperor!]

Other anthems (such as the 'Marseillaise') are military of
themselves, and marching is part of the text. Patriotic emotion
increased the force of any of these lyrics during the war, however.

Many established songs enjoyed renewed popularity. A volume
of patriotic songs which may be considered typical in Great Britain
was, for example, published by Charles Sheard. The one-shilling
booklet is not dated, but references in some of the lyrics and the
title, *British War Songs*, point to mild opportunism at the very
beginning of the war. Most of the songs predate the war, but the
volume is of documentary interest. Beside 'God Save the King' and

'Rule, Britannia' are several confident songs, of which two refer
specifically to the war. 'The Union Jack of Old England' ('Britain'
was a less common term in spite of the other members of the
union) comments that:

> we know not when the dread carnage may end. . .[7]

but the second verse points to the rout of the Kaiser as a *fait
accompli*, with an interesting allusion to 1871:

> The Kaiser set his back up fine and large,
> And dared to defy all once more;
> But he very soon found that he would not get off
> As cheap as he got off before.
> The Englishmen, Scotchmen and Irishmen there
> Soon sent all the Teutons double-quick to the rear. . .

A revised version of 'Three Cheers For the Red, White and Blue'
refers to a 'flagstaff awaiting in Germania' (the name is required
for a rhyme on Britannia) on which the Union Jack will fly, but
'Good News from the War' is an all-purpose piece written in 1896.
Others are linked with the Boer War. Of particular interest is the
emphasis on the assistance to be offered by the Commonwealth
('Mother England's Sons', 'It's the English-Speaking Race Against
the World'), and also on American participation. The publishing
firm was an Anglo-American one, and presumably the songs were
designed also to encourage an American involvement that came
only much later. It is significant that one of the songs included is a
piece again from the Boer War, called 'America Looking On', the
thrust of which is

> though America stands by, it's you she's standing by,

which had become appropriate again with the outbreak of the First
World War. Only one song – again from the Boer War – deals with
volunteering. 'Private Smith of the Volunteers' catalogues the
virtues of Smith in a Kiplingesque celebration of the ordinary
soldier. In 1914 it was eminently re-applicable to a new call for
volunteers, and the text instructs him on how to behave in war:

> If your cartridges gave out, grimy Smith!
> You'd give one defiant shout, baffled Smith!
> Then your teeth you'd firmly set

And you'd fix your bayonet,
And you'd send it home, you bet, tiger Smith!

The repetition of the name throughout makes its own point.

In 1914 even songs from the American Civil War were given new durability by the gramophone record, and one example exploited throughout the war was the song 'Just Before the Battle, Mother', which also appeared on postcards, the lyrics printed beneath a picture of a soldier with his mother hovering above him. Sentimental postcards of this type were common, and this particular song, which expresses in archaic vocabulary ('if I am numbered with the slain') the fairly obvious idea that the mother will not forget her son, was ripe for revival. The mothers shown on these postcards are usually disproportionately old, white-haired, frail ladies unlikely to have sons of nineteen, but who did have a stronger emotional appeal.[8]

France and Germany, too, used songs from earlier wars. Germany took up another nineteenth-century song which would be used widely again after the Nazi takeover, Max Schneckenburger's 'Die Wacht am Rhein' [The Watch On the Rhine], which contains notes of war in its opening:

Es braust ein Ruf wie Donnerhall
wie Schwertgeklirr und Wogenprall. . .[9]

and concludes with a refrain of confidence for the Fatherland:

Lieb Vaterland magst ruhig sein
fest steht und treu die Wacht am Rhein.

[A call roars out like thunder, like the clash of swords and the crash of the waves. . . Dear Fatherland, rest easy, the Watch on the Rhine stands firm and true.]

It was to be parodied in both wars in English and German; the watch on the Rhine would be wound up. In the period after Jutland a German adaptation mocked the fact that the fleet had not put out to sea for a very long time:

Lieb Vaterland magst ruhig sein
Die Flotte schläft im Hafen ein. . .[10]

[Dear Fatherland, rest easy, the fleet is dozing in the harbour. . .]

Commercial songs were used for recruiting. Many of the earlier songs in English stressed the motif of playing the game, and the best known of these is presumably 'We Don't Want to Lose You, But We Think You Ought to Go', the musical equivalent of the recruiting poster. The verse links war with the 'cricket and other kinds of game' that the women have watched the men play, and the refrain describes how the men will be welcomed back. The refrain of a less familiar song from 1915, however – 'We're Glad You've Got a Gun' – is worth considering:

> Ah, we're glad you've got a gun, lad, glad that you're a sport,
> There's time enough for other games, time enough to court;
> We're proud to see you ready, to do what must be done,
> Your only aim to 'play the game',
> We're glad you've got a gun.[11]

The verses develop the idea that the young man should make war, not love, the latter being no use 'if the clank of German sabres down your village street should ring'. The idea of war as a game is familiar, and the lyric 'we' are presumably the older and supposedly wiser. No reason is given for joining up, or rather, for *having* joined up, since the song is addressed to a soldier. There is only a vague reference to doing what must be done, and the phantom of German sabres in the village – not in the city – street. Such songs were very numerous indeed, and most are now curiosities. George R. Sims, for example, who wrote the once much-recited, but now forgotten, original of 'Christmas Day in the Workhouse' (which spawned a version which *is* still familiar in which the workhouse-master is told where to put his Christmas pudding) produced in 1914 an unlikely war song. It begins with an image of fairies dancing in the moonlight, and putting mortals beneath their spell. It becomes clear, however, that Puck, the 'little English elf', is post-Shakespearian:

> He is going to fight for England and he wants you ev'ry one
> To join the little army that is out against the Hun.[12]

The refrain is aimed at recruiting:

> Won't you join the army. . .
> Won't you, won't you, won't you, won't you come and join with me. . .

The addition of 'with me' draws the listener into a collusive fiction with the singer, who was probably a woman. M.R. Turner and A. Miall note that one of the lines is adapted from an earlier patriotic piece, and also that the music plays with the audience before it develops into a military two-step. The allusions to Puck (whose spells are a little ambiguous) and the echo of Lewis Carroll in the chorus ('won't you join the dance') are less than comfortable.

The role of women in English songs is essentially supportive. Lena Guilbert Ford and Phyllis Nash wrote in 1915 a song urging those at home to write to the soldiers, and 'Tommy's Mail Day' is made by a letter from his mother and sister saying how proud they are of him.[13] Usually the addressee of such songs is an unnamed and all-purpose sweetheart, sister or mother, and sometimes she is comforted, as in a song by Ivor Novello and Edward Teschemaker:

> Now Mollie, dear, oh don't you fear,
> And aren't you proud today,
> In khaki dressed he looks his best
> As everyone will say. . .[14]

Vanity recruiting was soon mocked by poets who experienced the reality which followed. Novello's best-known song, however, and probably the best-known English-language commercial piece of the war was 'Keep the Home Fires Burning', with words once again by Lena Guilbert Ford. It reassured the soldiers that the home fires still *would* be burning, and although the song is addressed ostensibly to those who have lost their 'lads', the soldiers could reassure themselves that there was indeed a silver lining to the dark clouds. The composition of the song in *tempo di marcia* meant that it could be used as a real march as well as an imitated one on stage. The verses are less well known than the familiar chorus; a 'nation in distress' calls, and

> we gave our glorious laddies;
> Honour bade us do no less.
> For no gallant son of England
> To a foreign yoke shall bend,
> And no Englishman is silent
> To the sacred call of Friend.[15]

Once again, the nature of that 'we' is unclear, and the men themselves, described *metri gratia* as 'glorious laddies', are treated as a kind of commodity, to be given away.

Patriotic songs in English stressed the necessity to fight in spite of parting from those loved, assured the soldiers that all would remain the same at home, and that they themselves were gallant and glorious, certain to defeat the enemy. A prize song, 'The Trumpet-Voice of Motherland is Calling', which won a hundred pounds for Albert W. Ketelby in 1914, contains all the ingredients: the trumpet calling to England (in spite of a Union flag on the sheet cover), a 'braggart madman' or 'Prussian prig' for whom one should not give a 'potsdam', Belgium, mothers, sweethearts, fame – and the assurance that 'right is might' without consideration of the possibility of a reversal of that sentiment.

Although the enemy is sometimes just 'the Hun', there are frequent references to the Kaiser. He is a braggart 'German War-Lord' in another song from 1914, 'Here's to the Day', which mocks the concept of 'der Tag', and carries the subtitle 'We've Got a Mailed Fist Too' on a cover depicting Jellicoe's flagship. There was a clear feeling that this was the Kaiser's war and he is mocked in cartoons, poetry, and songs (though prematurely in 'Belgium Put the Kibosh on the Kaiser'). The American show song 'When You're All Dressed Up and No Place to Go', copyrighted in 1913, was provided with additional material for British use and appeared in the Francis and Day songbook for 1917 with lines like:

> We are all at sea about the German War.
> How did it start, one asks, and what is it for?
> I'll tell you how, by heck! And you know it's so –
> The Kaiser was all dressed up and no place to go.[16]

The song predates the entry of the USA into the war, and criticizes Woodrow Wilson for his non-intervention policy as being 'too proud to fight' even though his army and navy are also 'all dressed up'. Further verses criticise Lord Haldane for pro-German statements. The song was included in one of the many albums still produced throughout the war of the best songs from individual publishing houses, beside such well-known songs such as 'A Broken Doll' or 'Every Little While'. Other songs also reflect the war, including a marching song which this time won a hundred-guinea prize in a competition run by the publisher. 'Taffy's Got His Jennie in Glamorgan' ('Ev'ry Tommy's Got a Girl Some-where') is not very original (it begins 'Tramp, tramp, British boys are marching'), but its theme is a reduction into stereotypes of the motif of the girl left behind. It reassured the soldier of her faithfulness, thus sustaining morale. The copyright is 1915, but its presence in a work which actually appeared in 1917 reminds us that lines like

> Cheer! cheer!
> Britain, Home and Beauty!
> Left, right, forward, what a game!
> All the rank and file
> Wear that sunny smile. . .

represented a commercial music standard not restricted to the early years. The collection even contains a comic song with reference to the war. Sam Mayo's 'The One-Man-Band' is a patter song with the mild sexual innuendo that typified certain music hall lyrics. Eve criticizes Adam for not being in the army, but unlike some of the unfortunates blackmailed by white feathers, Adam has an excuse:

> 'Oh why aren't you in khaki, pray?'
> . . .
> 'It's green fig leaves or none at all,
> For when leaves turn khaki, down they fall!'

Patriotism, sentiment, and reassurance are sometimes combined, as in the hundred-guinea specimen cited above. All aspects of the war could be reflected in music hall, musical shows, and even in pantomime. *Puss in Boots* at Drury Lane in 1916 – with text once again by George R. Sims – included a song praising the women who have given up demanding votes and have buckled to and taken on men's work. This was a major social effect of the war, and Sims notes the phenomenon of

> The smart little girl in blue
> Who snips your ticket
> At the railway wicket,
> And the girl who drives the motor too. . .[17]

The quality of verse may be low, and the adjective patronizing, but, as a social comment reflecting the war, lyrics of this sort (and the context) need noting.

Another major song publisher, Feldman, brought out an album

in 1918 with the same variety. 'There's a Ship That's Bound For Blighty' has as its motif the recurrent assurance that the war will end and all will be well, and 'When the Bells of Peace Are Ringing' could belong to the 1940s as well as 1918. 'Ten Days Leave' once again uses comic innuendo. The context of performance and reception must again be considered for songs like this, performed in music halls and heard – and presumably enjoyed – also by soldiers on leave. The humour does not mock the soldier nor the dead, but is often akin to that of Bairnsfather's Old Bill: rueful, resilient, and not reflective. 'Ten Days Leave' follows Tommy as he picks up a French girl, gets drunk, comments to a Salvation Army Captain that the latter is 'a long way from his billet', and attends a concert of songs so miserable that he wonders if he is at an inquest. But he goes back cheerfully, even if his advice to a would-be volunteer has a nice irony:

> His brother said, 'I'm joining up, because it is essential;
> Should I get in a Scotch or in an Irish regimental?'
> Said Tommy: 'If you're wise you'll try and get in the
> Prudential. . .'[18]

Commercial songs were designed, once the need for immediate recruitment was past, to sustain confidence – in British superiority and in the facts that the Kaiser was a figure of fun, dark clouds did have silver linings, and the home fires would be burning when the soldiers did come home. Sometimes they reflected events of the war, though not always real ones. The distortion of a fantasy story that turned eventually into the 'fact' of the Angels of Mons became the theme of a waltz. More realistically, Herbert Russell and Frank Lambert composed what is effectively a hymn for airmen in 1918 called 'Upward, Trusty Brothers' which contrasts with the ironic fatalism sometimes seen in the songs produced by members of the RFC themselves (though they, too, gloried in flight):

> Upward, trusty brothers!
> Angels guard your flight!
> Know what e'er betide you,
> God will guard the right.[19]

Given the survival rate for the early fighter pilots, one cannot but wonder how this was taken by those involved. Many popular song successes of the period had nothing to do with the war beyond the fact that they were taken up by soldiers and sometimes provided with new sets of words – 'If You Were the Only Girl in the World' or 'You Wore a Tulip' are illustrations. Theatres did make whole shows from the war, however, and the link with the Bairnsfather cartoons was made concrete when the Oxford Theatre put on in 1918 a show called *The Better 'Ole*, which contained not only a sentimental war song – 'From Someone in France to Someone in Somerset' – but also demotic pieces parallel to those composed by soldiers, 'I Wish I Was in Blighty' and 'I'm Sick of This 'Ere Blooming War'.[20]

Many commercial songs written for the music halls were adopted by soldiers and survived. In a collection with the title 'Songs That Won the War'[21] a few predate 1914, others date from the period of early enthusiasm. Thus 'The Army of Today's All Right' – is a comic song assuring the listener that the army can now be called complete since he, the singer, has joined. Like this, many are essentially recruiting songs, including some of the best known: 'Pack up Your Troubles in Your Old Kit Bag' (whose chorus Owen took as an ironic title) dates from 1915, and 'Here We Are Again' has a 1914 copyright, and expresses its early optimism with:

> ...when [Tommy's] walking through Berlin
>   He'll sing the anthem still,
>   He'll shove a Woodbine on and say
>   'How are you, Uncle Bill. . .'

Two songs signal the First World War to the modern mind. 'Tipperary' was actually written in 1912, and was sung even in the army before the war. A newspaper report on the arrival of the BEF in France mentioned it, and it sold well, becoming a standard in community singing. It is probably not quite true to claim globally that 'troops came to loathe it' or 'were nauseated by it'.[22] Doubtless it was heard too often, and became simply boring, but although its triviality seems inappropriate to the war in which it is now so firmly embedded, it became a war song just as much as any regimental march. Certainly, it was seen as such immediately after the war, and even earlier; in 1916 the cartoonist Captain Bruce Bairnsfather commented:

When Tommy went out to the Great War, he went smiling, and

singing the latest ditty of the halls. The enemy scowled. War, said his professors of kultur and his hymnsters of hate, could never be waged in the Tipperary spirit. . .[23]

The song as such tells of an Irishman wanting to return to his own country. But in its reception by soldiers from England in 1914 the emphasis was – as has been pointed out – on the farewell to Picadilly, Leicester Square, and so on, as well as on the abstracted notions of 'it's a long way to go' and 'my heart's right there'.

Linked with that song is another commercial favourite, usually dismissed for its banal lyrics, though in this case they are certainly war lyrics. 'Goodbyee' dates, however, from 1917, and became popular at the end of the war as a comic song. Only the first verse applied the *goodbyee* to someone leaving for war; the others refer to soldiers in comic situations, and the piling up of farewells is heightened comedy:

> Goodbye old things, cheerio, chin chin
> Napoo, toodleoo, goodbyee.

Yet the text contains references to convalescents and to a POW escaping. The reference to the silver lining ('in the sky-ee') mocks the genuine confidence of 'Keep the Home Fires Burning', and all in all it is more in the spirit of the song 'Oh it's a Lovely War', copyrighted in 1917.

Some of the songs most frequently sung in the war years predate 1914 quite considerably, yet still have a claim to be considered as lyrics of that war. One example is 'The Trumpeter', written in 1904 by J. Francis Barron and J. Airlie Dix. It achieved perhaps its greatest popularity in performance and recordings during the war, though it remained known in a version by Peter Dawson after the war. It may be considered in the light of a wartime recording, in which it was given a quasi-natural context by Raymond Newell and Ian Swinley.[24] Their recording opens with a conversation before battle, behind which the bugle call motif of the music is played. There is an inconsequential but cheerful conversation, which then gives way to the song itself, and after it is a hymn-like addition which asks the 'God of peace' to 'make all wars to cease'.

The lyric is not without literary value, and this may account for its lasting popularity. Unlike other evocations of the trumpeter (even Edward Thomas's 'The Trumpet'), this text condemns war by implication. The strophes are balanced, each one opening with a question to the trumpeter. The first call is the reveille, rousing men up – as songs rouse them – to be ready to fight. This is followed by the charge but, although the trumpeter urges the soldiers on, he remains aware of what is being faced, and suddenly comments

'And it's *Hell*', said the Trumpeter tall.

The early printed versions indicated that this line (which is outside the rhyme-scheme, although it gains effect from a delay called for by the music) was optional. By the time the song was performed in the First World War it was very much part of the effect.

The last call is faint, and the song voices the possibility of death as the trumpeter sounds the rally, to which not all will respond. In the wartime recording, the song is followed immediately by a roll-call in which many names go unanswered. The balance of the strophes and the development of the point in dramatic terms, as well as the dialogue between the trumpeter and a voice outside the poem, are all effective. Some of the diction is a little forced, with gratuitous elision and rustic forms ('my trumpet goes a-speakin''), and war as such is presented in terms of thundering hooves and flashing sabres – but this is countered by the sudden reference to war as hell. At the end, the summoning of the soldiers can refer to the survivors after battle or to the dead; the trumpeter sounding 'come home' anticipates Gabriel, who is referred to in the last line. The song is against war insofar as it presents a reality of death, and there is no indication of heroism in the piece. Within the song the general validity of the trumpeter's call is not questioned; there is no criticism of war leaders (as in Sassoon) or even of the futility (as in Owen). However, the absence of glory is not negligible; the enquirer may have been seeking a call to glorious battle at the beginning, but at the end he is aware that war is death. The development of the song sketches, in a sense, the course of poetic attitudes to the war: recruitment and arousal, awareness of war as hell, and then death. The fact of war is, however, not questioned; the soldier does not go beyond the simple

Trumpeter, what are you sounding now?

Elsewhere, the situation was similar. In French, a pre-war song that had not been particularly successful (and which originally had

74

little to do with the war and had less substance, even, than
'Tipperary') the unremarkable (if lively) 'Madelon', maintained its
popularity once the war had started right until the end (when there
was even a 'Madelon de la Victoire'). Beside the ready supply of
early 'death or glory' pieces Pierre Saka has noted an heroic strain
present throughout the war; he cites a song by R. Mercier which
treated the bloody defence of Verdun 'avec la plus belle
assurance'.[25] The verse varies the 'awake' motif nationalistically:

Mais tout à coup la coq gaulois claironne
Cocorico! Debout petit soldat. . .

[All at once the cockerel of France begins to sound, Cockadoodle
doo! Up, a little soldier. . .]

but it ends with a more serious couplet:

Le soleil luit, partout le canon tonne
Jeunes héros voici le grand combat

[The sun is up, the guns are roaring, young heroes, here is the
great battle]

and the refrain uses the slogan of that battle:

Et Verdun, la victorieuse
Pousse un cri qui porte la bas
Les échos des bords de la Meuse
Halte-là! On ne passe pas!

declaring to the barbarians at the gates

C'est ici la porte de France
Et vous ne passerez pas!

[Verdun, the victorious one lets out a shout which carries as far
as the Meuse! Stop! They shall not pass! . . .This is the gateway
of France, and you will not pass it!]

Germany, too, produced at the beginning of the war songs
reflecting the 'hurrah-patriotism' seen in poetry. Some simply
praised the military, as in the much-parodied show song:

Der Soldate, der Soldate,
ist der schönste Mann bei uns im Staate
Drum schwärmen auch die Mädchen sehr
für das liebe, liebe, liebe Militär. . .[26]

[The soldier, the soldier, is the finest man in all our land; and that's why all the girls are crazy about the lovely, lovely, lovely military man. . .]

If the initial resistance by Belgium had looked as if it would put the kibosh on the Kaiser, the eventual German victories under General von Emmich and his staff officer, Ludendorff, were celebrated fully. A Catholic priest produced a song about the fall of Liege at the beginning of August, in which Liege is seen as a woman embraced by Emmich, taken by force (but giving in) although she had once wanted to marry someone else – a Frenchman. The only superficially averted rape imagery is of some interest:

> Herr von Emmich mag nicht spassen
> Tat sie um die Taille fassen;
> Fraulein Lüttich schrie vor Lust,
> Und sie hat sich ihm ergeben
> In dem Jahr, in dem wir leben,
> An dem siebenten August.

[But von Emmich isn't in a joking mood, and took her by the waist; Miss Liege cried out with delight, and surrendered herself to him in the year in which we are living, on the seventh of August.]

The position with America was somewhat different. The popular musical theatre was used as a platform to encourage entry into the war, especially after the sinking of the *Lusitania*, and performers like Harry Lauder went on propaganda tours, although with limited success.[27] But Woodrow Wilson was re-elected in 1916 with the claim 'he kept us out of the war'. Ian Whitcomb has pointed out that the composers of popular songs in America concentrated until 1917 on the inevitable songs of Dixie. Certainly, American commercial songs were sung to and by soldiers in Europe, including even 'I Didn't Raise My Boy to be a Soldier' (which was scorned by Theodore Roosevelt and later changed to 'I'm Glad. . .').[28] When the United States did enter the war, the patriotism that had flourished in Europe earlier reappeared, and once again a popular song gave rise to a catch-phrase in George M. Cohan's 'Over There' – 'We won't be back till it's over over there'. Claims have been made for a printing of over five million copies for that work.[29] Songs spoke of knocking the hell out of Heligoland, or

76

– in anticipation of a later work – of hanging the clothes on the Hindenburg line. Major songwriters such as Irving Berlin found themselves in the army (some, like Cole Porter, had volunteered earlier) and wrote songs reflecting not only the mood of patriotism but also the soldiers' grumbles about their situation, in camp if not in the trenches ('Oh How I Hate to Get Up in the Morning'). Berlin's military show in June 1918 ended its run with the cast marching out to embark to the tune of 'We're On Our Way to France', a curiously theatrical, though genuinely emotional, echo of the mood of 1914 in a war that was nearly over.[30]

It is not always clear to what extent commercial songs of any country influenced the soldiers, although music hall songs enjoyed great currency, even if new words were provided for many from time to time. Music hall entertainers visited the troops, who responded with enthusiasm, and Harry Lauder, whose son had been killed in 1916, describes performing under fire.[31] The soldiers' own songs constitute one of the most important, if neglected, areas of war poetry. The combination of lyric and melody is important, and in many cases the melody is still known. Hymns and folk-songs were adapted, and so were popular tunes which still survive in their own right. 'What a Friend We Have in Jesus', 'If You Were the Only Girl in the World', 'Sous les Ponts de Paris', 'Loch Lomond', 'Morgenrot' and 'Muss i denn' all acquired new texts. The lyrics were a response to the war from within, and frequently made their point in a memorable and concise fashion, or with a sentimentality which is not excessive because it is applied to themes well able to support it, like longing for home, or fearing death. Soldiers' songs offer the most functional of all war poetry. The commercial songs have a limited role in their encouragement to enlist, but the songs of the soldiers bore the burden of sustaining and cheering in a situation that was, for anyone not involved, genuinely unbelievable. The adaptation of the popular songs 'They'll Never Believe Me' (of the beauty of the sweetheart) to apply to the horrors of the trenches is hardly surprising.

The songs sung by the soldiers fall into a number of categories: they could be patriotic, not in the general sense of stressing a concept of nation, but at least of asserting the superiority of their forces over the enemy; they could be sentimental, looking back to the homeland; perhaps, most important, they could relieve feelings either by verbal attacks on immediate superiors, or on the conditions under which they lived. Horrors are coped with by being put into words, and the songs also express a general desire to see the end of army life. The last category would include, of course, songs about all aspects of soldiering, with emphasis on drinking, sex, and simply being there.

Many of the lyrics borrow their structure from earlier pieces. Sometimes these are folk and patriotic songs (such as 'Rule, Britannia'), but it is hardly surprising that music hall pieces and hymns are the favourite sources. The latter were known at home and in the rituals of church parade, and the postcard verses of the war included, too, illustrated versions of hymns placed into a wartime context. At the beginning of the war a set of cards printed the three verses of Wesley's 'Jesu, Lover of My Soul'. The first verse is beneath a picture of a young soldier (complete with an unlikely sword) praying before battle. The second accompanies a picture of a very young wounded soldier illuminated by a kind of spotlight on a very tidy battlefield, his head cradled by a spotless Red Cross nurse. The final verse has a picture of the young man, cleanly bandaged – no blood is visible in any of the pictures – attended by another spotless nurse, who is reading the Bible to him. The images have a comforting eroticism: the nurses are pretty, the soldier handsome and not obviously wounded. The Lord will provide each mildly wounded man with his own Red Cross nurse. That particular hymn seems not to have been adapted, but other favourite pieces were either provided with entirely new or with largely different words.[32]

Music hall songs were themselves adapted, and even 'Tipperary' was treated in a mildly risque manner:

> That's the wrong way
> To tickle Marie. . .[33]

'Apres la guerre fini', (which has as an alternative line 'Mam'selle Français beaucoup picanninies') is based on a French music hall tune that was a commercial success in 1914, 'Sous les Ponts de Paris'.[34] The popular show tune 'If You Were the Only Girl in the World' gave rise to 'If You were the Only Boche in the Trench/And I had the only bomb', a parody which is more grimly realistic than most. Here, as elsewhere, the tension between the sentiments of the original and that of the recasting makes a point of its own. 'When You Wore a Tulip' uses the acoustic relation between tulip and tunic, and some of the phrases of the original, most notably the 'I' and 'You' juxtaposition to transform a tuneful love song into a war song that is an indictment by the soldier of those who were not involved:

> I wore a tunic, a dirty khaki tunic
> And you wore your civvie clothes.
> We fought and bled at Loos, while you were on the booze,
> The booze no one here knows.
> Oh, you were with the wenches, while we were in the trenches
> Facing an angry foe.
> Oh, you were a-slacking, while we were attacking
> The Germans on the Menin Road.[35]

The contrast between the man serving and the 'slacker' is stark and bitter, and like some poetry it uses specific names – Loos, the Menin Road – clearly setting it in the Ypres campaigns. The name Loos evokes 'booze', providing first a contrast and then a grievance of the situation at the front itself. The present tense is important and gives an actuality to the indictment. Not every adaptation is as effective, and others that are effective cannot be classified as war lyrics apart from the fact that they came into existence during the war. The revisions of George Sims's unfortunate 'In the Workhouse Christmas Day' are inventive, and the 'harem' version plays neatly on the literal understanding of a familiar expletive ('balls!') even if it was customarily avoided in actual singing, thereby drawing attention to the word. Finally, commercial war songs could themselves be parodied. 'Pack Up Your Troubles' was revised with reference, for example, to the lice in the trenches, with the advice:

> Wrap both your elbows up around your back
> And scratch, scratch, scratch. . .[36]

More significantly, 'We Don't Want to Lose You' provoked a well-deserved response:

> Now we don't want to hurry you
> But it's time you ought to go,
> For your songs and your speeches
> They bore us so.
> Your coaxings and pettings

Drive us nigh insane:
Oh! We hate you and'll boo and hiss you
If you sing it again.[37]

National differences in soldiers' war lyrics are only of degree. The self-irony of some of the English songs is less common elsewhere, and German collections show a wider range of military pieces than elsewhere. Some of the soldiers' songs express very simply the superiority of the singer's army over that of the enemy:

Unser Wilhelm hat gesagt
Lasst sie uns nur kommen.
Deutscher Michel hast du das
Denn noch nicht vernommen?
Steckt sie alle in den Sack
Russen und Franzosen
England und das Belgierpack,
Klopf sie auf die Hosen![38]

[Our William has said, let them all come! Spirit of Germany did you hear? Catch them all and put them in the bag, Russians, French, England and the Belgian rabble, beat the seats of their pants!]

Others, though, were more pointed:

England, du schlechtes England,
Du machst so was, das ist kein Spass,
Dum-Dum-Geschoss tust' fabrizier'n
. . .
Wart nur, wart, du Seepirat
Die Straf' wird hart.[39]

[England, you wretched England, what you are doing is no joke, making dum-dum-bullets. . . wait, you pirate, there'll be a hard reckoning.]

In English, the frequent and lively abuse was aimed at the Kaiser more often than at the enemy:

Poor Kaiser Bill is feeling ill,
The Crown Prince he's gone barmy.
And we don't care a fuck
For old von Kluck
And all his bleedin' great army.[40]

80

The name of the German Commander at the Marne was too happy
a concidence to miss that particular rhyme. Self-mockery appears
in a verse set to the tune of 'The Church's One Foundation', the
first lines of which vary to cover all branches of the services
(*Tommy's Tunes* contains seven versions, the *Airman's Songbook*
several more):

> We are Fred Karno's army
> The ragtime infantry.
> We cannot fight, we cannot march,
> What bleeding use are we?
> And when we get to Berlin
> The Kaiser he will say,
> Hoch hoch mein Gott
> What a jolly rotten lot
> Are the ragtime infantry.[41]

Karno was a comedian whose act was based on the idea of general
incompetence; his troupe included at one time Charlie Chaplin,
who appears himself as commander of the army in one version. It
will be noted that however incompetent, the supposition is that
they will still take Berlin, and in some texts the Kaiser praises the
ragtime army. Worthy of note is the contrast again between the
solemnity of the tune and the joviality of the attitude expressed. A
different tone is found in an ANZAC version, however, which
makes a serious point:

> We are the only heroes
> Who stormed the Dardanelles,
> And when we get to Berlin
> They'll say 'what bally sells!'
> You boast and spite from morn to night
> And think you're very brave,
> But the men who really did the job
> Are dead and in their grave.

The enormous ANZAC losses at the Dardanelles (and the strategic
inadequacies that caused those losses) are treated with a justified
bitterness. Songs reflected the war on all fronts, and there are
pieces which refer to Allenby, for example, containing slang Arabic
picked up in Palestine.[42]

German songs adopted, too, the tone of professed incompetence, however, once in the same rhythm as that of 'Fred Karno's Army':

> Wir sind die lust'gen Brüder
> Von der MG-Kompagnie.
> Und wenn wir exerzieren,
> Dann stimmt die Richtung nie.
>
> . . .
>
> Wir haben zwei Paar Stiefel
> Da ist kein Absatz dran
> Und wenn wir exerzieren
> Zieh'n wir Pantoffeln an.[43]

[We are the merry lads of the machine-gun crew, and when we are drilling we never get our aim right. . . We have two pairs of boots, but they are so down-at-heel that when we are drilling we put slippers on.]

Songs in English are very often critical of army life. Such songs could refer to the immediate superior, and it is highly significant in the first case cited here that the word 'sergeant' was interchangable with 'Kaiser':

> We haven't seen the sergeant for a hell of a time.[44]

and:

> You've got a kind face, you old bastard
> You ought to be bloody well shot. . .

and, with very many variations:

> If the sergeant steals your beer, never mind

or to higher officers:

> One staff-officer jumped over
>   another staff-officer's back. . .

or to the actual commanders:

> Jean de Nivelle
> Nous a nivelé
> Marchand
> Nous a marchandé. . .[45]

[Nivelle has worn us down, Marchand has sold us up the river. . .]

or to the men perceived to be behind the war:

> Wir kämpfen nicht fürs Vaterland
> Wir kämpfen nicht für Gott
> Wir kämpfen für die reichen Leut',
> Die Armen schiesst man tot. . .[46]

[We are not fighting for the fatherland, nor are we fighting for God; we are fighting for the rich folk, the poor ones all get shot dead. . .]

Life in the trenches was another target, although some details are no longer immediate, as in references to the inevitability of plum and apple jam in English or to other sorts of jam in German songs. One brief song sums up the whole of the English trench experience concisely and ironically:

> I like to hear the news from the Dardanelles
> I like to hear the whistle of the Alleyman's shells.
> I like to hear the rifle fire,
> I like to see the blinking Alleymans retire.
> I like to hear the click-click of the spade and pick
> (The French they are no bon)
> Look out, look out, the gas clouds are coming:
> Go get your respirator on.[47]

or from the other side:

> Es gibt kein schöner Leben, als in den Schützengräben
> Vor dem Feind zu liegen, Tag und Nacht.
> Wenn die Kugeln singen und Granaten springen,
> Dass die ganze Gegend ringsum kracht. . . .
>
> Keine Federbetten, keine Toiletten
> Und des Kriegers taglicher Bedarf,
> Wer sich will rasieren, braucht nur gehn spazieren,
> Den rasiert sogleich der Russe scharf. . .[48]

[There's no finer life than in the trenches, in face of the enemy day and night. The bullets sing and shells explode so all around is noise. . . . No beds and no toilets and the daily needs of the fighting man, if anyone needs a shave he just needs to pop out, and a Russian sharpshooter will shave him right away. . .]

American songs were milder, and looked at the problems of training:

> They took him on the parade ground
> To march, to rush, to crawl,
> The first was bad, the second was worse,
> The third was worst of all. . .[49]

It may be noted that this verse is couched in objective terms, rather than coming from the mouth of the soldier himself, and lacks spontaneity.

Drinking and sex are regular themes. The two songs cited at the head of this chapter – one from each side of the trenches, both in pidgin French – give an idea of the preoccupation of the soldier, and the French 'Cri du Poilu' has the much-repeated chorus: 'une femme!' Many of the songs were obscene, and are usually omitted from printed collections. It is a comment on the history of taste that criticism was levelled at novels in particular for using four-letter words, when their real theme was killing and wounding on a massive scale. Brophy and Partridge's collection from 1930 contains the tantalizing entry:

Mother Hunt
An eight-line snatch more witty than the run of soldiers' songs. But this gay and ribald commentary upon an old lady's misfortunes can hardly be printed here.[50]

One lyric of the First World War that remained well known through another war documents the career of 'Mademoiselle from Armentières', who hadn't been kissed for forty years. That verb is unlikely to have been the original one, and Brophy and Partridge leave a gap. They also comment that the melody is that of a French music hall tune. There are a great many variations on what is effectively a rhymed couplet with the first line repeated twice (interspersed with the refrain 'parley-voo') and almost unlimited extension, as also with 'The Quartermaster's Stores', where the format is, if anything, simpler still. The song could in one version provide a catalogue of places of the war, now sometimes requiring a gloss:

> Mademoiselle from dear old Pop. . .

referring to Poperinghe, which has not remained familiar. In another it could merely refer to the soldier's interest in the wine purveyed by the lady of the title (with echoes of 'La Madelon'), or indeed, in her daughter. It could also become an objective narrative of the activities of the enemy:

> A German officer crossed the Rhine
> skiboo! (parley-voo!)

Sometimes three officers were involved with the women and the wine, but once again the enemy was interchangeable with the superior officer:

> The sergeant-major's having a time
> (parley-voo!)

The same format, rigid yet versatile, was used for critical comments of all kinds, including a familiar one:

> The general got the croix de guerre
> (parley-voo!)
> And the son-of-a-gun was never there. . .

'Son-of-a-gun' is again a print avoidance.[51]

Songs often covered several themes. There were a number of blues concerned with the First World War, making the point that blacks were drafted, but were not given benefits of citizenship, and one comments, too, on the sexual situation. The blues form in its typical twelve-bar shape repeats the first unit, and the second responds to, or counters the first:

> The women in France hollerin',
> I no compris. . .
> Women in America hollerin',
> 'Who wants me?'[52]

That same song, 'Trench Blues', is at times defiant:

> We went to Berlin,
> Went with all our will. . .
> Lord if the whites don't get him
> The niggers certainly will. . .

'He' is the Kaiser, who is named in other verses, and over whom triumph is proclaimed at the end of the song. But it ends:

Wind a-blowin',
Big bell sadly tone. . .
Many a soldier, Lord,
Is dead and gone.

Certain extremely well-known songs merit special attention as
war lyrics, reflecting different aspects of war. None has a known
author, and all exist in different versions. All of them ask questions
overtly or implicitly about the nature of war, but they are rarely
included in anthologies. They represent the worm's-eye view, that
of the soldier who questions the war neither morally nor politically,
but wishes it would end so that he can go home.

Arguably, one of the best-known English war songs is that set to
the hymn tune 'What a Friend We Have in Jesus'. The tune itself
has a powerful melodic line and an expressive rhythmic pattern
which doubtless encouraged soldiers to adapt the existing words.
During the First World War new lyrics set up a tension between
their own irony and the knowledge of the actual text. Probably the
best-known version runs:

When this bleeding war is over
Oh how happy I shall be,
When this bleeding war is over,
No more soldiering for me.
No more church parades on Sunday,
No more queuing for a pass,
You can tell the sergeant major
To stick his passes on the wall.[53]

The avoidance of the rhyme in the last line is traditional, again
making the real rhyme even clearer. The reference to church
parades is a nice link with the hymn, something exploited in the
film of *Oh What a Lovely War*, although there a different version was
used. That alternative version has a gentler but surrealistic
humour:

When this bleeding war is over
Oh how happy I shall be
When I get my civvy clothes on,
No more soldiering for me.
No more church parades on Sunday
No more putting in for leave

I shall kiss the sergeant major
How I'll miss him, how he'll grieve!

Yet another version has as its second couplet the confident:

When this ruddy war is over
And we come back from Germany. . .

The rhymic emphasis on the first word in the hymn is still emphasized by the dotted quaver: *when*. The lyrics express dissatisfaction with the war and with the pettiness imposed by the immediate superior, but it does not raise larger questions of right or wrong, nor criticize leaders, nor the enemy. The song has a symbolic significance, in that it is a displacement of a religion that was finished by the experience of the trenches for a great many. Although all kinds of details are mentioned, church parade is the one constant in all versions, even in the Second World War.

It is possible that the opening phrase owes something to the American Civil War, in which 'by far the most popular sweetheart separation song' on both sides was called 'Weeping, Sad and Lonely', also known as 'When This Cruel War is Over'. Charles Carroll Sawyer's words (the music was by Henry Tucker) are interesting in that they admitted small substitutions (of blue for gray, for example), to be appropriate for either army.[54] The song itself spawned parodies ('When This Cruel Draft is Over') and imitations, one by Stephen Foster, with lyrics by George Cooper, which was again sentimental, but in which the rhythm matches the First World War piece well:

When this dreadful war is ended
I will come to you again. . .

There is also, it must be added, a flavour here of the boarding-school song:

This time next week where shall I be?
Not in this academy. . .

The adjective applied to war varies. In the older American songs, war is cruel or dreadful, and this is mirrored in English texts sung as 'When this lousy war is over', a nice choice in the context, and clearly pejorative, as is 'rotten'. Alternatives are 'blasted', 'bloomin'', 'ruddy' (avoidances for 'bloody'), and the very common 'bleeding'. It can be assumed that the other common adjective was also employed, although all of the abusive adjectives lose effect by the fact that they were employed, as has been pointed out, simply as neutral linguistic indicators, implying nothing much more than that a noun comes next.

Quotation of the text in a trench newspaper of December 1918 and an anonymous postcard printed during the war also bear witness to the familiarity of the piece, and to the way in which comic bitterness merged into a diluted end-of-term feeling. The card is headed 'Battalion National Anthem', and lists in five strophes the unpleasant tasks that will be no more. It has one or two additional interesting points: after the war

> NCOs will then be navvies
> Privates own their motor cars.[55]

Irving Berlin played on this class reversal after the war in 'I've Got My Captain Working for Me Now', and the point was made seriously in novels. Socially even more significant here are the lines

> When next the country has a war on
> We'll find a job that brings more pay.

The verses end with an attack on those who promised fame and glory in the war, none of which the ordinary soldiers have seen. Nevertheless, there is still a promise that when the Kaiser has been defeated the troops will sing this song:

> When we've finished with the Kaiser
> At the Palace we shall sing
> THE BATTALION NATIONAL ANTHEM
> Twice a night. God save the King.

The first strophe makes the derivation clear, however, even if the lines are rearranged, the words are now generalized to 'we', losing some of the personal feeling of other versions, and the adjective for war is a new one:

> When we get our civil clothes on,
> Oh how happy we shall be.
> When this gory war is over
> No more soldiering for me.

The English tradition contained many songs making it even

more specific that the soldier wished to be somewhere else:

> Far far from Wipers [Ypres] I long to be
> Where German snipers can't bother me. . .[56]

Or (with ironical relation to the American Civil War tune 'Tramp, Tramp, Tramp the Boys Are Marching' in the melody):

> I don't want to be a soldier
> I don't want to go to war
> I'd rather stay at home,
> Around the streets to roam
> Living on the earnings of a — —

The last words are either 'lady typist' or (making the avoidance of the real rhyme word even more narrow) 'high-born-lady'. Clearer still is the declaration 'I don't want me bollocks shot away', but perhaps clearest of all is:

> Oh my, I don't want to die
> I want to go home. . .

The song was adapted in the Second World War, as indeed were most, given that their message is generally applicable, and that by putting feelings into words they help make the situation bearable.

The many popular songs in the period of the First World War which ask that the singer be taken back to Dixie were modified, too, with 'Dixie' being replaced by 'Blighty'.[57] It is possible to form a picture of life in the trenches from soldiers' doggerel: 'Nobody knows how tired we are/ And nobody seems to care', 'Hush, here comes a whizz-bang', 'Apple and Plum', 'Bombed (gassed) last night and bombed the night before. . .' A German soldiers' song, too, made the point very clearly that being killed was an absolute, and that it did not matter much how and why and for what:

> Lieg ich einst im Massengrab
> Ist mir alles schuppe
> Ob ich einen Zug geführt
> Oder eine Gruppe. . .[58]

[If I finish up in a mass-grave I don't give a toss whether I commanded a company or a troop. . .]

Another well-known German song is located in the Argonne Forest, not far from Verdun. 'Argonnerwald um Mitternacht'

[Midnight in the Argonne Forest] was sung from 1914, based on a song referring to Kiau-Tchou,[59] and various versions exist. In contrast to the French song of Craonne this earlier piece has some nationalistic elements, although they are essentially sentimental:

> Argonnerwald, um Mitternacht
> Ein Pionier stand auf der Wacht.
> Ein Sternlein hoch am Himmel stand
> Bringt ihm ein Gruss aus fernem Heimatland.

[Argonne Forest, midnight: a Pioneer stood guard. A star high in the skies brought him a greeting from his distant home.]

This static picture develops into a narrative of battle, which soon changes to the present tense. Here an enemy is mentioned:

> Granaten schlagen bei uns ein
> Der Franzmann will in unsere Stellung ein. . .

[Shells burst upon us, the Froggies want to take our trench. . .]

Franzmann is a normal slang designation and is not expanded. The bravery of the German soldiers is stressed in a strophe that is, however, not always present, and which can be replaced by one describing the entry of a soldier into heaven. The last strophe, however, is frequently cited independently, and is elegaic:

> Argonnerwald, Argonnerwald
> Ein stiller Friedhof wirst du bald.
> In deiner kühlen Erde ruht
> So manches tapfere Soldatenblut.

[Argonne Forest, Argonne Forest, you will soon be a quiet graveyard; in your cool earth rests the blood of many a brave soldier.]

Some versions have 'Heldenblut' (hero's blood) in the last strophe, and the Pioneer is also variable. After the war the song was adapted to refer to the struggle of the Spartacists, but in its original version it is noteworthy that the climax is the death of the soldiers. German songs adapting the folk-song 'Morgenrot' stress this as well; the patriotic element is not forced and included only in farewell. A version from 1918 begins:

> Abendrot, Abendrot
> Leucht' es mir zum frühen Tod.

Vieles Blut ist schon vergossen,
Ach, wie liegen sie geschossen
Auf dem weiten Leichenfeld. . .[60]

[Sunset, sunset, lights me to an early death. So much blood has already been spilled, oh how they lie shot down on the field of corpses. . .]

Close to this in English is the song given by Brophy and Partridge the title 'The Old Barbed Wire', which consists of a series of questions and answers – if you want to find the sergeant, the quartermaster, the sergeant-major and the CO, they are, variously, lying on the canteen floor, miles behind the line, boozing up the privates' rum, and down in the deep dugouts. The last verse forms a bitter contrast, however:

If you want to find the old batallion
I know where they are
They're hanging on the old barbed wire.
I've seen 'em, I've seen 'em,
Hanging on the old barbed wire. . .[61]

Perhaps the most bitter in its reflection of reality and of the war as such, and of great importance, is the French 'Chanson de Craonne', [Song of Craonne], described as a 'rare example of a song produced from a collective and spontaneous inspiration', and banned for a long time. It was based upon the tune of a sentimental waltz by Adelmar Sablon, 'Bonsoir m'amour' [Goodnight My Love].[62] The song of Craonne, which the French took in May 1917, attacks the insistence by Nivelle on continuing to hurl troops against the German lines in the Aisne campaign on the Chemin des Dames. The song is a protest, and the verses contain phrases like 'c'est bien fini' (it's all over), as well as inviting 'messieurs les gros' (the big boys) to take their turn; if they want to make war, they should pay with *their* skins. The chorus is a general indictment of the cannon-fodder mentality:

Adieu la vie,
Adieu l'amour,
Adieu à toutes les femmes.
C'est bien fini,
C'est pour toujours
De cette guerre infame.

91

C'est à Craonne
Sur le plateau
Qu'on doit laisser sa peau
Car nous sommes tous condamnés,
Nous sommes les sacrificiés.

[Farewell life, farewell love, farewell all the women. It's over forever with this wretched war. At Craonne, on the plain we have to lose the lot, for we are all condemned, we are the sacrifices.]

Objective adaptation was possible ('Qu'ils ont laisse . . . ils sont tous condamnés, ce sont les sacrificiés'), but the basic version has the force of involvement. The devices used are simple but effective: the repeated 'Adieu', and the general finality of 'C'est pour toujours' is picked up and given a specific sense of place in 'C'est à Craonne', the name giving for the modern ear a reality to the piece which is not affected by the fact that the place is not now easily identified. There is, finally, no ambiguity at all about the notions of men condemned or sacrificed.

Equally worthy of consideration as war poetry is a song from a different culture which questions the nature of war with an interesting image. The Polish song 'Wojenka' [Madame War] admits no enemies but war itself. It originated in the Polish legions after 1915 and has a simplicity not unlike 'Where Have All the Flowers Gone'. It was sung by Polish forces in both wars, and exists in different forms, with extra verses sometimes added.

Wojenko, wojenko, cóżeś ty za pani?
Że za ciebie idą
chłopcy malowani. . .

Wojenko, wojenko, szanuj swych rycerzy:
Kto ciebie pokocha
W krótce w grobie leży!

W zimnym grobie leży, zdala od rodziny,
A po nim zostaje
Cichy płacz dziewczyny.[63]

[War, war, what kind of fine lady are you, that young men in the bloom of youth go after you? War, war, take care of your warriors: whoever loves you will soon be in a grave, lying in the cold grave far from his family; and left behind a girl is weeping.]

In a significant variant, the verb 'to go' is replaced by *giną* 'perish', making the image of destruction more forceful. War is seen to be inexplicable but irresistible. Some versions of the song add to the elegaic conclusion a more vigorous marching element, although it seems likely that this is a later addition:

> Maszeruje wiara, pot się krwawy leje,
> Raz, dwa, stapąj bracie
> To tak Polska grzeje!

[Faith marches on, blood and sweat flows, One, two, stamp, brothers, that keeps Poland warm.]

The image of the elusive lady pursued by all the young men is an evocative one, even ambiguous; but the addition does not fit the context.

Other songs look at the nature of war. The enemy may be referred to, usually in slang form as Boche, Alleyman, and so on, but is rarely described. The soldiers coped with their immediate situation in various ways, however, often with a comic-ironic (but vocal) resignation. In the British trenches an adaptation of a 1913 sentimental song by Harry Dent and Tom Goldburn, advised 'never mind' in all cases:

> If the sergeant steals your rum
> Never mind![64]

or far worse

> When old Jerry shells your trench
> Never mind!

a situation rather different from the broken heart occasion of the original song. The trench newspaper *The 'New Church' Times*, which succeded the *Wipers Times* printed in May 1916 a version with the heading 'Minor Worries' which began:

> If the Hun lets off some gas
> Never mind!

and continued to enumerate a whole range of possible misfortunes:

If your trench is mud knee-high. . .
If you're whizzbanged day and night. . .
If a sniper has you set. . .

and so on. Songs like this underscore the impotence of the ordinary soldier. A German song, cited in a work of the Second World War, expresses the point more philosophically, emphasizing the fact that the situation in which the men found themselves could simply not be changed:

In dem Bache schwimmt ein Fischlein
Das ist glücklicher als ich.
Glücklich ist, wer das vergisst
Was nun einmal nicht zu ändern ist.[65]

[In the streamlet swims a fish, and he is happier than me. You are happy if you can forget about things you can't change anyway.]

Sometimes, this impotence brought about a reduction of the poetic expression to a minimum, even to the level of simple repetitive nonsense ('I shall be whiter than the whitewash on the wall. . .'), and Erich Maria Remarque's comment that the patriotism of the ordinary soldier lay in the fact alone that he was there was expressed in songs with ever-recurrent lyrics, of which

We're here because we're here because we're here
because we're here. . .[66]

is the best known. This is not a nonsense piece, however, and gains effect from the tune, since it is sung to 'Auld Lang Syne', used at the end of things – a dance, or a year. The monotony of the repeated 'we're here because we're here' short-circuits any questions of responsibility and focuses entirely on a situation that could not be changed by the individual. It also short-circuits poetic considerations, but it was sung very widely, and summed up the situation of the greatest number of soldiers, while taking the poetic form beyond the memorable to the deliberately unforgettable.

The home fronts on both sides, too, had songs other than those produced for the halls or for recording, and one from Ireland (and perhaps therefore with an additional edge) exists in versions which indicate sympathy for the volunteers on the one hand and attack the notion of fighting for Britain on the other. Those verses of the song that are not, in fact, directed specifically against the war have an elegaic tone, a home-front response far from the rousing send-offs or the promises that the home fires will still be burning. The song is known as 'Salonika':

> Me husband's in Salonika
> I wonder if he's dead?
> I wonder if he knows he has
> A kid with a foxy head?
> . . .
> When the war is over
> What will the slackers do?
> They'll be all around the soldiers
> For the loan of a bob or two. . .[67]

Other verses are obscene. Variant verses of the kind attacking the war include:

> They taxed our pound of butter
> And they taxed our ha'penny bun
> But still for all their taxes
> They can't beat the bloody Hun. . .

There are many songs in Germany, most notably at the end of the war, which make directly anti-war points. Usually they are adaptations, and the most effective are those which attack pro-war propaganda by using their tunes and lyric framework for new motifs directly opposed to the original. Thus, the patriotic song cited already which praised the soldier as the 'finest man in all the land' was adapted in 1917 at the time when blockades were affecting food supplies to refer to the ersatz (turnip) jam then available:

> Marmelade, Marmelade
> Ist der schönste Frass im deutschen Staate.[68]

> [Jam, jam, the finest nosh in all of Germany.]

Food shortages occasioned other songs. The folk-song 'Morgenrot', already mentioned, gave rise at the end the war to a home version which spoke of the food available in France and England. It concludes:

> Morgenrot, Morgenrot
> Ohne Karten gibt's kein Brot.
> Hetzen muss man, rennen, laufen,
> Um sich ein paar Gramm zu kaufen
> Und am Ende ist man tot. . .[69]

[Red of dawn, red of dawn, you can't get bread without coupons. You have to struggle, rush and run to buy a couple of grammes, and at the end, you're dead. . .]

A well-known soldiers' song, that of the 22nd Division, which summed up the whole war year by year, and told how the soldiers went out in masses, and were buried in masses, indicates how in 1918 the great hunger left everyone with only dry bread:

> Da blieb nichts and'res übrig
> Als wie der Heldentod.

[Nothing was left except to die a hero's death.]

Even the song that was to become the national anthem, 'Deutschland über alles', was parodied, and here the target was the rich, who *did* have food. The dialect and the slang terms are difficult to imitate in translation:

> Deutschland, Deutschland, schwer in Dalles
> Schwer im Dalles in der Welt,
> Wenn die Marmelad' nit alles
> Brüderlich zusammenhält.
> Eier, Butter, Wurscht un Schinke
> Sin nur fir die Reiche da
> Nur mir arme, arme Schlucker
> Gucke zu und kreische: hurra!

[Germany, Germany, up to its ears in debt and trouble, up to its ears in it in the world, but jam holds us all together in brotherly fashion. Eggs and butter, bangers and bacon are only there for the rich. All us poor buggers can do is watch and wave the flag!]

Other songs, like 'The Watch on the Rhine' received similar treatment, and these songs embody important social points, matching the criticism in soldiers' songs against the profiteers behind the war. Beside the widespread English slogan suggesting that the Kaiser should be hanged, Wilhelm II's departure to the Netherlands occasioned in German:

O Tannenbaum
O Tannenbaum
Der Kaiser hat in Sack gehaun. . .

[O Christmas Tree, o Christmas Tree, the Kaiser has jacked it
all in. . .]

to the well-known carol tune, and also – a song sung apparently on
the long march back from the fronts in 1918:

Vidi vumbumbum
Der Kaiser ist in Holland nun

. . .

Drum Mädchen weine nicht
Und sei nicht traurig,
Mach deinem Landsturmmann
Das Herz nicht schwer.
Denn dieser Feldzug
War auch kein Schnellzug
Und Marmelad' juchhe
Die gab's grad gnua. . .

[Tiddly-om-pom-pom, the Kaiser's off in Holland . . . so don't
cry, my girl, don't be sad, and don't upset your soldier. This
campaign wasn't like an express train, and there was – hurray –
always enough turnip jam. . .]

A final German song, its first line and tune again from the 'Watch
on the Rhine', is clear in its contrast between Germany as such
(personified by Michel, the sleepier equivalent to John Bull, Uncle
Sam or Marianne), and the Kaiser as the embodiment of a
patriotism that had dominated the earlier period of the war:

Es braust ein Ruf wie Donnerhall,
Es sitzt ein Mann im Schweinestall,
Der einstmals war von hohem Stand
Und Wilhelm II. sich genannt.
Er floh nach Holland hin geschwind,
Mit Stab und Hofnarr, Weib und Kind.
Das nennt man Lieb' fürs Vaterland,
Wie er's im Krieg so oft genannt.

. . .

Der alte Michel brummte sehr,

Denn er fand all sein Geld nich mehr.
In Holland aber geht's in Sekt und Wein
Und lässt den Michel Michel sein. . .

[A call resounds like thunder, a man is sitting in the pigsty who was once of great rank, named William II, he made a quick getaway to Holland with his staff, his court jester, his wife and kids. That is what is called patriotism – what he spent the war proclaiming. . . Poor old German Michel grumbled away because he couldn't find any of his cash. But in Holland there is champagne and wine, and Michel's problems are his own. . .]

The lyric responses to the social and socialist revolutions in many of the countries which followed on from the First World War go well beyond this study.[70] Post-war soldiers' songs and music hall songs, however, became nostalgic very quickly in England and France, while in Germany the patriotic songs were revived after 1933 for a new purpose. In America, though, the songwriter Billy Rose placed several questions into the 'spirit voice' of the Unknown Soldier, and although he asserts that he would die for his country again if necessary, he wonders if the profiteers and the kings are satisfied, and whether the orphans and the bereaved are ever in need.[71] Those points, too, are valid ones.

4

Tomorrow the Whole World
Fascism and the lyric

Wir haben niemals den Krieg gewollt,
haben dem Feind, der ihn brachte, gegrollt
freuten uns an Arbeit und Frieden.
Aber das war uns nicht beschieden!
Wir erlebten Kampf, Sieg, Rückzug, Sieg,
Todgefahr – nun wollen wir Krieg!

Wilhelm von Scholz, 1944[1]

The consideration of the popular war poetry in the Axis
countries during the Second World War presents a range of
problems. Some are pragmatic: it is not always easy to lay hands
on original material, and the post-war anthologies tend, unsur-
prisingly, to ignore them. Even if the charge of revisionism need
hardly be levelled at an objective interest in the reflection of the
war in the poetry and songs of Nazi Germany, Mussolini's Italy or
Vichy France, there remains a natural reluctance to promote their
ideas in any way at all. Thomas Rothschild's excellent anthology of
political lyrics in German excludes, programatically, all reaction-
ary, militaristic, and nationalistic lyrics, for example, and thus all
Nazi lyrics are excluded,[2] although he does not deny their
documentary interest.

Wars are, however, fought by two sides, even when the
ideological basis for war on one of those sides is unacceptable. The
word 'popular' is again the sticking point, however, since in this
case 'popular' may mean material not genuinely loved, but widely
known and sung because the regime wanted it to be. *Mein Kampf*
was in terms of dissemination a much printed and much owned
book; it was presumably hardly a much loved and certainly not a
much read book. The simple presentation of Nazi ideology in the
party-line lyric can be functional war poetry with a quite specific
and militaristic intent. German material, poetry and song, is not
difficult to find,[3] but texts are less readily available for Italy or

99

Vichy France, especially in comparison with the wealth of partisan or Free French material.

Verse in the service of the Fascist regimes was encouraged and widely published, and these regimes recognized more clearly than most the benefit of placing ideas into songs. The principle that men will argue in speech, but will sing in harmony was well taken, especially as in song ideological tenets could be compressed into emblems. The lyrics of the Fascist regimes reflect the idea of war as well as the war itself, since the material concerned dates at least from 1933. The critical problem, however, is not unlike that of establishing the 'good' war poem in the First World War. Objective or moral good cannot be applied to a poem with an immoral or unacceptable aim, but linguistic subtlety and poetic skill in a Nazi poem may still be analysed. How the poem makes its point, and the degree to which it could have affected the war effort by its portrayal of war are the questions which have to be asked.

Although much of the Fascist poetry is from the period between the wars, it feeds upon what was perceived as the shame of 1919. Nazi Germany interpreted the fighting of 1914–18 as a testing, from which a new nationalism emerged. Further, the patriotism of the verse in the Fascist period added nothing except excess. Usually a poetry of attack, it exaggerated and employed on a wider scale than ever before familiar trappings of patriotic poetry. The motifs of national awakening, of flags and trumpets had all appeared before, notably in English poetry in 1914, but never on such a scale, and not as part of an official standardization of ideas. It is of interest, however, to note where techniques overlap and where they diverge. Praise of leaders is, for example, found on both sides even in the Second World War, although there is a clear difference in degree between the endless panegyrics on Mussolini, say, as the new Augustus come to rule the world and the presentation of Churchill as the man of the moment, even when 'unflinching, indomitable, his spirit saved Britain and so the world' (thus the legend on a bronze victory medallion of 1945). Indeed, critics like Albrecht Schöne have demonstrated clearly the proximity of poetry in German eulogizing Hitler to that in praise both of Lenin and of Stalin.[4]

What we may for convenience term 'Fascist war poetry' has several recurrent themes. Poetry and songs saw the leaders of the various Fascist regimes as embodying ideals, which included war, and they underlined the necessity to fight if and when war came. These lyrics are not only by establishment poets (some of them high-ranking party men like Baldur von Schirach), but also by workers and peasants in Germany or Italy: the Fascist movements were ostensibly socialist worker movements, and popularity in this general and social sense was policy. The question of reception, however, is more complex. As some modern German writers have pointed out in their recollections, some of the Nazi material was and is difficult to forget. Lyrics that are reinforced by their own simplicity, by firm melodies, strong rhythms and dissemination that is both loud and frequent make for memorability, whatever the intrinsic poetic qualities. The Fascist war poetry worked.

In Fascist lyrics, then, war is explained or more often glorified, but never rejected, and the early view of the First World War as a holy war is revived. Poetry of suffering, because it was equated with defeatism, could not be published during the Reich. From the inception of the Nazi state in Germany (and from the rise of Mussolini even before that) came instead a flow of lyric in support of war as part of an ideology that included acceptance of the Führer-principle and the glorification of the leader-figures. In the case of Mussolini, the lyric proclaimed the reconstitution of a Roman Empire whose armies would rule the world; in that of Hitler, the confirmation of an empire that was to last a thousand years, which would bring all Germans back under a single rule and march to victory against its enemies, be they Jews, Communists, or those who opposed the will of the leader, all the while protesting that Germany was simply retaking what was rightfully its own. The consolidation and furthering of an ideology through songs which compress the basic elements into a series of fixed symbols (and which, indeed, stress that anyone who is not in favour is an enemy) is a technique long used in religions, so that the quasi-religious nature of many of the lyrics of the Reich is hardly surprising.

The popularity of the lyric as a propaganda vehicle in the era of the dictators is underlined by the many ways in which lyrics were placed before a wide public. Not only was approved poetry published widely, but songs formed a vital part of the various movements. There were songs for the Giovanezzi, for the Hitler Youth, for the SA and the SS, and later for the youth movement in Vichy France. A child's first reading book published in Germany in

1940 with official approval has a telling passage headed *Jungvolk* — the most junior branch of the Nazi youth movement, for ten- to fourteen-year-olds:

> Da kommen sie mit den braunen Hemden. . . Wir grüssen den Wimpel und rufen: Heil Hitler! Wie stramm sie marschieren! Wie hell sie singen: Unsere Fahne flattert uns voran![5]
>
> [Here they come with their brown shirts. . . We salute the flag and shout: Heil Hitler! How well they march! How loudly and clearly they sing 'Our Banner Waves Before Us!']

The Hitler Youth marching song is not cited *in extenso*, but a knowledge of it is presumed. The reader is a primary one, and the following page has counting-out and nursery rhymes. It is not surprising that there was a reaction by some youth elements, whose protest was not strictly political, but whose use of English or American popular songs was (sometimes savagely) repressed.

There was, too, a carefully nurtured tradition of *Sprechchöre* in Germany, choral speaking with all the force of a football crowd, giving what has been termed the 'sledgehammer effect', and approved writers such as E.G. Kolbenheyer produced poetical works specifically for this purpose.[6] As war poetry in the sense of poetry as incitement to war, the directness is difficult to match, although in the Fascist countries as amongst the Allies there was full use of the musical as well as the dramatic film. The German cinema used musical films to underline blood and soil nationalism, and in Italy Mussolini was with Verdi and with a literally operatic grandeur.[7]

Finally, and it is again a method used on both sides, the lyric was used as propaganda in its purest sense in aerial bombardment. One example indicates that such propaganda could be subtle: in the autumn of 1939 a poem appeared which looks like an anti-war piece. It is, indeed, not entirely clear whether it is intended as a poem, although its imagery and form point to this. It is in French, and has slight echoes of Verlaine's 'Chant d'Automne':

Automne

Les feuilles tombent
Nous tomberons comme elles.
Les feuilles meurent parce que Dieu le veut. . .

[Autumn. The leaves fall, we fall as they do. The leaves die because God wills it. . .] .

The final part is in the same vein:

> Au printemps prochain personne ne se souviendra
> plus ni des feuilles mortes ni des poilus tués.
> La vie passera sur nos tombes.

[Next spring no one will remember, not the dead leaves nor the fallen poilus. Life will pass by our tombs.]

The link between the dead leaves and the dead poilus is maintained, and the pathos in the move from the autumn (when it is natural for leaves to fall) to spring (when the dead do not rise but life goes on) is clear. The poetry of the passage – the sound-echoes and the balance of the leaves and soldiers, as well as the climax on life and the tomb, which brings back the unity of the first person plural – is striking. The imagery of the leaf falling is underlined further by the fact that the whole piece was printed on a leaf shape, a falling autumn leaf making a more real image of death. At the foot of the work is a death's-head with a poilu helmet.

But the poem is not complete: two middle lines pick up the idea that God wills the death of the leaf:

> Mais nous, nous tombons parce que les
> Anglais le veulent.

[But we, we fall because the English want us to.]

This was a propaganda sheet dropped by the Germans on French troops at the beginning of the war, designed to affect the morale of the French by implying that it is not their war but that of the English, who implicitly equate themselves with God. The first person pronoun underscores the fact that these are thoughts put into the heads of the French. Nor is there any doubt that this is functional poetry, given its dissemination. It is of a more subtle kind than many aerial drops, some of which merely caricatured Hitler; noteworthy here is the poetic use of a language and imagery associated with anti-war poetry, and indeed, this *is* an anti-war poem, designed to stop the fighting by undermining morale. In 1941, incidentally, British aircraft dropped similar 'falling leaves' – in this case oak leaves, which are used in German military decorations and found frequently as an heroic motif in art in Nazi Germany. Again the wording can be accepted as poetry:

> In Russland decken gefallene
> Blätter gefallene Soldaten
> Und Schnee deckt die Blätter
> die gefallene Soldaten decken. . .[8]

[In Russia fallen leaves cover fallen soldiers, and snow covers the leaves that cover the fallen soldiers. . .]

Similar poetic images are on both sides being used to underline to military or civilian audiences the fact that war kills and therefore that the war in question should be stopped. The reasons behind the two are different, and what remains is the moral issue, affected on both sides now by historical hindsight. In their time and contexts, both may have been effective.

Fascist poetry is official. Prohibitions on writing, the *Schreibverbot* and the principle of literary standardization, *Gleichschaltung*, ensured that the only poetry was that encouraged by the regime. The literary techniques of Fascism have been well documented and widely discussed.[9] Avoiding argument by assertive statement, the stimulation of existing emotions, the pinpointing of a supposed or real enemy (who is often tagged by a stereotype image or a pejorative term), repetition of individual points, selectivity, the big lie, and the implication that anyone who does not believe is a criminal – all these occur in the poetry. They are not, of course, the exclusive property of Fascism. J.A.C. Brown comments that 'the basic idea was to build up strong in-group attitudes and feelings on our own side accompanied by opposed attitudes of hatred towards the enemy as a dangerous out-group, a mechanism which appears to be almost innate in man when faced by frustrations and anxieties.'[10] Although 'our own side' is variable, the Nazi machinery in particular supported its own assertive statements of racial purity, of the need for living space, of the quasi-religious Führer-principle, of mastery and of the glory of a new war that would obliterate the shame of Versailles and usher in a new Reich that would last a thousand years by a poetry categorized by a well-defined and limited vocabulary and diction.

That vocabulary – which critics such as Hubert Orłowski have analysed in detail – underlines constantly a belief in war by reiterating terms like 'flag' (*Banner, Fahne, Fanal, Flagge*), or concepts like 'sacrifice' (*Opfer*), or Walther Darre's blood and soil nationalism (*Blut und Boden*), or fire and flame (*Flamme*), or the idea of a German mission (*Sendung*), or the much repeated key words of Hitler himself: the triad of race, empire, and leader (*Reich, Volk, Führer*). Attendant adjectives include not only German (*deutsch*) but the religious and mystic borrowings of holy, elevated, and eternal (*heilig, hehr, ewig*), as well as iron (*eisern* or *ehern*). The words themselves are frequently archaic or associated with a romanticized medievalism, and support endless combinations and juxtapositions, especially with general military terms – *heiliger Kampf*, 'holy struggle', *ewige Front*, 'eternal front-line'. Ideas of marching, of battle and of struggle make much Fascist poetry into war poetry because it uses the vocabulary of war. Once again, some of these motifs are invoked in patriotic poetry of the First World War on both sides, but it is again a question of degree and of exclusivity.[11] Similar key words and slogans recur in Italian verse (plays on *vittoria*, 'victory' are frequent, linked with the name of the king of Italy), and there are variations on the same religious-mystic concept of a blessed mission which link with the Christian name of Mussolini. In Vichy France the figure of the former military leader Pétain gives rise to an emphasis on his leadership, while there is much use of the terms which replaced liberty, equality, and fraternity as a slogan, the ideas of work, family, and homeland.

Most striking of all features in the functionality of Fascist lyric is the idea of unity embodied in a particular use of the 'we' voice which is positive and homiletic. One of the Nazi poets, Heinrich Anacker, combines all the techniques in a rallying poem that is pre-war in fact, but sounds like a call to arms rather than a call to political unity. He begins with the 'we' voice and uses this stance to inculcate an outsider feeling, a suggestion that there is something odd about those not part of the communal 'we':

> Wenn wir singen, marschieren
> mit hartem Schritt und Tritt –
> was, bist du, Bruder, nicht dabei?
> Auch dir gellt heiss ins Ohr der Schrei:
> 'Auch du, auch du musst mit!'[12]

[When we are marching and singing, with firm step and tread –

what, are you not with us, brother? The cry is urgent in your
ear, too: 'You must join, too!']

In the climax of the poem the outsider acquiesces to what is an
inner force as well as a cry from outside, and agrees:

> 'Auch ich, auch ich will mit.'

['I too, I too want to join in'.]

The technique is not dissimilar to the pressure put on young men
to join up in the First World War, but the insistence on the
isolation of those who do not belong is particularly strong.

The glorification of the leader elevates Mussolini or Hitler to
imperial status and views them either as sent by God or as God-
like figures themselves.[13] The position of Pétain is a little different –
he is seen as the old warrior returned to save his people in their
hour of need, and the Vichy national anthem, 'Maréchal nous
voilà' pledges itself to the aged soldier directly. Once again
Japanese material is not readily available, but given the cult of a
god-emperor in any case, the additional building up of these ideas
is presumably less necessary. All this contributes towards a general
encouragement to war.

The expression of complete faith in Hitler is present from the
earliest stages. Baldur von Schirach's manifesto for youth in 1934
declared that the young 'may not always be able to reason out the
motives for its unconditional allegiance to the Führer – that is the
way of youth. But when the question 'why' is put, it will always
find the cry with which the Hitler Youth follows the Führer all his
ways: 'The Führer is always right! Our life for the Führer!"[14]
Countless lyrics of the period bear witness to this acceptance of the
leader principle. A well-known poem, written before the war by
Herybert Menzel, born in 1906 and committed to Hitler as a writer
of lyrics and spoken cantatas for the SA, is nevertheless clearly a
poem of war:

> Die Welt gehört den Führenden,
> Sie gehn der Sonne Lauf.
> Und wir sind die Marschierenden
> Und keiner hält uns auf.
> Das Alte wankt,
> Das Morsche fällt,

Wir sind der junge Sturm.
Wir sind der Sieg!
Spring auf, marsch, marsch,
Die Fahne auf den Turm!

Der Kerl muss nicht geraten sein
Den unser Lied nicht packt.
Ein Kerl muss bei Soldaten sein,
Gleich schlagt sein Herz im Takt.
Das Alte wankt
Das Morsche fällt.[15]

[The world belongs to the leaders, they follow the sun's course; and we are on the march, and no one will stop us. Old things are about to tumble, what is rotting will fall. We are the young storm, we are victory. Up, march, march, plant our banner on the castle walls. A lad who is not gripped by our song must have something wrong with him. A lad should be with soldiers – at once that will have his heart beating in step. Old things are about to tumble, what is rotting will fall.]

The poem is one of attack, not defence. The castle is being stormed and the banner will be planted victoriously. Newness, and the attack on what is crumbling are also key concepts, as is the idea that there is something wrong with anyone who does not agree. What links this with the war is that it is specifically military, demanding that every young man should be a soldier to bring him into line. The adverb 'gleich' towards the end means 'at once', but also has the idea of equality and uniformity in it.

The same year – 1936 – saw the publication by a younger poet, Gerhard Schuhmann, born in 1911, of another clearly military 'Lied der Kämpfer' [Song of the Warriors], in which the commitment to Hitler as the leader is clear, whilst the vocabulary remains military. This is again a war poem in spite of its date and although it actually describes the rise of the Nazi party to political victory. The last strophe reads:

Die Vielzuvielen sind versprengt, verlaufen,
Vom Feuer blind, das über uns gebraust.
Die heut marschieren in den erznen Haufen,
Wir fragen nicht. Wir sind des Führers Faust.[16]

[The enemy masses are dispersed and scattered, blinded by the fire that roars above us. Those of us now marching in the iron columns do so without questioning. We are the fist of the Führer.]

The total and explicitly unquestioning self-abnegation to become an instrument (or rather, a part of the body) of the leader was promulgated through poems of this sort – it is entirely typical – in the years leading to the war, to inculcate obedience when that war came.

Not all of the poetry concerned with the glorification of the leader can be viewed as war poetry, although leadership by a Führer, Duce, or Maréchal was almost inevitably military. Lyrics about Mussolini in particular, though, try to make clear the prized adulation by the workers and the peasants, something shown in a collection published in Italy just after the invasion of Abyssinia. Filippo Fichera's investigation of the presentation of Mussolini and Fascism in Italian dialect poetry (which has a preface by the Futurist Filippo Marinetti) is a massive compilation of adulatory poetry presenting Mussolini as the new Augustus and the creator of a new Roman Empire, the whole accompanied by a slightly hysterical commentary. Poems greet the invasion of Abyssinia with the exclamation 'Oh gloriose milizie' and there are triumph songs in praise of Victor Emmanuel, Mussolini, and of the 'glorious victory' in Addis Ababa.[17] Mussolini himself is seen time and again not only as Augustus, but as Cicero, Marcus Aurelius, and many others. Poetic tributes such as that by a Veronese lady named Aida Pimazzoni carry the praise even higher:

> Duce, Duce, Taumaturgo,
> Redentor del mondo intiero. . .[18]

[Duce, Duce, great healer, saviour of the entire world. . .]

and, indeed, the commentator is himself somewhat excessive apropos of a poem by one Bachisio Asili, seeing Mussolini as 'il redentore della Patria, il salvatore della casa Savoia per la salute di Roma Eterna e di tutta l'Umanità',[19] 'redeemer of his fatherland, saviour of the House of Savoy for the well being of Rome Eternal and of all of humanity'. These *canti dialettali* include, incidentally, not only the many Italian dialects and the Italian of the Engadine, the Tirol, Dalmatia, Monaco, Corsica, Malta as well as Tripolitania, Somalia, Eritrea and Tien-Tsin, but also of America, a linguistic imperialism of some breadth, which reminds us of some of the reasons for the continuation of isolationist policies supported by voting groups in the USA before 1941. The collection includes verse in a curious Italo-American 'Sicilianized' dialect, 'nel dialetto inglese sicilianizzato di New York'. The anonymous material is thematically much like the rest of the poetry, but even in this most curious of popular poetry the trappings of Fascism are quite clear. The language is in fact English, although it might not seem so at first glance:

> Itali hev in Ti, di olmàitti Dux,
> di nìu Sisa Augustus immortal;
> in is Fassism hev di Làif end Lux
> end av Jòstis di Fleg iuniversal.[20]

Marshall Pétain came to power later, but the poetry associated with him is precisely similar to that associated with Mussolini or Hitler. Special elements introduced include his role as the victor of Verdun (to which grudging references are also made in anti-Vichy poems), but the notions of acceptance of the leader and the presentation of Pétain as the saviour of France as well as its symbol and incorporation are also found. The Fascist leaders all made much of the comparison with historical greatness, Mussolini using imperial Rome and Hitler figures from the Germanic past. Pétain is associated with Joan of Arc and Roland, both of whom, incidentally, were widely used by the Free French as well (and both of whom were actually defeated, though Roland – invoked also in German lyrics – embodies the idea of a hero's death in a just cause). Pétain, however, was celebrated in the national anthem which replaced the 'Marseillaise' in the Vichy period:

> Maréchal, nous voilà
> devant toi le sauveur de la France,
> Nous jurons, nous tes gars
> De servir et de suivre tes pas
>
> . . .
> Tu nous a redonné l'espérance
> La patrie renaîtra. . .[21]

[Marshall, we are here before you, the saviour of France, we swear, we your men, to serve you and follow your footsteps . . .

you have given us hope again, our fatherland will be born again. . .]

All the by now familiar attributes of leadership are there in André Montagnard's lyric, and the title incorporates the first person pronoun. W.D. Halls cites a song designed for the youth movement in Vichy France which takes the leader a stage further:

> vous qui venez
> Ainsi qu'un envoyé de Dieu
> Sauver la France bien-aimée. . .
> Oh! vous dont la vieillesse
> Egale en sa noblesse
> De Jeanne d'Arc la jeunesse. . .[22]

[. . . you, who come like one sent by the Lord to save France the dearly beloved . . . you, whose age is equal in nobility to the youth of Joan of Arc. . .]

The quasi-liturgical tone, (*benedictus qui venit*. . .), the idea of 'one sent by God' and also that of a saviour are all patent, as is the link with Joan of Arc and the idea of France as a favoured land. The military overtones in the reference to the saint, and the play on youth are also clear, here aimed at the young audience. Halls notes, in fact, that references to Pétain's advanced age were later dropped from poetic panegyrics.[23]

With Hitler there is a wealth of material, and lyrics glorify his military aims, underline the unity between people and leader and thus make his will theirs, and culminate again in apotheosis. Heinrich Anacker, one of the best known of the Nazi poets and writer of innumerable songs and poems for the Hitler Youth and the SA, drew not without skill a picture of the rise of Hitler in 'Der Führer spricht' [The Führer Speaks], praising that power of oratory which was mocked (because it was feared) in satirical verse in English. Four quatrains are linked by anaphora, the first three historical: 'Der Führer sprach. . .' ('The Führer spoke. . .') – first to a small group, although this brought forth *Kampfgeschrei* 'battle-cries' as well as applause. This is then extended to the city and then to Germany as Hitler shows himself to have the strength to master fate. The final strophe of the poem, written just before the war broke out, echoes another celebrated Nazi piece which will be considered later, that which has the familiar refrain 'today

Germany belongs to us, tomorrow the world', with an echo of 'gehören', 'belong' in the verb 'hören', 'listen', which is used in this climactic verse:

> Der Führer spricht. . . Und heute hört ihn die Welt!
> Millionen ahnen seine hohe Sendung,
> mit Deutschlands Recht auf Freiheit steht und fallt
> des Völkerfriedens strahlender Vollendung![24]

[The Führer speaks . . . and today the whole world listens! Millions feel his mighty mission, with Germany's right to freedom stands and falls the glorious consummation of the peace of nations!]

While the *unio mystica* of people and leader is often stressed (in such pieces as Baldur von Schirach's short 'Hitler'),[25] a piece by Josef Weinheber, 'Dem Führer' [To The Führer], which appeared in a collection with the same title published in 1941 in a series for soldiers, shows a clear support of the war. Weinheber was an older poet whose reputation was furthered by the Nazis, and who was ultimately to commit suicide in 1945, apparently aware of the implications too late. The poem is in honour of Hitler's fiftieth birthday:

> Deutschlands Genius, Deutschlands Herz und Haupt
> Ehre Deutschlands, ihm solang' geraubt,
> Macht des Schwerts, daran die Erde glaubt.
>
> Fünfzig Jahr und ein Werk aus Erz.
> Übergross, gewachsen an dem Schmerz.
> Hell und heilig, stürmend höhenwärts.
>
> Retter, Löser, der die Macht bezwang,
> Ernte du auch, dulde Kranz und Sang:
> Ruh in unsrer Liebe, lebe lang![26]

[Germany's guiding spirit, Germany's heart and mind, the honour of Germany, of which she has so long been deprived, the might of the sword, believed by all the earth. Fifty years and a work of bronze. Gigantic, grown through pain. Bright and holy, storming heavenwards. Redeemer, saviour, controller of power, reap, too, suffer these wreaths and songs, rest in our love, live long!]

The religious overtones become commonplace. An unattributed
'Song of the Faithful' in an anthology distributed to German
households at Christmas 1939, written, according to Goebbels's
preface, by a member of the Hitler Youth, speaks of Hitler laying
his loving fatherly hands upon his people to heal their wounds, and
concludes:

> Darum ist unsre Liebe auch so gross,
> Darum bist du der Anfang und das Ende –
> Wir glauben dir, treu und bedingungslos,
> Und unser Werk des Geistes und der Hände
> Ist die Gestaltung unsers Dankes bloss.[27]

[Therefore is our love so great, and therefore you are the alpha
and omega – we believe in you, faithful and unconditionally, and
the work of our spirit and of our hands is just the expression of
our gratitude.]

Even without the liturgical allusion, the religious overtones are
clear, as they are in Alice Fosterling's eulogy of Braunau am Inn,
Hitler's birthplace, as if it were Bethlehem. To the modern reader
perhaps the most tasteless of all is Fritz von Rabenau's adaptation
of 'Silent Night', which appeared in a volume called 'Christmas in
the Third Reich' published in 1934. In spite of its early date, it still
anticipates the militarism of Hitler's state:

> Stille Nacht, heilige Nacht,
> Alles schläft, einsam wacht
> Adolf Hitler für Deutschlands Geschick,
> Führt uns zur Grösse, zum Ruhm und zum Glück,
> Gibt uns Deutschen die Macht. .[28]

[Silent night, holy night, all is calm, wakeful is only Adolf Hitler,
watching over Germany's destiny, leads us to greatness, to fame
and to happiness, gives power to us, to Germany. . .]

There is a clear movement from Hitler as a Christ-figure to Hitler
as a replacement for Christianity. It is implicit in the text just
mentioned, is at its clearest in a Hitler Youth song dating from
1934 which replaces by the militarism of National Socialism any
traces of the *miles Christiani*, just as the swastika (*Hakenkreuz*)
replaces the cross (*Kreuz*):

Wir sind die fröhliche Hitler jugend,
Wir brauchen keine Christentugend,
Denn unser Führer Adolf Hitler
Ist stets unser Mittler. . .[29]

[We are the merry Hitler Youth. We don't need your Christian
virtues. Our Führer Adolf Hitler is all we need to intercede for
us.]

In the same song there is a reference to Horst Wessel as a better
model than Christ.

Justification for the treatment of the poetry and song of the
Third Reich as war lyrics is provided not only by the forward-
looking militaristic tone of much of the poetry, but by the express
linking with the First World War. Nazi ideology saw the 1914–18
war as a time of greatness and of individual heroism, a 'bath of
steel', and its culmination in Versailles as a tragic and shameful
fact which could be obliterated only by another war.

The process of standardizing the view of the First World War in
literary terms was emphasized in May 1933 by the consigning to
the fire of the works of writers like Remarque – 'for treachery
towards the soldiers of the front'. Collections of poetry much like
those which appeared at the beginning of the First World War now
began to appear, and one which may serve as an example was
published in 1934 (with a second edition the same year) by
Diederichs in Jena under the title of *Volk im Kriege* [A Nation at
War] in their 'Deutsche Reihe' [National Series]. It was provided
with an afterword by Peter Diederichs claiming that the concentration was upon poems reflecting the 'great inner experience' of the
First World War.[30] Interestingly, some of the poems are anonymous,
from newspapers or similar sources. The layout of the work and the
selection is deliberately positive, although a final section – entitled
Klage und Vermächtnis, 'Lament and Testament' contains such
poems as Georg Trakl's 'Grodek', a bitter and apocalyptic poem
culminating in an awareness of the generations who will now be
unborn. For the most part, however, even this section points
onwards to the new day, and stresses the message of the dead of
the First World War in the words of a worker poet pressed into
service by the Nazi movement, Karl Bröger:

Nacht um Nacht sich in meiner Seele brennt
Tief der toten Brüder Wille und Testament.

Wieder hör ich die Stimme voll dunkler Kraft:
'Klagt nicht – schafft!'

[Night after night the last will and testament of my fallen
brothers burns into my soul. I hear again the voice, full of dark
power: 'Don't weep – act!']

It is easy to see how this sentiment could be adapted to a new
notion of revenge. The idea of the omnipresence of the dead of the
First World War is not unfamiliar, of course, though the idea of
keeping faith now undergoes a new and specific development.[31]
The *Volk im Kriege* anthology contains great emphasis on the virtues
of comradeship and on a basic nationalism even in poems which
portray events of the war realistically. Thus Reinhold Braun's
'Fliegerkampf' [Dog Fight], ends with the words:

Ich lebe!
Ich lebe und sterbe,
Dass nicht verderbe
Deutschland, mein Deutschland!

[I am alive! I live and die so that Germany, my Germany may
not perish!]

Nor is it accidental that the anthology should begin with a poem
by the Expressionist poet Heinrich Lersch, who was wooed by the
Nazis as a 'worker poet'. It is a good indication of the links
between the wars that his 'Fahneneid' [Oath Before the Flag] was
first published in 1916; but every word suits the Nazi ideology. The
link with the heroic earlier generation, which in 1916 meant the
victors of the Franco-Prussian War, had a new set of implications
in 1934. The insistence on victory in some of the lyrics of the
1914–18 war was reapplicable, and familar phrases recur: 'honourable war', 'noble victory', 'holy fatherland', 'holy war'. It is clear
how pieces like Hanns Johst's 'Der Sturm bricht los!' [The Storm
Begins!] can be a war poem of two wars, arising from one and used
both as a reminder and as pointer:

In allen Strassen steht dunkle Wut.
Das Volk ist eins! Unser Volk ist gross!
Heiss, heilig fordert es Blut!

Wir atmen verhalten –
Der Sturm bricht los!

[Dark anger is in every street. The people are united! Our people are great! Fiery, holy, they demand blood! With bated breath. The storm begins!]

Diederich's afterword to the collection begins:

No period has shown more forcefully than that of the Great War that poetry is in essence the expression of shared popular feelings. Immortal expression was given to the shared and communal German experience by what broke forth from within the people in a language suddenly made free. War poetry contains for us the immediate witness to that heroic feeling of self-awareness that enabled Germany to carry out deeds of unheard-of greatness in the battle against enemy superiority.

The unity of feeling, then, is stressed (*Volk* is, with its derivatives, an emotive term and difficult to translate), and the view of war poetry as such as intrinsically nationalist and heroic is one that persists.

Other collections make the bridging of the two wars even clearer. H. Böhme's *Rufe in das Reich* appeared in 1934 too,[32] and includes work by most of the best-known Nazi poets. To stress their unity of ideas, the writers are not named on the text pages. The arrangement of the anthology is significant, however: it includes a section on the spirit of Langemarck and another on Versailles (Irmela Linberg has a poem called 'Hass', [Hate]). Other headings are crisp evocations of tenets of Nazi ideology: 'Wille zur Wende' [The Will to Change], 'Volk will zu Volk' [People Want to Join Their Own], 'Der Führer', and a religious section which contains a 'German Our Father' with the lines

Vater versuche
Uns nicht mit Versöhnung. . .

[Father, lead us not into the temptation of reconciliation. . .]

With the war itself, the reference back to the earlier conflict increased. One anthology of selections from trench magazines bears the title-page legend:

Die Frontsoldaten von 1914–18 ihren Kameraden von 1939–40

115

[Front-line soldiers of 1914–18 to their comrades of 1939–40]

A preface describes the material – prose and poetry – as the legacy of the First War to the front-line soldiers of the Second, stressing the unity of the two generations and referring to the poetry as expressing a depth of experience from which heroic deeds arose.[33] Similarly, Oskar Wöhrle could publish in 1940 (when he himself was nearly fifty) a volume which may again stand for many like it, entitled *Kamrad im grauen Heer* [Comrade in Uniform]. The 'grey' of the title refers to the field-grey equivalent to khaki, and the cover was patterned with oak leaves. *Feldpost* editions of collections like this existed, with fold-over flaps for posting.[34] Wöhrle's collection includes somewhat contrived pieces in which a soldier bids farewell to his girl, but another, with the title 'Tröstung' [Comfort], expresses the idea familiar from the *Song of Roland* onwards that death in battle is a path to heaven, although Wöhrle hedges his bets somewhat in 'Mythe' [Myth] and sees Thor carrying the dead heroes to Valhalla. There is less emphasis on specifically ideological points (to which serving soldiers might not have responded), but most of the pieces are patriotic in a sense that is familiar from poems of all sides in the First World War. In the 'Ode an Deutschland' [Ode to Germany], the notion of 'Vaterland', *patria*, does attract the adjective 'holy', but more typical of the book is the expression of readiness to fight at the start of the war in a poem called 'September 39'.

The poem begins with a clear link to the First World War:

> Und wieder dieses dumpfe Dröhnen
> der schweren Züge durch die Nacht. . .

[And once again that dull roar of laden trains in the night. . .]

but follows this with a reference to the million marching steps of the soldiers 'den Grenzen zu' (to the borders), implying that the war is not one of invasion, but of defence. Comradeship is stressed, but no ideals are given to justify the conclusion:

> Auch wenn jetzt kein Befehl uns riefe,
> wir müssten mit! wir müssten mit!

[Even if there were no order commanding us, we should still have to go! Still have to go!]

The invocation is of the *patria* alone:

Vaterland, du sollst mich segnen!
Schenke mir die höchste Kraft,
Auch dem Tode zu begegnen.

[Fatherland, bless me, grant me the greatest strength that I may even face death.]

Wöhrle's 'Soldier's Breviary' – his subtitle – contains other poems which call for unquestioning obedience in war, and in one of these the speaker goes comforted into the battle after he has had a vision of the dead friend with whom he is thereby keeping faith. The awareness of death is acceptable in the Nazi lyric if it is not defeatist. The message as war poetry is that the soldiers must fight and will win, though not all will return.

One poem at least in Wöhrle's collection is worthy of mention finally in literary terms. 'Sand aus Soldatenschuhn' [Sand From the Soldiers' Boots] looks forward to the return of the soldiers – again designated as *wir* and thereby generalized – who before coming indoors tip the sand and dirt from half of Europe out of their boots. This forms a mound on which 'a regiment of flowers', especially the forget-me-not, can be planted, and the earth will itself become a testament:

Sie soll uns Heimgekehrte
samt Kind und Kindeskind
der guten Kamraden erinnern,
die draussen geblieben sind.

[It must remind us, who have come back, and our children and our children's children of the good comrades who didn't come back.]

The simplicity of the poem makes it effective, and it could take a place in any war anthology, although language and context are against it.

Individual poems concerned with the war appeared throughout the Third Reich on postcards and in soldiers' magazines just as in the First World War. Poetry produced in Germany during the Third Reich that was not about war in any sense – that was, for example, about nature – is often close to the *Blut und Boden* idea,[35] even if all poetry that is not about Fascism has sometimes been taken as implicitly anti-Fascist. Any poetry not specifically pro-Nazi might, of course, have hidden allusions which might have been picked up at the time, but it is almost impossible to gauge how far this dangerous technique of *contrebande* poetry was ever used, or if it was effective.

Humorous or light verse also appeared. One collection, with the title *So oder so ist das Leben* [Life Is Like That, or Like That],[36] by Achim von Winterfeld and published in 1943, is for the most part unexceptionable whimsy, but in the collection there is what might nevertheless be called a war poem. 'Der böse Nachbar' [The Nasty Neighbour] recalls a political piece by Ogden Nash about the polite Japanese in the next garden who bows, and takes over.[37] Winterfeld's piece refers to Germany, however, and underscores an attitude to the conflict:

> Ein Volk beginnt was aufzubaun,
> da lugt der Nachbar übern Zaun
> und neidet ihn das Aufgebaute,
> das er da übern Zaun erschaute.
> Er meint voll Grimm: 'Der wird zu mächtig,
> das ist ja einfach niederträchtig!
> geht's ihm so weiter von der Hand,
> dann drückt er mich glatt an die Wand!'

[A nation begins to build itself up, then a neigbour peers over the fence and envies what has been built and what he has seen, and thinks angrily: 'He's getting too powerful, that is suspicious. If this goes on, he'll try and flatten me!']

This leads to conflict and eventually to war:

> und ehe man's noch recht bedacht,
> ist alsobald ein Krieg entfacht. . .
> Niemand kann friedlich aufbaun auf der Welt,
> Wenn es dem bösen Nachbarn nicht gefällt. . .

[And before you know where you are a war has broken out. No one can build in peace in the world if the nasty neighbour doesn't like it.]

Words like 'Volk' and the concept of building up (by which we might understand the annexations and invasions) make it clear that the poem can serve as a justification for war. It is a poem designed to help convince a population at war that the war was nevertheless one of defence and not of aggression.

The home front in the Third Reich was well provided with party-line verse. A poem has been cited already from the chrestomathy issued to less well-off households under the auspices of the Winter Aid programme in 1939, a work with a preface by Goebbels, a frontispiece of Hitler and the title *Ewiges Deutschland. Ein deutsches Hausbuch* [Eternal Germany. A German Book for the Home], and most of the poems included underline the party's ideals. Many are in praise of Hitler, who is quoted throughout, or of the German homeland. There are anecdotes and verses from the Franco-Prussian and the First World War, and the whole is an interesting repository of material aimed at popular appeal. Once again, it is not clear how much was actually read, but the digest format probably means that some of the poems were indeed read by those who did not normally read or buy poetry books proper. It contained such pieces as 'Der Preis' [The Prize] by Ludwig Finkh, a poet who was well over sixty by the outbreak of war (he lived until 1964) and who spent much time promoting the myths of racial purity. His poem closes with the lines:

> Aber wir haben für dich gestritten
> Deutschland, und mit dem Führer gelitten.
> Das ist unser Preis.[38]

[But we have fought for you, Germany, and suffered with the Führer. That is our reward.]

The effects of *Gleichschaltung* after 1933 can be seen in more orthodox anthologies of poetry. The examples are again fortuitous, but we may compare two volumes of poetry from 1929 and 1934 respectively. The first is of modern lyrics, *Kristall der Zeit*, [Crystal of Our Times] edited by Albert Soergel, with a comprehensive selection, including the Expressionists, Jewish poets like Stefan Zweig, but also some of the poets later approved by the regime. Only a few years later came Rudolf Mirbt's *Ein deutsches Herz*, subtitled 'ein Volksbuch' [A German Heart – a Book for the People]. Admittedly it covers a wider range and includes early and classical poetry, too. But its extensive modern representation excludes Jews and most of the Expressionists, but includes material by many of the Nazi poets, including Baldur von Schirach. The sections into which the work is divided end with 'Volk und Vaterland', ('Nation and People'), 'Deutsches Soldatentum',

('German Soldiers'), and 'Junge Mannschaft' ('Young Manhood') –
all of which contain a good number of Nazi lyrics.[39]

The clearest expressions of Fascist ideology in lyric form are in
the official songs written for the various Nazi units. Soldiers, too,
were encouraged to sing and books were issued of suitable songs,
but here the ideological aspects of Fascism are less prominent. The
Chorliederbuch für die Wehrmacht [Army Songbook] carries a statement by Hitler stressing that 'German song lives within us, and
wherever we are it can suddenly conjure up before our eyes the
eternal homeland, Germany and the Reich.'[40] However, the songs
are largely from earlier periods (including the First World War) or
are folk-songs. Even the song given the title 'Das SS-Treuelied'
[The SS Song of Loyalty] – the text prints the runic lightning-
flashes for SS – is adapted from a song from 1814 and is little more
than an expression of comradeship and mutual trust. Other songs
with a copyright from the NSDAP itself prove to be relatively
neutral in tone: 'Wenn die bunten Fahnen wehen' [When the
Bright Banners Flutter] is actually about ships setting off, for all
that the keyword 'Fahne' arouses different expectations. There is a
clear difference between material in collections like this and
material produced for the Nazi units. The extreme elements of
party ideology are avoided in favour of a stress on the nobility of
the aims of the movement and the assertion of loyalty to it.

Many of the Nazi songs stress the revival of Germany after the
First World War. Dietrich Eckhart's 'Deutschland erwache!'
[Germany, Awake!] is a much discussed example, and the staccato
form and the absence of reasons for why Germany is to be
awakened have long been noted.[41] The idea of awakening is
common, as indeed it was in Britain in 1914, and the Nazis used
the rhymed slogan 'Gebt Hitler die Macht – Deutschland erwacht'
[Give Hitler Power, Germany is Awakening]. It could be linked,
however, with other aspects of Nazism:

> Deutschland erwache aus einem bösen Traum
> gib fremden Juden in Deinem Reich nicht Raum.
> Wir wollen kämpfen fur Dein Auferstehn,
> arisches Blut soll nicht untergehn.[42]

[Germany awake from your bad dream, let no outsider Jew into
your Reich. We are going to fight for your renewal, Aryan blood
shall not disappear.]

The bad dream is of the lost war, the idea of preparedness to fight is evident, and coupled with the idea of Aryan blood having to struggle against complete destruction ('untergehn'). The idea of renewal or resurrection – again part of the post-Versailles doctrine – is once more quasi-religious. Heinrich Anacker, another of the best-known poets of the Reich, speaks in his 'Deutsches Ostern 1933' [German Easter 1933] of Germany having been crucified, and Germany's mothers having been wounded to the heart; but however heavy the stone might have been, Germany has rolled it away by its own efforts so that

Auch Deutschlands Grab ist heute leer[43]

[Germany's tomb is empty too, today]

A further song from before the Second World War became very much part of it, and was often cited in the Allied countries, too. It contains a programmatic military statement, a clear view of the enemy, and again refers to the idea of Germany's renewal or revival from the debris of Versailles. Hans Baumann's song 'Es zittern die morschen Knochen' [Brittle Bones are Trembling] requires examination here on the grounds of its popularity throughout the period of the Third Reich.[44] It was written in 1932 and the lyrics were adapted at various times, the word 'gehört' ('belongs to') becoming 'hört' ('listens to') at one stage, although the first version was that which was most widely sung. The idea of victory and the theme of marching are present and the contributions made by these motifs to the success of the song have been noted by the critics who have discussed the work. Interestingly, the compilation *The Mind and Face of Nazi Germany*, which appeared in London in 1942 and cites in translation a number of Hitler Youth and other songs, includes only the last line of the refrain, which was the message taken from it.[45]

Es zittern die morschen Knochen
der Welt vor dem roten Krieg.
Wir haben den Schrecken gebrochen,
fur uns wars ein grosser Sieg.

Wir werden weitermarschieren
wenn alles in Scherben fällt,
denn heute gehört uns Deutschland
und morgen die ganze Welt.

[Brittle bones of the world are trembling in the face of the red war. We have smashed this terror, and it was a great victory for us. We shall march ever onwards, even if everything crashes down in pieces; for today Germany belongs to us, and tomorrow, the whole world.]

The Communist enemy is clear in the text, although this too had to be adapted for the period of the Hitler – Stalin pact. The poem was very widely reprinted, and the authorship was something of a burden to Baumann after the war (a parallel to Lissauer and the 'Hymn of Hate'); he was awarded the Gerhart Hauptmann prize for a play submitted anonymously, and then deprived of it when the identity of the writer was found to be that of the composer of the notorious song.

Of the so-called 'worker poets', Heinrich Lersch, always an uneasy bedfellow of poets like Anacker, produced in 1934 a poem 'Soldaten der braunen Armee' [Soldiers in the Brownshirt Army]. The poem demonstrates the effects of militaristic generalization in the lyric if the adjective 'red' replaces 'brown', but other elements in the verse make the standpoint clear:

> Wir sind die Soldaten der braunen Armee,
> Die Kolonnen der eisernen Zeit,
> Unser Vormarsch ging durch Blut und durch Weh
> Im bittern Brüderstreit.
> Doch wir kämpfen für Freiheit und ewiges Recht,
> Für Deutschland, das neu sich erhebt:
> Denn wir bekennen uns zu dem Geschlecht,
> Das vom Dunkel in das Helle strebt!
> Die Augen auf, dein Bruder naht,
> Der Werkkamerad, der Arbeit Held;
> Wir sind des schaffenden Volks Soldat,
> Die hämmernden Brüder der Welt.[46]

[We are the soldiers of the brownshirt army, the troops of the age of iron, our march has taken us through blood and tears in the bitter strife between brothers. But we are fighting for freedom and our eternal right, for Germany, newly rising up. For we declare ourselves men of the kind that strive for the light out of darkness. Eyes forward, your brother approaches, your fellow worker, hero of labour. We are the soldiers of working people, brothers of the hammer in the world.]

Many phrases point to Nazi ideals: the age of iron, and of course the image of a renewed Germany. The links with the war also remain clear, and the entire tone is military – army, fighting, marching, troops, and comradeship are all stressed, and the piece is yet again in the first person plural form. Like so much else, the dominating Third Reich themes make this into a war poem by linking the loss of the First World War with the foreshadowing of the Second.

The link between the wars is often explicit. The SA poet and associate of Goebbels Hans Jürgen Nierentz wrote a poem with the title 'Als Deutschland stürzte' [When Germany Fell] which appeared in a collection edited by another major writer of the Reich, Will Vesper, *Die Ernte der Gegenwart* [Harvest of the Present], the third edition of which was published in 1943.

> Als Deutschland stürzte, waren wir noch Knaben.
> Wir waren jung, und hatten kein Panier.
> Der Sieg lag draussen vor dem Feind begraben.
> Deutschland war Nacht. Und Deutschland waren wir.
>
> Wir fielen mit im Schmerz des jähen Falles,
> und waren mit zertrümmert und zerschellt
> und liebten Deutschland, Deutschland über alles,
> und hatten nichts mehr lieber in der Welt.
>
> Doch da das Volk, das dämmernde, das fahle,
> noch zagend zittert und verwundert steht,
> bauen wir der Treue eine Kathedrale,
> die ragend über dem Jahrhundert steht.[47]

[When Germany fell we were still boys, young and with no banner to follow. Victory was out there, buried in the face of the enemy, Germany was in darkness, and we were Germany. We fell too, in the pain of the hard collapse and were ourselves broken, and we loved Germany, Germany above all, and loved nothing more than that in the whole world. But whilst the defeated, pallid people stand there trembling and baffled, we are building a cathedral to loyalty that rises up above our century.]

The familiar first person plural address implies unity of effort. The poem is about the war that was lost, but the enemy are not perceived as having taken the victory, rather that victory as an absolute concept lies buried. The implication is that a German victory is retrievable. The patriotic stress on Germany already sounded three times in the first strophe is reinforced in the second with an echo of the national anthem adopted in 1922, and the last strophe introduces those ideas of renewal and of positive building which typifies so much of this poetry. That it is a cathedral is part of the deliberate exploitation of religious connotations.

Clearest of all is Anacker's 'Gegen Versailles' [Against Versailles], which contains the explicit demand that they should 'zerreisst das Papier unserer Schande' ('rip up the paper of our shame'). On posters concerned with the *Anschluss* vote in Austria in 1938 it was claimed that Hitler had 'torn up the *Diktat* of Versailles' piece by piece. Anacker's poem concludes with the line 'wir marschieren, marschieren, marschieren' ('we are marching, marching, marching').[48]

The marching dead of the First World War are merged with those who died in the early stages of the Nazi movement. Baldur von Schirach used the motif,[49] and the best known illustration, and one of the best known of the Nazi marching songs was that by the notorious Horst Wessel, the SA man killed in dubious circumstances but made by the party into a hero. That the song he wrote was viewed as extremely dangerous because of its (even if manufactured) popularity is made clear by Brecht's and other parodies. References to Horst Wessel and his song are frequent, and he himself was put forward in romanticized form as a role model.[50] The song itself is simple, stresses solidarity and looks forward to the takeover by the Nazis. This was not a war poem when written; the battle it describes is for political supremacy within Germany. Nevertheless, it was used as a war song, and the sense was reapplied to the greater battles. Its imagery made this very easy to do:

Die Fahne hoch! Die Reihen dicht geschlossen!
SA marschiert mit ruhig festem Schritt.
Kameraden, die Rotfront und Reaktion erschossen,
marschiern im Geist in unsern Reihen mit.

Die Strasse frei den braunen Bataillonen!
Die Strasse frei dem Sturmabteilungsmann!
Es schaun aufs Hakenkreuz voll Hoffnung schon Millionen.
Der Tag für Freiheit und fur Brot bricht an.

Zum letzten Mal wird nun Appell geblasen!
Zum Kampfe stehen wir all schon bereit.
Bald flattern Hitlerfahnen über allen Strassen.
Die Knechtschaft dauert nur noch kurze Zeit.

[Raise the flag! Close ranks! The SA is marching calmly and firmly. Comrades shot down by the Red Front and by the reactionaries are marching with us in spirit. Open the streets to the brownshirt columns, open the streets to the SA man. Already millions are looking with hope towards the swastika. The day of freedom and bread is dawning. Roll-call has sounded for the last time. We are all prepared for battle. Soon Hitler's flag will fly over all the streets. The time of servitude will not last long now.]

Günter Hartung has shown the ancestry of the song,[51] and its techniques are patent. The immediacy of the movement and the familiar concept of the dawning day are both present, and the entire tone is military. It must be remembered that in the song the last two lines of each strophe are repeated, and indeed, that this is a song for marching, about marching. The first strophe was also repeated at the end. It was difficult to forget, and the tune is a vigorous one.

J.M. Ritchie points out[52] that it is unusual for the enemy to be as clearly delineated as in this lyric. In songs and lyrics of the Reich, though, specific references *are* found to what the movement saw as its ideological enemies, the Jews and the Communists, and, later, to the actual enemies in battle. The denigration can be quite straightforward. The poem by Baumann and the 'Horst Wessel Lied' both attack the Red Front quite clearly, as do Italian equivalent songs, such as that of the blackshirts, the 'Camicia nera'. Those directed against Jews contain particularly horrific lyrics, many of them exceptionally crude:

schmiert die Guillotine
mit dem Judenfett. . .[53]

[grease the guillotine with the fat of Jews. . .]

Similar examples could be multiplied. The detailed anti-Semitic material of the early years of the Nazi movement is not war poetry as such, of course, and indeed, as Schöne has commented, this kind of crass material (though it surely continued to be cited and cannot be ignored) was played down in *printed* sources in favour of a 'steely romanticism'. It is, indeed, not found in contemporary popular anthologies to any extent. What *is* there – and this is more insidiously dangerous – is the tagging of 'the Jew' as the enemy in the simplest of terms, linked often with the blood and soil ideology as the foreigner within Germany. Nevertheless, *The Mind and Face of Nazi Germany* did cite in 1942 the very well-known lines:

> When Jewish blood spurts from the knife
> Then things go twice as well. . .[54]

A separate category of war poetry deals with actual events, such as the occupation of Austria, of the Sudetenland, or with the Allied forces and their leaders. The lyrics concerned with the initial Nazi expansionist moves are bound up, of course, with the ideas of *Lebensraum* and of the pan-Germanic unity.

This expansion was celebrated and reinforced by the official poets. Josef Weinheber celebrated the takeover of the Saar, Agnes Miegel that of Danzig and the east, Richard Nordhausen the *Anschluss* of Austria in a poem called 'Die Ostmark kehrt heim, Marz 1938' [German-Austria Comes Home, March 1938], and Josef Moder eulogized the 'Sudetendeutsche Heimkehr' [Sudeten-German Homecoming] in the same year.[55] Nordhausen published in the popular periodical *Kladderadatsch* a celebration of Hitler's breach of the Munich agreement and the taking of Bohemia and Moravia which bears analysis as a poetic justification of what was, in fact, an act of aggression, a clear example of the use of the lyric form (two linked sonnets) and its attendant concentration of ideas in the service of the war that had now effectively begun. The two sonnets bear the title 'Hakenkreuz überm Hradschin' [Swastika over the Hradcany Palace]:

> Urdeutschen Raumes blühendes Gelände,
> nur deutsche Arbeit bracht's in Glanz und Flor,
> doch immer wieder warf durchs offene Tor
> der ewige Hussit des Hauses Brande.
>
> Ein sinnlos Wuten ohne Ziel und Ende,
> das sich im Chaos stets von neu'm verlor!
> Jetzt aber reckt die Flagge sich empor,
> die Flagge der gewalt'gen Schicksalswende.

Verschwören sind mit Seele und Gemüt
ihr alle Deutschgebornen, Haupt und Glieder;
wo diese Flamme, diese Flagge glüht,
da loscht sie niemand, holt sie niemand nieder.

Die Flagge weht! Zukunftsgedanken ziehn
auf Adlerschwingen über den Hradschin.[56]

[The blossoming land, ancient German territory brought to
flower by German labour alone – but time and again the eternal
Hussite has thrown a burning brand through the open door.
Stupid ravings, without a goal or aim, always ending in chaos!
But now the banner rises up, the banner of the mighty turn of
fate. All you Germans born are heart and soul part of this, with
all your self. Where this flame and this flag shine, no one will
douse it or tear it down. The flag waves in the wind. Thoughts of
a future soar on eagle's pinions over the Hradcany Palace.]

The build-up is skilful. The sonnet opens with the stressed notion
of ancient German territory, reinforces this with another 'German'
in the next line and shows us a land in flower, contrasting it at
once with the wanton destruction of the house (though the idea of
the torch at the temple door is hardly new) by the Czech – tagged
as 'der Hussit' in a phrase which recalls *der ewige Jude*, the
'wandering Jew', literally 'eternal Jew', used to mean 'ever-
present'. Note that the door is open, so that the Czechs are
presented as aggressors – Ritchie and others have commented on
the technique in Nazi poetry of accusing others of what the
movement was itself most guilty.[57] The second quatrain again
offers a contrast: the chaos claimed for pre-Nazi government in
most of the invaded countries is set against the 'new turn' –
'Wende' is another keyword in Nazi poetry – and the flag
symbolizes the new government. What is actually offered is not
described, of course, but the flag and the its attendant stock motif
of the flame (which comes somewhat oddly after the accusation of
wanton arson) unite the German-born (before the First World
War). The flag then becomes that of the future over the centre of
government in Prague.

The second of the two sonnets makes clear that this is still a war
poem, even though the outbreak of war was some months away. It
anticipates reaction, whilst reasserting the familiar concepts of a

holy, thousand-year Reich, the Führer-principle, and the idea of victory in spite of any enemy:

> Sie bauscht sich stolz und frei in Gottes Winden,
> Ordnung und Frieden sichert sie fortan;
> in ihrem starken Schutz wird jedermann,
> der guten Willens ist, Genüge finden.
>
> Die letzten Nachtgespenster müssen schwinden,
> nun tausenjähr'ges Recht den Sieg gewann;
> lässt dem geliebten Führer, der den Bann
> zerbrach, uns immer inniger verbinden!
>
> Ob dann die Welt sich gegen uns empört,
> deutsch bleibt das Land, kerndeutschem Volk verhiessen,
> denn was in Ewigkeit zum Reich gehört,
> kann ihm kein Feind, kein Teufel mehr entreissen.
>
> Im Winde Gottes Zukunftsmelodien!
> Die Flagge Hitlers über dem Hradschin!

[The flag billows proud and free in God's own breezes, and ensures from now on order and peace. In its firm protection all men of good will can find satisfaction. The last few nightmare-figures have to disappear now that the justice of a thousand years has won the victory. May our beloved Führer, who broke the old spell, bind us ever more closely together. No matter if the world rises up against us: the land is German, granted to a solidly German people, and what has always belonged to the Reich can be taken from it by no enemy, no devil. In the breeze of God's songs of the future, Hitler's flag is over the Hradcany Palace!]

The religious underlay is again quite clear – God's breezes stand at the beginning and the end, and the liturgical allusion to peace brought to all *hominibus bonae voluntatis* is unsurprising. The third quatrain takes the typically aggressive stand of attacking and vilifying those likely to object, and the final couplet, which links with the first sonnet, is again assertive. The swastika is flying over Prague, and nothing can be done. This is more than patriotic or ideological-tendentious poetry. It anticipates war, and its skill *as* poetry illustrates the point that poetry (specifically war poetry) can be both functional and – in the wrong hands – dangerous in its concentrated persuasiveness.

Once the war began, soldiers' songs tended towards a simple encouragement based firmly in the view that victory was certain. Such songs included the march 'Von Finnland bis zum Schwarzen Meer' [From Finland to the Black Sea],

> Von Finnland bis zum Schwarzen Meer
> Vorwärts, vorwärts nach Osten
> nun stürmen wir.
> Freiheit das Ziel
> Sieg das Panier
> Führer befiehl,
> Wir folgen Dir.[58]

[From Finland to the Black Sea, onwards, onwards to the East we are storming – Freedom the aim, victory our banner, Führer command, we will follow you.]

This is the refrain, and the last part is repeated. Tanks rolled firmly over Africa, and the same confidence was there on another front:

> Kamerad, wir marschieren im Westen
> mit dem Bombengeschwader vereint,
> und fallen auch viele der Besten,
> wir schlagen zu Boden den Feind.
> Vorwärts, voran, voran,
> über die Maas, über Schelde und Rhein,
> marschieren wir siegreich
> nach Frankreich hinein. . .[59]

[Comrades, we are marching westwards, together with our bomber squadrons, and even if many of our best men should fall, we will still hammer the enemy into the ground. Onwards, on and on, over Meuse, Scheldt and Rhine – we are marching on to victory into France. . .]

The reference to bomber support indicates that this is from the Second World War, but just as the names and the destination recall the First World War, so too it plays on the notion of revenge against an enemy victorious only twenty years or so before.

The soldiers themselves sometimes produced more specific

sentiments. In 1942, Corporal Fritz Wildmoser published in the *Münchener Feldpost* the following 'Worte an den Tommy' [Some Words to Tommy] which demonstrate, in dialect, a simple battle mentality addressed directly to the enemy:

> Du brauchst bloss kommen, mia wart'n scho,
> aber liab tät'st ausschaug'n, guater Mo!
> Was glaubst, wie mia dich zuaricht'n tat'n
> zuerst mit'm G'wehrkolben und dann mit'm Spat'n.
>
> G'rad neihaun tät'n ma auf euere Kopf,
> damit's euch einmal vergeht, ös Tropf,
> einen G'fangenen z'fesseln und z'schikanier'n
> oder unser Münchner Städtl z'bombardier'n.
>
> Bei einem neuen Gastspiel am Atlantikwall
> nur keinem Bayern in die Hande fall,
> denn da hast dich g'waschen, mei liaba Mo!
> Du braucht bloss komma, mia wart'n scho. . .![60]

[Just come on, we're ready and waiting, but you'd best look out, man. You'd better believe what we'll do to you, with our rifle stocks and then with spades. We'll just set to and bang your heads, you dolts, to knock out of you the idea of chaining up or mucking about with a POW, or bombing our own little Munich. In any new fun and games at the Atlantic Wall mind you don't fall into Bavarian hands, or then you've had it. Just come on, we're ready and waiting. . .!]

The promise of attacks with gun butts and spades sounds much like the trenches, although references later to the Atlantic Wall and to the bombing of Munich fix it in a later period. Propaganda about the treatment of prisoners seems to have had its effect here, too, but the main note struck by this poem and verse of its kind is a somewhat old-fashioned 'up and at 'em'. Far more political is another marching song, 'Wir stürmen dem Siege entgegen' [We Are Storming On to Victory], with the refrain:

> Wir stürmen dem Siege entgegen
> zu säubern Europas Haus
> und schlagen mit hammernden Schlägen
> die Briten zum Lande hinaus.[61]

[We are storming on to victory to purify Europe's house, and with hammer-blows we are driving the British out.]

On the other front, the catchy song 'In einem Polenstädtchen' [In a Little Polish Town] was widely sung, though now it had new implications. Rudolf Leonhardt prints a set of words to the same tune which mocks the fall of Poland as 'Es gab einmal ein Polen' ('Once there was a Poland'),[62] but adds that it was not sung. Whether or not this is accurate is impossible to determine, however.

One of the best known of the marching songs, however, was the so-called 'Engellandlied' (which uses an archaic or sailors' song form of the name England). This was, in fact, written at the beginning of the First World War by Hermann Löns, and set to music only in 1939 at the instigation of the Nazi controller of the German radio. Assisted by broadcasting, it became popular. Löns himself wrote prose and verse of a conservative nature, and this song might merely be a song of parting, but the singer is leaving specifically to fight. The extended form of the name lays emphasis on it, just as its climactic position had done in Lissauer's 'Hymn of Hate'. The song owed its popularity, perhaps, to the similarity of much of the lyric with sentimental songs of farewell in a different context, a type which still crops up in German popular music from time to time. Here the phrase 'leb' wohl mein Schatz' recalls such well-known pieces as 'Muss i denn zum Städtele hinaus'. The chorus runs:

> Gib mir Deine Hand, Deine liebe Hand,
> leb wohl, mein Schatz, leb wohl,
> denn wir fahren gegen Engelland.[63]

[Give me your hand, your lily-white hand, farewell my darling farewell, for we are setting off against England.]

The sung version repeats the 'farewell' several times, and heightens the point of the verse by repeating also the 'denn wir fahren', ('we are setting off'). But in the second strophe the context is clear:

> Unsre Flagge, und die wehet auf dem Maste,
> Sie verkundet unseres Reiches Macht,
> Denn wir wollen es nicht länger leiden,
> Dass der Englisch-Mann darüber lacht.

[Our flag flutters at the masthead in the wind, a sign of our Reich's power, for we will suffer the Englishman to laugh at us no more.]

To leave the word 'Reich' is a little unfair: Löns meant the Kaiser's empire. However, the text suited the Third Reich, and it was functional in the intent to keep up the spirits. But there is a considerable gap between simple statements of belligerence and poetry and song underlining tenets of Nazi ideology, to the extremes either of anti-Semitism or of Hitlerian apotheosis. Some soldiers' or sailors' songs even adopt a humorous approach. The traditional sailors' song 'Das kann doch einen Seemann nicht erschüttern' [A Thing Like That Can Never Shock a Seaman] was adapted early in the war as the basis for a Churchill-Chamberlain taunt. It uses English words as an additional point, as well as the colloquial style with the Low German flavour expected from a sea song:

> Wie gern Herr Churchill uns blockiert,
> you see it now looks black.
> Das deutsche U-Boot torpediert
> ihm seinen Frühstücksspeck.
> Ihn selber trifft ein jeder Schuss,
> die Welt zu rulen ist jetzt Schluss.
> Die Nordsee ward ein deutsches Meer,
> nu kiekste hinterher.
>
> Das muss den ersten Seelord doch erschüttern,
> jeder Streich macht ihn weich, macht ihn kleen.
> Wir werden ihn auch weiterhin zerknittern,
> siehste woll, siehste woll Chamberlain.
> Am Meeresgrund liegt mighty ships
> wir kriegen ihn noch an den Schlips. . .[64]

[Mr Churchill loves to blockade us, but you see it now looks black. German U-boats torpedo away his breakfast bacon. Every shot hits him amidships, so much for ruling the world. The North Sea became a German sea, look at that. A thing like that must surely shock the First Sea Lord, every blow softens him and puts him down. We'll go on crumpling him, look here, Chamberlain. The mighty ships are at the bottom of the sea, and soon we'll have him by the collar. . .]

War poetry in the Third Reich in particular and in the other Fascist countries too was used programatically and functionally.[65] It is a poetry in favour of war, and the inbuilt conciseness of the poetic form, regardless of the level of the language, which can be elevated and poetically skilful (though seldom abstruse, of course, for fear of obscuring the message) makes an ideal medium for putting across and reinforcing views about war without the necessity of reasoned argument, especially by the use of emotive recurring ideas. War is not killing and maiming (though heroic death is possible and even perhaps worthwhile); rather it is marching to victory behind a flag. The lyrics of the Third Reich did not admit of defeat in any sense. With deliberate uniformity it imposed a view of the First World War which stressed rather the iniquities of Germany's treatment at Versailles, and that in its turn demanded a particular view of the new war even before it came.

Popular war poetry can have conceptual implications that are sometimes forgotten. The propagandist use of poetry can be documented on both sides in the two wars, but here it is at its most extreme in style. The Nazi war lyric is a poetry of excess, exaggerating motifs found regularly enough in all patriotic poetry in the First World War and earlier. Nations are asked to awaken because the tyrant's heel is on their shore; flags, drums, trumpets, marching, the dead of other wars, even praise of the leaders, are all found as individual elements in most patriotic war poetry. The extent, the totality, and the uniformity of their use in Nazi and other Fascist lyrics is quite different, however. For the modern reader, the war poetry of the Nazis – and a good part of it *is* war poetry – has an extremely powerful memorial and warning function, and it should not be ignored. It provides an object lesson in the functionality of the lyric form when it is used systematically as a weapon in an immoral cause. The extreme shows us that a war poetry of incitement can work.

5

There is No Need for Alarm
Poems of the Allies, 1939–45

I don't allow nobody for to dictate fings to me
Excepting p'raps the missus — still that's 'ow it ort to be
Arthur Victor and Ernest Longstaffe, 'My England'[1]

It has been pointed out that poetry in English in the Second World
War differs from that of the First in its lack of a sense of 'deep
moral outrage' at war as such and its stress on the need to get on
with the job.[2] The range is just as vast, however, but there are
some areas of war poetry, particularly in English, that merit more
consideration than they have been afforded. One such is that
represented by A.P. Herbert, who said of his own work that it
made 'small appeal to Apollo. But it may be of some assistance to
Mars when he compiles his annual report.'[3] Patriotic lyrics of the
1939–45 period, too, may not be dismissed with a chichéd reference
to the 'Kipling-Newbolt School'. Many of the poets concerned,
whose works were purchased and read, belonged to a generation
who had written already about the First World War, and some of
them had fought in it.

As was the case with the First World War, the lyric form was
used in all kinds of contexts. Beside the many posters reminding a
civilian population that walls have ears tags like 'tittle-tattle lost
the battle'[4] are both memorable and useful. Both Anne Harvey and
Susan Briggs cite a comforting little piece for children on
'Embarkation Leave' in which

> Sheila carries daddy's gas mask
> Peter carries daddy's gun. . .[5]

and its inclusion in anthologies is justified by the purpose served at
the time. Though designed for children, the verse makes clear that
the mother is deliberately trying to play down the problems of
parting, and also acknowledges implicitly that the child is aware of
the seriousness of the situation. It is certainly a war poem.

The moral issues with the Second World War are clearer, and the dismissal of patriotic poetry in English is harder. Precisely as with the First World War, however, we may consider beside lyrics designed to help a home population to cope with and, indeed, ultimately to win a war the material produced by soldiers to help themselves to cope. The division is now not nearly as clear cut, however, as bombing and the threat of invasion put civilians into the front line. In English and other poetry of the Second World War a series of themes may be distinguished that echo, though not always to the same degree, those of the First. There is pure patriotism, in some senses even with a hatred of the enemy that recalls Lissauer. Hitler is attacked in precisely the same way as the Kaiser. There is a stress on home and beauty not restricted to home poetry, and some very widely read sentimental verse, as well as resignation and humour in soldiers' poetry.

Poetry was presented to the public in a great variety of ways, and the anthologies were particularly varied. The Readers Union collection *Fear No More*, for example, has comments in its (anonymous) preface on the great desire for poetry at the beginning of the war: 'they asked for poetry as hungry people ask for bread, not to escape circumstance, but to be able to hold it'. The work contained verse like:

> Let Goliath have his say
> David won, and will today. . .[6]

If there were reasonably priced anthologies of highly competent poets – as in the *Modern Reading Library* two-and-sixpenny edition of poems by John Hall, Keith Douglas, and Norman Nicholson in 1943 – there were also less demanding collections, such as *Poets in Battledress*, which claimed

> Nothing . . . except that it may be of interest as representative of the reactions of a group of people who love and who are trying to write poetry whilst engaged in the same phase of the universal struggle.[7]

Any doubts as to where the war poets might be could have been cleared by a glance at the soldier collections, including anthologies of poems from the desert, from India, and from Italy. The last contains 71 poems selected from 596 submitted, all written during the first nine months of the Italian campaign. The companion volume, *Poems from the Desert*, had a brusque foreword by Field Marshall Montgomery and Sassoon's introduction to the Italian volume gently praises poets who are 'both ancient and modern in their technique'.[8] Regimental magazines, too, bear witness to how much was still being written within the forces. Attention must be paid as well to verses which fall within the oral tradition, but which once again served a purpose as war poetry in that they helped maintain morale within a particular set of circumstances.

Poetry of circumstance is not the same as occasional poetry written without real engagement. There are special difficulties with the concept of popular poetry in the occupied countries. War poetry in these countries or by their forces in exile had a clearly enhanced function in providing encouragement towards the war effort often under difficult conditions. Within the occupied countries there were clandestine writings ranging from straightforward patriotism to poems of human experiences, but popularity was on an inevitably small scale. Poems often went unpublished, although French *contrebande* poetry appeared in print with the patriotic sentiments covert or allusive. Many of the forces of governments in exile – Czechs, Poles, Dutch, Yugoslavs, Belgians, Norwegians, and the Free French – had their own publications. The best known, the French, can point to underground literature in France, and to journals like *La France Libre* in Britain.

It was made quite clear to the British soldier, however, precisely what he was fighting for this time. The Army Education Directorate produced from 1942 a series of pamphlets known as BWP, *The British Way and Purpose*, which in the very first issue described the Nazi ideal of world domination by the master race and went on:

> We are out to lick the Nazis for what they have done to the Poles, the Norwegians, the Dutch, the Greeks and the rest, and for fear of what they are likely to do to the rest of the world, including ourselves, if they win. . .[9]

The engagingly direct tone is echoed in the music hall monologue, a lyric form virtually (though not entirely) moribund by the war. Victor and Longstaffe's 1941 piece at the head of this chapter is a late example. Once more in a not quite consistent Cockney with occasional stylistic breaks (such as the reference to the mailed fist), the message is perfectly clear:

> Old England ain't a country what's ruled by Gestapos,
> By blokes dressed up in uniform and goodness only knows.
> You sees a copper now an' then but if you ain't on the twist,
> They treats you matey an' polite, there ain't no mailed fist,
> An' I want to keep it just like *that*!

Some of the references are direct:

> Old England ain't a country of Heils and raise yer arm
> An' you can 'ave a pint at night and never do no 'arm,
> An' if you 'as a drop too much an' runs the guv'ment
>   down,
> There ain't no concentration camps around an English
>   town.

The conservative working-class England in which a man can have a pint in peace is what is being fought for, and the speaker moves into the homiletic 'we' to say that 'we treasure it an' are fighting for it, too.'[10] The patriotism of defence is far more specific than it was in the First World War, and it is accepted that civilians as well as soldiers are involved. Another piece from the same year, by Longstaffe with Percy Nash and Nosmo King [Vernon Watson], praises the symbolic civilian after the Blitz:

> The British fighting forces are a pattern to the world. . .
> But courage isn't only found beneath a uniform,
> Our wonderful civilians too have stood up to the storm.

The civilians are portrayed as in the front line, facing the 'fearful carnage and the terror of the raid' but the piece ends somewhat incongrously with an expression of sentiment that could have come from the earlier war:

> So let us all with grateful hearts each night and ev'ry morn,
> Fall on our knees and thank our God, that we are British
>   born.[11]

Divine providence has given the audience the natural equipment to withstand the suffering. It is worth noting, incidentally, that this monologue does at least refer to 'Britain' rather than to England.[12]

Patriotism of the kind produced in 1914 is difficult to find in its more extreme forms, although Brooke and Kipling did have their heirs (and it would be an interesting study to consider poems which actually linked the two wars). In 1940 Dorothy L. Sayers wrote:

> Praise God, now, for an English war —
> The grey tide and the sullen coast,
> The menace of the urgent hour,
> The single island, like a tower,
> Ringed with an angry host. . .[13]

Eleven similarly hymn-like stanzas follow, and the reference to 'the English War' is justified by an emphasis on the defence of the southern coast: Drake's drum is still beating in the work. Elsewhere, in fact, Dorothy Sayers went to some pains to justify herself. In a lecture delivered in 1941 and published in Macmillan's war pamphlets, she commented at length on the manner in which England is the focus of enemy attention. Well aware of the Celtic presence (since, she says somewhat acidly, they 'continually point this out'), she is able to joke about the 'legendary Scotsman' who altered the German 'Gott strafe England' to read 'Britain'. 'It is England', though, 'who is the object of hymns of hate: "Wir fahren gegen Engelland". The real enemy is England, and that peculiarly English conception of the State which the rest of Britain has assimilated, and to which it so magnificently works.'[14]

There is sometimes almost a feeling of satisfaction that Britain was fighting alone.[15] This is coupled with a direct echo of the 'Hymn of Hate' by Alfred Noyes, whose 'On the Eve of Invasion' rests upon the rhythms of the National Anthem:

> Comes now the thunder-shock;
> Now, as they rave and mock
> Stands the unshaken rock,
> England!
> Lies have but fleeting breath.
> Out of this night of death,
> Wakes the strong voice that saith,
> 'England again!'[16]

Patriotic poetry of the Second World War, just as in the First, uses symbolic devices as shorthand. In English, St George is again found frequently enough. A.P. Herbert celebrated 23 April 1944, and Fay Kershaw compared the tank soldier to the knight in armour in a verse which appeared in a *Poetry Review* supplement after the war.[17] Herbert also recalls Boadicea as a national heroine at one point, but there are fewer heroes than in French, say, where the symbolic protection of St Joan, Roland, or Charlemagne was sought by Free France and Vichy alike. More often, English popular poetry stresses the innate virtue of Englishness, as does E. Storey, whose poem on the Northumberland Fusiliers is included in the *Return to Oasis* anthology:

> At Alamein they stood at last, though their ranks were sadly depleted,
> But you see, they came of English stock, and an Englishman's never defeated.[18]

There are echoes of McGonagall, but it is impossible not to be struck by the confidence of the inserted 'you see', making the whole into a statement of fact.

The allied forces provide plenty of examples of patriotic poetry. The Soviet forces were supported by rather repetitive nationalistic verse along the lines of:

> Slava, slava geroyu-narodu
> Slava Armii Krasnoi yevo![19]

[Glory, glory to the heroic homeland, glory to its Red Army!]

That of the exiled forces was often a firmer call to action, however. Louis Aragon's 'Prélude à la Diane Française' echoes the 'Marseillaise', and was included in the famous *L'honneur des poètes* collection in 1943:

> Entendez, Francs-Tireurs de France
> L'appel de nos fils enfermés
> Formez vos bataillons formez
> Le carré de la delivrance
> O notre insaisissable armée.[20]

[Listen, riflemen of France, to the call of our captured sons, form your batallions, form a square for freedom, our inconquerable army.]

Material not by French poets, but by those who felt themselves particularly involved appeared in a variety of forms, as for example the 'Ode to France' of the novelist Charles Morgan, an eight-page pamphlet from 1942. Morgan condemns the 'evil day' on which

Verdun is betrayed, but foresees a day 'as yet unknown' when the martyred France will rise from the tomb in apotheosis and 'beat down Satan'. The anthology of verse for and about France edited by Nancy Cunard in 1944 contains many more examples, praising Marianne and citing the 'Marseillaise', as well as using heroes of the past.[21] To take a less widely distributed example of reaction to occupation, the Polish soldier Antoni Boguslawski produced a volume somewhat optimistically entitled *Mist Before the Dawn* in London in 1942 with some vigorous patriotic verse. The preface, by F B. Czarnomski, explains that the poet himself knew 'only the rudiments of English', but worked with L.L. Gielgud, who had 'only the average Englishman's knowledge of Polish' – a nice euphemism – through the medium of French. Boguslawski himself was over fifty in 1942 and Czarnomski's preface notes with some charm that 'as a cavalryman [he] was not called upon to take an active part in the Battle of Britain'. Nevertheless, the modest collection is still a functional call to resistance not unlike Cammaerts's Belgian 'Carillon' of 1914:

> God is our Shield and Buckler – yours, and mine
> Our friends, the friends of Poland; our Divine
> Assurance, Victory! For the unsubmitting
> The golden road to Victory will shine![22]

François Mauriac, speaking of France, underlined the general value and functionality of the poets in exile during the war. 'The voices of these beloved poets . . . helped France not to lose heart when she was tied to the executioner's post. They sang, and she believed once again in her genius. . .'[23]

In English, attitudes to the enemy in lyrics intended to inform public opinion in support of the war effort can be jingoistic. Robert Hewison refers in his *Under Siege* to Lord Vansittart who remained preoccupied with the 'Hymn of Hate' and returned like with like in prose and verse at great length.[24] Less violent, but still forthright, is the work of A.P. Herbert, whose writing was aimed at a wide audience through popular newspapers and magazines. Herbert's work is not generally thought of as war poetry, but its importance in its time, and its skill within its own terms makes it worthy of detailed study. After some pre-war pique aimed at the 'Hun' (still used in home-based poetry rather than the soldiers' 'Jerry'), Herbert commented in 1939:

'We have no quarrel with the German nation' –
One would not quarrel with the trustful sheep:
But generation after generation
They cough up rulers who disturb our sleep.[25]

The attitude hardened as the war progressed. In October 1942 he rejected the name 'Jerry' as too amiable for

The man who thinks of things to do in concentration camps,
The man who beats and tortures. . .

He also became more critical of those who had accepted Hitler:

I know what you will say,
That only Hitler's hateful, and the rest are sheep astray.
But they created Hitler, they would kneel at Hitler's nod –
We must not call them 'Jerry' till they choose a better god.[26]

As the war progressed, attempts to exonerate Germany received short shrift. The notion of economic necessity for the war is, for example, summarily set aside in June 1943:

We had two million unemployed, but did we go to war?[27]

In 1944 Herbert rejected even the phrase 'Nazi tanks' – 'it is the GERMANS we must thank'. Like Vansittart, Herbert took issue with Bishop Bell over attitudes to the bombing of Germany. It is interesting to compare recent views of the bombing to two verses of Herbert's, one entitled 'Berlin' and dedicated 'To a Bishop', the other 'To a Bomber'. The aggression is muted and self-conscious, but it is pefectly clear:

I do not 'gloat'. But when I see
What they have done to all mankind,
Whatever you may think of me,
I manage not to mind.

and

Heed not the sighs and sermons,
Go, gallant lads, again.
Let some folk think of Germans –
We think of Pole and Dane.[28]

By the end of 1944 he was considering attitudes towards a defeated

Germany. He objected to the proposed provision of 'Buns for the Huns' on the fourth anniversary of the outbreak of war, and speculated on whether the 'softies' would prevent 'us' (the first person plural had been established in the poem as 'we can take it') from 'rubbing their noses in it'.[29]

Two further poems demonstrate Herbert's attitude by the end of the war. In 'Broken Glass' in April 1945, he focuses upon one small aspect of the destruction:

> We are still growing glass where the roses were.
> Each little piece I pluck from a flowerbed
> Is a piece of Hitler, soiling the English spring.
> For each I cry a curse on a German head,
> And when I remember Aachen − I laugh and sing.[30]

Attitudes to the bombing of German cities may have changed with historical hindsight, but Herbert's view was not unique in its time. Once some of the details of the extermination camps had become clear, Herbert rejected the German people both as beast and as brother in a poem subtitled 'Buchenwald' and now referred to 'germans', without the capital letter, speculating that in the future they would regret only what Hitler had *failed* to do.[31] This attitude would continue in popular publications for a very long time – one thinks of Osbert Lancaster cartoons and the policy indeed of the *Daily Express* well into the 1960s – but it is less common in soldier poetry. There are mockeries of the Nazi leaders, but not much on the Germans as such, who are simply 'the Hun' or more often 'Jerries'.[32]

Two long poems may conclude these comments on the image of Germany presented during the war, both written in 1942 by Olga Katzin as Saggitarius of the *New Statesman*. In September 1942 the German love of ceremonial was the starting point for a sustained condemnation of the Third Reich:

> The Germans love processions; there will be
> One more procession when the war is done.
> That they may know what triumphs they have won
> As the Third Reich advanced to victory.

That opening is repeated. The procession here, however, is that very familiar one of the marching dead, on this occasion those who have been conquered – in Norway, the 'butchered hostages of

France', the dead of Greece and Crete, the Slavs, and – as we move towards an emotional climax – the children murdered in the Reich. The final group is of special interest:

> And last, returning to their capital,
> Those Germans, suspect in the German cause,
> Who were enlightened in the Third Reich laws,
> And died unseen, and had no burial.

Herbert's poetry rarely acknowledges good Germans. Saggitarius (though without full knowledge of the extermination camps) draws together the allies who have suffered in their struggle against a Reich which is both identified with and separated from the concept 'German'. The Germans are to watch, in fact, what 'they' have done, and the silence of the 'triumphal procession' is to be broken only when

> . . .death will cry aloud the German name
> Bringing the harvest of the Third Reich home.[33]

In October of the same year Saggitarius published a considerably more extensive piece with the title 'Who Shall Wash the Rhine' (the title is from a satire by Coleridge) which was later reprinted as the conclusion of the *Targets* collection. Although it stems from the middle of the war, it ties together a number of themes already raised within a broad view of the war as such. The first section of the poem presents St George, not as a hero figure, but as not having made a sortie into the Continent since France fell in 1940, and assailed on one side by the Vansittartists who want the Germans eradicated root and branch, and on the other by those who stress the greatness of the German soul, now enslaved by the Third Reich. Some of the rhymes are neat and comical:

> One side declares that it rejoices
> To hear in the Third Reich two voices,
> The other hears in tones yet clearer,
> One voice: 'One Reich, one folk, one Führer!'

The second section declares that the German character is all too well known, having been described and having described itself from Tacitus onwards. Saggitarius sees Faust's comment that 'two souls reside in my breast' as German greed, rather than as a split,

143

while their minds (a somewhat less original joke) cannot be cleared of Kant. The Germans

> Drew strength from joy and joy from toil,
> Up to the eyes in blood and soil. . .

Nazi phrases and concepts are regularly mocked. The Germans of the Third Reich (the first two empires are dismissed as an aping of antiquity and as a statesman's coup) are seen as sheep following a black sheep, but there is a fear that history will repeat itself with a Fourth Reich. In contrast with some of the poems from the very beginning of the war, St George will not be called upon to deal with the problem of Germany alone:

> For as he could not, to be candid,
> Knock out the dragon single-handed,
> Without assistance in his quest
> From Champions of the east and west,
> Once they have set its victims free
> They'll have as much at stake as he.

A conclusion dismisses both Vansittartism and blanket forgiveness, to ask:

> Will every country have a plan
> Except the land where it began?
> Or will at last some power divine
> Make Germans wash their river Rhine?[34]

The poem has breadth, and both its humour and its historical allusions are interesting. The effect differs from that of the quick-thrust verse of Herbert, but it is noteworthy in its considerations of the world after the war.

The idea of functional opposition is seen particularly clearly in a quite different area again rarely included in anthologies and surveys, partly because it does not fall into any national category: the Yiddish poetry of the East European Jews. Yiddish poetry is clearly relevant to a consideration of responses to the Holocaust, but the war poetry produced in Yiddish by partisans is equally interesting; it was, of course, not popular in the same manner as a squib by A.P. Herbert. Usually it was not published at all at the time, was written under terrible conditions, and was sometimes lost until after the war. Defiant poetry against Hitler was composed even inside the concentration camps, and Ruth Rubin cites one example:

> Lomit zayn freylekh un zogn zikh vitsn,
> Mir veln Hitlern shive nokh zitsn![35]

[Let's be cheerful and tell each other jokes. We'll still live to sit and mourn for Hitler!]

The irony of the Jewish ritual phrase *shive zitsn* in the context of Hitler is clear. The poetry of the partisans is more strictly war poetry, however. One of the leading modern Yiddish poets, for example, Abraham Sutzkever, survived the Vilno ghetto, and while fighting as a partisan produced poems which were published just after the war in a collection called *Di festung* [The Fortress]. Some of these clearly have the intent of encouraging the partisans in fairly simple verse, although their audience was small at the time of writing, and their function, when ultimately published, one of memorial, rather than of action. Some of the titles indicate the partisan themes – 'Baglaytlid baym avekgehen in valt' [Song to Go With You into the Forests] – or the aim: 'Zing nit kayn troyriks' [Don't Sing Sad Songs]. The refrain of a poem written in the Vilno ghetto in April 1943 may illustrate the point:

> nit vartn barut,
> mit blut far blut
> a nem ton dem ayzen![36]

[Don't wait calmly. Blood for blood − grab the iron!]

A further area of war poetry that rarely features in anthologies is that of the German lyric against the dictators and the Nazi war effort. Some of the material is *émigré* poetry, and some was again published after the war. Poetry by German POWs collected after the war, however, often distanced itself from the guilt in some respects: 'wir waren nur Soldaten' – 'we were only soldiers'.[37] Outside Germany, however, was a wealth of cabaret material, songs, and poems, the most often discussed perhaps that of Bertolt Brecht, in whose 'Alfabet', for example, 'A' is for

> Adolf Hitler, dem sein Bart
> Ist von ganz besondrer Art.
> Kinder, da ist etwas faul:
> Ein so kleiner Bart und ein so grosses Maul.

[Adolf Hitler, whose moustache is very strange. There's something wrong there, boys! Such a little moustache for such a big gob][38]

Less well-known *émigré* material included poetry published in journals such as *Orient*, a weekly that appeared in Haifa in 1942 and 1943, co-edited by Arnold Zweig, or in *Das Wort* in Moscow. The aim with this poetry may be no more than to provide an outlet for feelings shared by others – in this case German-speaking refugees. In the *Orient*, poems mocked Hitler or the 'Nazi Gangsterreich'. Hermann Vallentin in particular contributed many pieces, usually parodies of known poems such as Heine's 'Lorelei', the Jewish authorship of which was an embarrassment to the Third Reich, and which therefore gained extra irony when used against Hitler. Thus Hitler himself shrugs off the bombing:

> Die Luft ist frei – nur wenn's dunkelt,
> Schleicht mal ein Bomber sich ein,
> Wenn's dann auch ein wenig funkelt,
> Das sollte schupp uns sein.[39]

[The airways are free, but at night-time, a bomber or two gets across, but even if a few sparks fly, we really must not give a toss.]

If Germany does not win – Hitler continues – the waves can swallow it up, though it will be fault of Churchill, not the Lorelei. Meanwhile, however

> . . .heissts noch schreien und singen
> Heil Hitler! Hallelujah!

[the word is still: screech and sing – Heil Hitler! And Hallelujah!]

Still another parody of the same song has Hitler complaining:

> Wenn die Alliierten verschlingen
> meinen Welteroberungsplan
> Dann haben's mit Dollar und Pfunden
> Die Radfahrer getan.

[And if the Allies swallow up my plan to conquer the world then it will have been done, by dollars and pounds, by the cyclists.]

Not the Lorelei, but the cyclists: the reference is to an old joke, which in its briefest form runs: 'The Jews are to blame for Germany's troubles.' 'No, the cyclists.' 'Why the cyclists?' 'Why the Jews?'

Ernst Linz even has a poem in English, parodying the old rhyme 'Ten Little Nigger Boys'. 'Ten Little German Boys' disappear one by one for various reasons, only to be reunited in a concentration camp at the end. Thus:

> Five little German boys –
> One asked: 'What is the score?'
> He meant the British air attacks.
> Then there were four.

Of the various parodies, Vallentin's skilful and far-ranging adaptations in particular demand knowledge of the originals, but have the effect of mocking German culture implicitly whilst overtly making their point, as when Goethe's 'Erlkonig' with the father on horseback becomes a poem about Rommel's equally fatal journey (by tank this time) to El Agheila.

As might be expected, the Japanese are discussed less frequently in British poetry, although A.P. Herbert recalls with dissatisfaction earthquake aid sent to a Japan which now shows scant gratitude.[40] A Japanese statement in February 1941, well before Pearl Harbor, did attract attention, however. A Japanese spokesman commented that Japan had the heart of a dove, wishing to lay the egg of peace, but Britain and the US had laid the snake's eggs of Singapore and Guam in the Pacific nest. Two poetic responses at least were offered to this statement, one by Saggitarius and the other by Alfred Noyes. The former, 'Poor Madam Butterfly', concludes with an ironic attack on the Axis as such:

> Whites should be wiped like vermin
> From Oceania's map,
> Except, of course, the German
> (An honorary Jap),
> For, favours past forgotten,
> Her love-call they decry,
> They say her egg is rotten.
> Poor Madam Butterfly![41]

The squib works well, and the overtones of Madam Butterfly, and even of the popular song 'Poor Butterfly' add to the effectiveness of

147

the notion that Japan's egg of peace is a rotten one. In contrast, Noyes is heavy handed in his use of mock-oriental English ('Mellica' for 'America'). But the oddity of the Axis in racial terms is played up again, noting Japan's antagonism towards China and Hitler's 'yellowness':

> Somebody want to keep East all yellow.
> That's why he kill John Chinaman. See?
> That's why Hitler the velly best fellow.

With hindsight, the ending of the poem is interesting, threatening Japan with attack by the American fleet, something which will reduce their ships to junks. With Pearl Harbor and Hiroshima still in the future, Japan could be viewed as somewhat comical, playing second fiddle to Hitler's war efforts.

Just as Mussolini, Hitler, and Pétain were lauded in innumerable verses in their own languages, popular writers in English such as A.P. Herbert took them as targets. The Nazi leader was referred to either by name or as 'der Fuehrer', the designation (like Mussolini's 'Duce') becoming an object of mockery. There is, incidentally, a distinction between the ways in which Hitler and Mussolini are treated, the latter attracting a more general contempt from the earliest stage. A verse by Herbert in 1940 makes interesting reading in view of later presentations of Hitler. The poem is addressed to the 'Top Wop' and speaks directly to the 'dear old Doochy', but concludes:

> The Prussian is a valiant hog
> And even Hitler's some renown;
> But you are just a dirty dog,
> And, dirty dog, we'll do you down.[42]

For all that, Herbert reminded Hitler on the latter's fifty-first birthday in April 1940 that Napoleon died at fifty-two, a nice counter to adulatory Nazi celebrations of the event.

At a time of serious fear of invasion, there is a note of anxiety in poems referring to Hitler. Herbert published in September 1940 a poem on 'Invasion', which was later reprinted in his alphabetical collection *ATI* – the signal meaning 'there is no need for alarm' – in which Hitler is not actually named:

Napoleon tried. The Dutch were on the way,
A Norman did it — and a Dane or two.
Some sailor King may follow one fine day;
But not, I think, a low land-rat like you.[43]

Napoleon is a little ambiguous, but the Dutch and the Danes were
allies by 1940, as were the Normans, so that Hastings and the
Vikings could be forgiven. Later verse by Herbert took a stronger
line. In January 1943 he sent new year greetings to Hitler, hoping
that 'Herr Chancellor' would get the merciful reward of a rope,
rather than of boiling oil.[44] Later in the same year Hitler is seen as
a 'petty pilferer', and thereafter Herbert's aim is to belittle him, as
in a poem of July 1944, not long after the abortive plot to kill Hitler
in Germany:

Kill Hitler? Why? A Himmler takes his place.
There'll be no rest till you destroy the race.
Besides, he'd be a hero if he died.
The thing is simple. Have him 'certified'.[45]

Mockery of Hitler in Herbert's verse can make light of real
dangers. In the wake of the V1 rockets Herbert postulated a V7,
which brought a fate worse than death:

'V7' is a flying gramophone
That fills the firmament with yells and screeches,
And in a voice more hideous than his own
Recites long passages from Hitler's speeches.[46]

The intrinsic link between nation and leader found neat
expression in a parody in April 1944. The fact that it is a parody of
a patriotic British song lends point to the poem, implying the
notion that 'There'll always be an England/And England shall be
free'. The rhymes used are the same, so that the recollection of the
original words is firmly established. Herbert's poem is once more
for Hitler's birthday, and the effectiveness lies in all the implied
contrasts – a birthday greeting that is not one, and a song which
denigrates the enemy, seeing them as sheep, who can furthermore
be disposed of fairly easily, and all the time with the underlying
strength implied in the original words:

There'll always be a Hitler
Beside the silver Spree

149

If Germans are such silly sheep
As Germans seem to be.

The final injunction is that the German race should be 'dumped in the sea', and the rhyme is predicated on an anglicized pronunciation of the river on which Berlin stands.[47]

Two longer poems by Herbert on Hitler deserve attention. As early as October 1939 Herbert offered an epitaph entitled simply 'A.H.',[48] and placed in Hitler's mouth – an unusual but effective conceit. He refers to his bones as the 'saddest . . . in earth,' because he was 'The mightiest might-have-been of all'. Instead of taking a crown, Hitler chose to be 'the world's Horatio Bottomley', which makes for an interesting conclusion. Bottomley was the celebrated patriot who wrote fervent anti-German pieces for *John Bull* during the First World War, but who was jailed for embezellment in 1922. The whole affords a nice parallel of the patriot gone to the bad, whilst over all a petty crook is compared to a national leader.

On 31 January 1943 Herbert commented specifically on Hitler as a demagogue in 'Der Fuehrer Speaks', and the opening of the first of two twelve-line stanzas still offers an interestingly qualified view of Hitler:

Ten years ago, poor sheep, I stole the flock,
And led you upward by ravine and rock.
I was not wholly bad or imbecile;
There was a fire in me that all could feel. . .[49]

The German people are again sheep, a faintly religious imagery that is carried over to the second stanza:

But madness took me, sheep, and I could not
Enjoy one mountain till I had the lot. . .

Still in Hitler's mouth, the conclusion makes fun precisely of his achievement. The adjective 'small', slipped into the penultimate line is notable, as is the attack on the Germans:

Cheers, my people, cheers!
Never before these ten tremendous years,
Has one small man disturbed so vast a space;
Nor has the world so loathed a single race.

Much use was made (not only by Herbert) of personal details, building up a picture of Hitler as a teetotaller, non-smoker, and vegetarian, the literary equivalent of that emphasis on hair and moustache that were a cartoonist's dream. The dictator allies of 1939 are all thoroughly un-British; not only are the 'teetotalitarians' ranting demagogues but worse, they are abstainers:

It seems that this here Stalin, like that Hitler, doesn't drink.
He doesn't smoke. He don't eat meat. Well, don't it make you think?
Mussolini lives on lettuces. His drinks no man can blame.
And Napoleon, so the paper says, was very much the same.[50]

Comic verse existed side by side with seriously intended longer pieces by establishment poets. Alfred Noyes's long poem 'If Judgement Comes' was published separately, and reprinted later in a collection, and it is an interesting literary curiosity. Noyes, who shares in some respects a poetic reputation with his alphabetic neighbour in many anthologies, Newbolt, was a prolific poet in both wars, known for his strong views against modernism in poetry and aspects of the modern world in general. His poetry – apart from occasional revivals of 'The Highwayman' – is not now generally read: his work 'lacks distinction of style or subtlety of feeling, but has a certain strenuousness'.[51] For all that, he *was* read and his verse appears regularly in anthologies throughout the interwar years. 'If Judgement Comes' stands out because of its length, approaching five hundred unrhymed pentameters. In the work, Hitler stands accused before history:

You stand there, in the dock, before the world
For Judgement, with the froth of your last lie
White on your lips, the red blood on your hands;
The blood of children plastered on your boots;
The blood of women, dust of their rubbled homes. . .[52]

Noyes provides a summary of the ways in which Hitler was viewed by the world, and before he is named we are given the externals, including the caricature forelock and moustache, which have, says Noyes, wrongly been taken as comical. The Chaplin link is reversed. Rather he is

> . . .bully to a prostitute; the pale,
> Blackmailing type of injured *maquereau*. . .

Hitler's demagogic hypnotism is linked with the 'witches cauldron'
of the 'bogus intellectuals' that Noyes attacked so frequently in his
prose, and the clear flaw of the work is its mixture of targets.
Nevertheless, the point is that Hitler is not a laughing stock; Noyes
contrasts the way in which the whole world misunderstood Hitler's
intentions with the statements of *Mein Kampf*. On this occasion the
German people are separated from Hitler and the plutocrats, 'like
Goebbels or yourself', and the ills of the wars are laid at the feet of
the statesmen. The overall image – repeated several times, – is of a
'blinded people', even though they goose-step 'across the graves/Of
innocent millions. . .' The poem concludes not just with a
condemnation of Hitler, however. Vengeance and justice are seen
as attributes of God, and the call is for mankind to change. The
view of war presented in close of the work is an interesting one; it
has in the past been noble and glorious, but now

> The name of 'War'
> Is but a name today, a cheating cloak
> For murder of the helpless multitude,
> By monsters in high places.

The answer that Noyes provides at the last is a specifically
religious one, that of individual faith which can deliver man from
the evil will. The whole resolves itself as a prayer against a Hitler
who is seen as an embodiment of original sin in a modern world.
The poem grinds some of Noyes's favourite axes, but for its view of
Hitler and the conceit of his being brought to (divine) justice
before the end of the war, it is not without interest, and it makes
the valid point that *Mein Kampf* should have been read more
carefully.

   Stalin was more problematic than Hitler, as pre-war admiration
(in some quarters, at any rate) was affected by the Russo-German
pact, and then the attack by Hitler which led to the USSR's joining
the allies. A poem by Saggitarius in 1941, based upon a report in
Asahi Shimbun to the effect that Stalin had wept whilst bidding
farewell to the Japanese Foreign Minister, mocks the problem of
the Communists' unsettled allegiances. Noting that a union of this
sort 'must be against someone for something, and if so, for what,

against whom?', Saggitarius went on to express the problems of the left:

> . . . Communists all the world over, already perceptibly dazed,
> Awaited in mute acquiescence their cue for a sound Party line.[53]

A.P. Herbert is dubious from the start about the unholy alliance, and in March 1940 saw the 'poor old twisted Axis' as a most unlikely combination, pointing out that Stalin could hardly be comfortable with *Mein Kampf* and its view of Russians any more than Mussolini could love the Comintern. The view is summed up with his customary felicity:

> A hates B, and B hates A, and C distrusts the two.[54]

Later on, of course, the attitude to Stalin could change, but even if Herbert presents him in the more familiar guise of 'Uncle Joe', it is not without an edge. 'Less Nonsense', the title poem of one of the collections, reminds us that while Stalin may be loved and lauded, nevertheless it was little Britain that bore the brunt in 1940.[55]

Attacks on Mussolini, referred to by Herbert as Top Wop, in contrast to the 'Duce' title, tend to see him as beneath contempt. In July 1940 Herbert was still able to admit Hitler's toughness, whilst commenting that at the thought of Mussolini one

> . . . really must expectorate –
> There's nothing else to do.[56]

Another of the establishment poets, George Rostrevor Hamilton, has a particularly neat epigram which provides a counter to the Italian propaganda verses lauding Mussolini as a second Caesar:

> This pinchbeck Caesar aping the sublime
> To Nero for his inspiration turns,
> And, from the Teuton leader taking time,
> Plays second fiddle while his country burns.[57]

Mussolini's own much publicized vision of the glory of the Roman Empire restored was inevitably satirized in English verse, and Saggitarius used the image of a bedraggled Imperial Roman eagle which is more like Poe's raven as it answers Mussolini's questions on his future victories with the word 'nevermore'. She also placed

into Mussolini's own mouth Mark Anthony's speech on the death
of Caesar, thereby setting up a series of referential and not
undemanding cross-currents. 'In Rome', says Mussolini,

> . . .must Romans welcome the Gestapo
> (For they are all, all honourable men)
> . . .
> Lest we inflame them, lest we make them mad. . .[58]

The motif of German dominance and the belittling of Italy is clear
once again.

Marshal Pétain also presented problems, although he was of
course mocked by French and English poets alike. The victor of
Verdun's new image invited attack; in the face of adulatory verse
in which the Marshal took up his pilgrim's staff

> Quand le Maréchal Pétain prend
> Son baton de pélérin,

resistance lyrics in poem and song referred to a somewhat different
kind of baton and to Pétain's celebrated sexuality. Herbert and
Saggitarius attacked Pétain (the former playing on his age and
presumed senility); and Nancy Cunard's anthology of poems in
English written on behalf of the Free French, *Poems for France*,
contains several specific attacks on Pétain, Laval, and Vichy
France. Lord Dunsany contrasts with Pétain the 'fine fierce blare'
of the 'Marseillaise' (which was not sung in Vichy France) and sets
the Spirit of France as embodied in Joan of Arc and Napoleon
against the 'phantom' of a crazy old man.[59] Ada Jackson, in the
same anthology, sees Pétain's story as a tragedy, and Sylvia
Townsend Warner contrasts the young of France with the aged
Marshal. A poem signed 'Zodiac', demands (on 14 July 1940) that
he be sent to the Bastille, and the same poet attacks Laval in a
poem 'To Marianne' which ends with a collection of battle-cries –
'The Carmagnole! Ça ira! Croix de Lorraine!' It begins with a
caricature of the Vichy leaders:

> What slobbering ape is this? What Caliban
> Has ravished France? What Emperor of Yahoos
> Usurps the land, leading his grinning crews
> Of Jackbooters to pillage what they can,
> The rest defile? While one that was a man

Like some poor harlot broken in the stews
Limping and whimpering his fate pursues
Down the dark alley-way, pétin-pétant.[60]

Pétain, referred to only allusively in the French pun (the proximity
of the aged general's name to the verb 'to fart' was exploited more
than once) is seen as having once been a man; but his subsequent
breakdown is seen as that of a harlot, an ironic emasculation, in
view of his supposed sexual behaviour.

If mockery was aimed at the enemy war leaders in poetry of all
kind (just like the Kaiser, Hitler made appearances in *Alice in
Wonderland*),[61] the allied leaders were praised. English poems refer
to the King and Queen, but there is a nice illustration of this in a
Commonwealth poem. In a poem in Xhosa, George VI is credited
with a personal victory over Hitler in a heroic panegyric that is still
a poem of the Second World War:

You thundered over Hitler. . .
Yes, you killed the man with the sullen face.
Hero of London, distinguished in battle. . .[62]

In English, however, the theme was more often Churchill, although
the imperial elevation and indeed apotheosis of the Fascist leaders
is hardly present. Nevertheless, A.P. Herbert pinpointed the
oratorial effectiveness of the war leader in his poem on Churchill's
birthday in November 1941, where he addressed him as

The Voice of old Britain at bay

and trusted that he might

live to hear History say
'This was their finest man.'[63]

As Herbert later noted in his autobiography, it was by no means
certain at that point that Churchill would be accepted by history
that way. Churchill's own speeches, of course – as here – provided
a great number of phrases. 'Give us the tools' provided a title for
Saggitarius, just as 'Some Chicken, Some Neck' did for a popular
song. Herbert addressed lyrics to most of the individual war
leaders – Chamberlain, de Gaulle, and Montgomery were praised,
and Chiang Kai-Shek received his versified tribute, as did
Roosevelt in a piece entitled 'Thanks, Mr. President' in 1943

(George Formby performed a song with the similar title of 'Thanks, Mr Roosevelt').[64] Saggitarius produced in 1942 a long poem praising all the allied leaders, each verse of which had as an afterthought the comment that the British, in spite of a 'Genius for Understatement' (the poem's title), were also doing their bit.[65] Exile forces cast their own leaders – de Gaulle, Sikorski, and others – in a more specifically patriotic role.[66]

Noteworthy among the poetic tributes to Churchill is a long piece by Cecil Roberts, *A Man Arose*.[67] It appeared in June 1941 as a fifteen-page booklet, with a dustjacket designed by J. Morton Sale carrying a picture of a lion defending itself against an eagle. A frontispiece reproduced a Cecil Beaton photograph of Churchill in at his desk, cigar in hand. More details of the work, and, indeed, the justification for examining it as a piece of popular poetry of the Second World War, may be found in the introduction to a second edition in 1952, once Churchill had been returned to power, and this time with the Beaton photograph as the jacket illustration. Cecil Roberts, a poet in the First World War and a prolific, but no longer widely-read novelist who died in 1976, wrote *A Man Arose* in March 1941 and read it to friends in New York, and then to Wendell Willkie, the Republican presidential candidate, who had long argued for American support in the war. He in his turn arranged for it to be broadcast, which it duly was at the end of March 1941, with repeats which reached a wide audience. Willkie concluded his own introductory remarks with the view that 'America must and will uphold the hand of Britain'.[68] The work was functional in its encouragement to the American people to join the war, and for those already fighting it made a clear statement on the situation as a whole, rather than just on Churchill. It is not even primarily 'about' Churchill in the sense that works on Mussolini or Hitler are 'about' their subjects. Roberts's poem was – thus the blurb for the 1952 edition – 'immediately recognized as a tribute also to the stirring courage of the British people.'

The work, in nearly two hundred lines of rhymed verse, opens with a picture of the days before the war. The British lion is slumbering, whilst the British people do nothing more than smile tolerantly upon Hitler and Mussolini, neither of whom is actually named:

> They smiled with tolerant humour while

> A hate-crazed creature, master of lies
> With arm aloft and throaty *Heil*
> Screamed at the soft democracies.
> They listened while the blacksmith's son
> Strutted and ranted, blackshirted, obese,
> Threatened the world with dagger and gun. . .

It is hardly surprising to see Hitler dubbed 'master of lies' in evocation of the devil; there is a dismissive tone about Mussolini as 'the blacksmith's son', however, which is at variance with the emphasis on the values of ordinary life in the rest of the work. Historical distance might cause us to pause just a little on 'obese', not only as a rhyme for 'democracies', but also in view of the girth of the dedicatee. Britain's complacent sleep, however, was to be disturbed by a voice, which is compelling, though not that of a demagogue,

> When in their midst a Man arose.

As yet, no name is given to Churchill. If Hitler is the master of lies and Mussolini a blacksmith's son, Churchill is 'suckled by the young, free West' – having, of course, an American mother – but still 'of lineage proud', with immediate reference to Blenheim and Malplaquet and to the Marlborough line, promising people 'blood, sweat and tears' to serve 'as a conquering creed'. The words used by Churchill in 1940, then, are set back into a British past.

The lines cited above contain the title of the work, and we may note the capitalization of 'Man', though it is not capitalized in the line which follows, introducing the section on Churchill's family background:

> A man arose, in England sired. . .

The only other times the noun is capitalized are at the end of the poem. There is first a reference to 'the holy spirit of Man', but then a reference to the 'Man of Sorrows, thrice-denied', invoked to comfort those who:

> . . .long in faith and valour stood
> to crush a monstrous creed of blood.

The resounding ending may link Churchill with Christ, but for all that, the work is really about the (albeit conventionally romanticized) British character. There are garden flowers at evening by the vicarage door, neatly spaced prayer books and a people who are

> Slow, trusting, worthy, free, kind-faced.

A war memorial lists the local men who left meadow and hill, and their cottage doors to die for England. The motif of keeping faith with the dead is extended, therefore, and those who fell in the First World War recall an even older conservatism, from an English (not British) village (not city).

The new men also fight, however. Roberts begins what turns out to be a eulogy directed primarily at the airmen with a reference to the celebrated debate at the Oxford Union in which the proposal that one should not fight for King and Country was accepted, an event given disproportionate coverage, even in poetry. Roberts dismisses it as a jest as the same young men now affirm their faith in the skies. Roberts employs an heroic diction: young men perform 'matchless deeds' in the clouds, or they fight, not in tanks in Africa, but:

> Where the hot desert wind of Libya blows,
> Upon the mountain heights where Grecian snows
> Untrammelled lie beneath the watchful star. . .

Nevertheless, the men are encouraged precisely by the voice of Churchill and by phrases which quickly became familiar quotations:

> Speaking these words, so knit, so tempered, true –
> '. . .so much owed by so many to so few. . .'

The Battle of Britain is thus evoked in a line which was in any case rhythmically effective. The power of Churchill's oratory is seen as the binding factor which roused not just England but in this case all of Britain and, indeed, the British Empire. Roberts's work comes to a climax in an image of Britain standing alone:

> . . .O pitying Christ!
> Thou see'st a fair land sacrificed,
> A valiant people holding breath
> Beneath a screaming rain of death;
> Unbowed, unbeaten in the hell

Of mine, torpedo, bomb and shell,
Around them ruin swiftly falls
On churches, towns, memorials
Whose loveliness a thousand years
Have touched with mellow grace of age;
And yet above the blood, sweat, tears,
They write for Time a deathless page. . .

Churchill's speech is echoed once again, and this time Roberts is
forced in his picture of the actual war to name the weapons of
modern fighting, which are destroying his ideal England, one
which has already lasted a thousand years, unlike Hitler's Reich.

Another work designed to help persuade America to join the war
and which enjoyed considerable popularity as one of the best-
known poetic works of its time is Alice Duer Miller's *The White
Cliffs*, a work whose patriotism is reinforced by narrative
sentimentality. Alice Duer Miller's work is now barely known, but
during the Second World War it was acclaimed as 'the most
moving piece of writing that has come out of the war', and as 'a
book which ought to inspire all lovers of freedom'. It was written to
inspire, and if at times its principal influence appears to be
Patience Strong, it can nevertheless rise to a genuine memorability.

The long poem – fifty-two cantos of irregular length and in
different verse forms – was first published in 1941, before America
entered the war. By 1944 it had reached its twenty-third edition
and nearly half-a-million copies. It was read on American radio,
and twice by the BBC, and in 1944 it was filmed by Metro-
Goldwyn-Mayer as *The White Cliffs of Dover*, with additional poetry
by Robert Nathan. A review of the film in the *New York Times*
provides a lead-in to the poem when it referred to 'such a tribute to
English gentility as only an American studio would dare to make',
noting that it offered a sentimental picture 'of frumpy old codgers
with hearts made of Bank-of-England gold'.[69] The film should
prove comforting, the reviewer concluded, for some Americans.
The poem must surely have proved comforting in giving an image,
albeit again romanticized, of what was being fought for. The
conservative image was underscored by the cover of the two-and-
sixpenny edition, which showed the White Cliffs themselves at
what must, from the boats in the foreground, have been a pacific,
but slightly remote point in history.[70]

The plot is simple. An American girl falls in love with an Anglo-Scottish gentleman and marries him at the beginning of the First World War. She has a son, but her husband is killed at the very end of the war. Her own father had pointed out faults in the English character, but she herself comes to admire them, and accepts it when her son, now grown up, goes to fight and perhaps (in the film certainly) to die in a new war. Sir Walter Layton, the former editor of the *News Chronicle*, and a wartime minister, stressed in an introduction the American admiration for 'the dogged defence put up by Great Britain against long odds', and underlined the work's initial function of persuading the heroine's people that it was their war, too. It can never be clear to what extent Miller's poem actually affected American opinion. Nevertheless, it *is* clear that it was a genuinely popular piece. The choice of verse form adds to the deliberately romanticized picture, and that verse is undemanding and therefore readily accessible:

> The English are frosty
> When you're no kith or kin
> Of theirs, but how they alter
> When once they take you in!

Even when of a higher quality, there is not much staying power, although the wedding in 1914 is well done:

> Percy, the best man
> As thin as paper and as smart as paint
> Bade us goodbye with admirable restraint,
> Went from the church to catch his train to hell;
> And died − saving his batman from a shell.

What matters in the work, however, is the image of England. Even in the poem some of the criticisms made of the film apply – that the England is upper-middle class, dull but very comforting. The reader is invited to empathise with the characters, and it is their England that is being defended. What is of some interest is the introduction of the New England father. He provides an *apparent* counter to the adulation of England by referring to the War of Independence, but he is no more than a devil's advocate, and the first-person narrator thinks back further to the first American settlers:

160

The tree of liberty grew and changed and spread,
But the seed was English.
I am American bred,
I have seen much to hate here — much to forgive,
But in a world where England is finished and dead,
I do not wish to live.

A famous poem by Keith Douglas – 'Aristocrats' – expresses a
kind of despair at the gentle and fatalistic upper or upper-middle
class; but Miller's treatment of the same class in a rather different
poem is more expressly functional.[71] A romantic novelette in verse
is an odd kind of war poem, but it encouraged the war effort by
portraying sympathetically a conservative society and thereby
implying that it was worth fighting to preserve it. The expectations
and stereotypes are those of an American audience, it is true, but
the popularity of the work in Britain is not insignificant, and
indicates acceptance of a conservative class tradition. A setting
socially above the bulk of the readership is a standard feature of
the popular romantic novelette, but in this case the feature is
exploited. The officer saved his batman, the son will save England.

Another long work, Francis Brett Young's *The Island* of 1944, is
of genuine epic length – some 450 pages of varied verse of a
remarkably consistent quality – and moves from prehistory
(including in passing such sections as the 'Song of the British
Grenadiers', with the refrain 'Malbrouk s'en va-t-en guerre'), to a
final section entitled 'Fantastic Symphony, AD 1918–39', which is
not ineffective in portraying the social divisions of the inter-war
years, and which shows too the rise of the dictators and the
reaction to them. There is an honesty in the acceptance of the fact
that Hitler's aims were not always condemned; Germans lap up
'stale Wagnerian stuff',

And England – God forgive her – half admires
Their cult! What restless Germany desires
Is equilibrium. Arson, loot and murder,
Seems an odd price to pay for Law and Order;
But that's their way. To persecute a Jew
Is vile; but lots of us are Aryans too,
And understand. . . .[72]

The Munich agreement was a false hope, and Hitler moves onwards until a 'chosen chieftain' leads Britain, promising

> no choice
> In all their toil but blood and tears and sweat.

But Britain marches again to the tune 'Malbrouk' (which is at least that of 'For He's a Jolly Good Fellow' even if it may not really be connected with Marlborough). The climax is the Battle of Britain, and the heroes are equated with those who fought against Rome with Caradoc, at Agincourt, or against the Armada:

> They were the seed
> Of the mild, unadventurous Middle Class:
> Plain-sailing folk, who neither knew the need
> That stunts the body nor the wealth that cankers
> The spirit, moderate in dream and deed:
> The sons of parsons, laywers, doctors, bankers,
> Shopkeepers, merchants, chemists, engineers,
> Whose loftiest endeavour was to live
> Within their calculable means. . .

The middle class is set against the master race. The description of 'our finest hour' is genuinely heroic, however; even if Britain were to fall her name and reputation are secured for all time.

Simpler idealizations of England are frequent in the popular writings of the Second World War. Unqualified references to home and homeland form a staple as serving soldiers remind themselves of the natural beauty that they are fighting for, and home poets reassure the reader that there will, indeed, always be an England. Admittedly, foreign political habits are cited sometimes to demonstrate how Britain is both different and saner; Herbert invents in a poem reprinted during the war a new political party that didn't have a shirt of a particular colour, but which adopted 'Pink Knickers' as its symbol.[73] For Herbert, too, the women at home are not just banking the home fires, but are working solidly in support:

> The shop, the sink, the kitchen, and the queue –
> Firewatching – gardening – the child – the chores –[74]

and, indeed, making other sacrifices, as is clear in Elsie Cawser's 'Salvage Song', one of the few genuinely funny war poems, though

THERE IS NO NEED FOR ALARM

it now needs historical footnoting. Her kitchen utensils, having been taken for their metal content, the housewife-speaker concludes

> So now, when I hear on the wireless
> Of Hurricanes showing their mettle,
> I see, in a vision before me
> A Dornier chased by my kettle.[75]

Harold Nicolson edited in 1944 a volume called *England: An Anthology*, which included contemporary work as well as older material. Brooke is there, but neither Sassoon nor Owen. A Second World War poem by Rostrevor Hamilton, however, offers an apparently apologetic, but in fact perfectly clear assertion of loyalty to England, right or wrong. The poem is called 'Bias':

> . . . forgive me if I turn my anger,
> Fresh and whole, against the stranger.[76]

The anthology, produced for the English Association, and, according to its preface, 'so redolent of English happiness, so resonant with English pride', ends with a poem from a 1922 collection by G.K. Chesterton that becomes now an epitaph for the fallen of a new war. 'The English Graves' contains some apposite references to Warsaw and Lorraine, but of the English dead it concludes

> They died to save their country and they only saved the world.[77]

The soldier poets made the conservatism very clear. The *Poets in Battledress* collection contains pieces like Dennis Birch's 'Dorset: Wartime', which is typical of very many others in the demand that there should be no change:

> Stay Dorset, stay; all that we fear is change.
> Stay so that when our present fears are over,
> We may come back and seek your peace again. . .[78]

Birch's wish is answered in poems such as one by Joyce Grenfell, who commented on a spring day in 1941 in the particularly English medium of the Shakespearian sonnet. Her picture is a familiar one, with aconites and crocuses, but the final couplet states

> I've known this day for thirty years and more;
> It will go on as it has done before.[79]

Only the title – 'March Day, 1941' – pins the piece down as a war poem in the first instance, yet it *is* a war poem, and a functional one at that, reassuring the reader that in spite of the problems indicated in the date of the title, things will go on unchanged.

The bombing of London and elsewhere called forth a great deal of verse, and here a pattern emerges of reflected reality, often couched in ironic terms, mixed with open defiance. That the civilian population precisely did *not* panic has been stressed,[80] and some of the poetry of the Blitz has been anthologized. The home front now becomes the front line, and many of the poems are by women. Catherine Reilly has a number in her *Chaos of the Night* anthology, and the realistic representation is present in Lois Clark's 'Picture from the Blitz', and the defiant ability to cope in Margery Lea's 'Bomb Story' (Manchester, 1942).[81] One single volume, however, can illustrate well the popular response to the bombing. Olga Katzin published as Saggitarius a collection of pieces in 1941 under the title *London Watches*, illustrated with post-bombing photographs by G. Wren Howard. The poems – which imitate well-known works and styles – joke about the bombardment, and echo the assertion that 'Britain can take it':

> And if people ask how we carry on
> When this is gutted and that is gone,
> And face the round of a working day
> Trim and jaunty and grim and gay –
> Well, Londoners know that they'll be quits
> *One* morning after the Blitz.[82]

Gog and Magog are invoked to lay low the wreckers, the bells of St Clements are mourned (though their ghostly echo survives), and the staff of the Oxford University Press continue to take tea in the ruins of Paternoster Row. Earth hath not anything to show more black from Westminster bridge, but at least we may be sure that the heart of the city is beating still and that Eros will return to Picadilly even if it takes years. The volume needs to be taken as a whole, since the photographs are integral, but as an expression of the defiance the work is an effective one, since it contains examples of war poetry that are both realistic and practical.

Also worthy of consideration as a whole work is a poem by Clemence Dane, dated 'Covent Garden, October 1940' and with the title 'Trafalgar Day 1940', which was produced by Heinemann as a shilling pamphlet, the verse printed in calligraphy (by George Mansell). The production of the booklet is itself an act of confidence after the Blitz, and the tone of the work is once more defiant:

> They have dropped a bomb on St Paul's –
> 'they', for their name shall not live.[83]

The central theme of the work is that the bombing wakens Lord Nelson, buried in the crypt, and he slips out, to mingle with the people of London, themselves 'stiff from a shelter bed'. His voice stirs the people, as he ignores the signal for retreat and utters the celebrated 'England expects'. The refrain line of the work, a poem of something more than 100 lines, is that 'they' (the enemy not dignified with a name) were unaware of how dangerous is it to waken the dead. On this occasion the dead of an earlier period return to keep faith with the present. The little work illustrates, like the Saggitarius volume, how poetry published in the immediate wake of the heavy bombing on London could strengthen in form and content the spirit of resistance, and both deserve to be better known.

As poems, these works compare with the cycle of poems by Paula von Preradovic in German on the bombing of Vienna, and published only after the war, or with that by Gerhard Kuckhoff on the bombing of Breslau.[84] Another side is represented, however, by poems concerned with the bombers themselves: aggressive in some of Herbert's verse, praising in lyrics like Noel Coward's 'Lie in the Dark and Listen', and descriptive of the dangers in P. Heath's 'We, the Bombers'.[85] Only after the war did Dresden – like Hiroshima – join the list of names which may stand alone to connote horror, and which have their own pity.

What heroes there are in the poetry of the Second World War tend to be found in lyrics connected with the war in the air. Randall Jarrell's 'The Death of the Rear-Turret Gunner', washed out of the plane with a hose, has a factual and unsentimental acceptance of horror that has its closest parallel in the songs sung by airmen, and a more bitter note is sounded in Walter Clapham's 'Requiem for a Rear-Gunner', who is married for a week before he 'flew to Nuremberg and died'.[86] The home-based popular poetry, and some of that by airmen themselves, however, simply praised, for example, the visible bravery of the Battle of Britain pilots. A.P. Herbert countered in July 1940 the view that these are not the men their fathers were:

> Yet . . .
> . . . while we heave a single sigh
> They shoot a brace of bombers down.

Another poem to a pilot concludes:

> You need no Medals, Crosses, Bars:
> Your name is written in the stars.[87]

The Battle of Britain inspired celebratory verse from established poets: George Rostrevor Hamilton refers to 'Young men, whose death redeemed us', and (though there is an edge to the title) 'Icarus', by Francis Scarfe in May 1941, still reflects the reality of the pilot's situation. In a poem by John Waller ('Airman') the pilot falls 'in glory', and there is much of this in the collection *Air Force Poetry* edited by John Pudney and Henry Treece in 1944.[88] An even clearer panegyric is seen in a piece by a writer who was in fact a specialist in medieval German literature, Margaret Fitzgerald Richey. The poem 'To the RAF' was composed in 1940 although it was published only in 1953:

> Sons of the air, Boanerges, sons of thunder,
> Dipped in a baptism of cloud and fire,
> Fleet-winged and sure, you strike our hearts with wonder.
> O brave desire,
> Wherewith we had dreamed alive the heroic days
> Of individual prowess, you outrun it!
> If from this transitory life can spring
> Promise of fame undying, you have won it
> With incomparable splendour of endeavour.[89]

That Richey was a medievalist is not irrelevant: she sees again in the air in the Second World war precisely the individual valour of the hero of the Middle Ages in her panegyric. Richard Spender's poem in commemoration of 'RGM' sees the lost fighter 'ennobled in proud robes of flame', and echoes Rupert Brooke's second sonnet on 'The Dead':

166

He leaves white
Unbroken glory, a gathered radiance,
A width, a shining peace, under the night.[90]

One major poet composed 'songs . . . not written in tranquillity
. . . never far from the sound of aircraft engines'. John Pudney's
poems were widely reprinted during the war and through the
medium of film and radio became known to a very wide audience
indeed. Heroism and reality are contrasted in one of his best-
known pieces – 'Combat Report', broadcast in 1941 – where the
thoughts of a pilot and a poetic commentary are in a markedly
different register, underlined typographically with roman and italic
in the printed form. Thus 'to ride the majesty of air' is set against
the realism of the final comment: 'that's how the poor sod died'.
Other poems by Pudney tread the same line between matter-of-
factness and poetic generalization. The fact of war is sometimes
accepted unquestioningly; Pudney agreed later in life that his
attitudes were at the time too simple – though hardly for him
alone. But his pilots empty their pockets before they leave, because
personalia clutter up 'somebody's head, somebody's heart', and
one of his key figures is a completely generalized 'Smith', who may
have been his friend, but of whose death, 'the less said, the
better'.[91]

One poem, however, makes Pudney very clearly a 'popular'
poet, and that brief poem is almost certainly the most widely
reprinted piece of the Second World War. Talking about the
amazing resilience of 'For Johnny' in 1976, not long before his
death (most of the obituaries commented on his authorship of it)
the poet noted its appearance in books of quotations, in *Hansard*,
and on several gravestones. It was broadcast early in the war, used
in the film *The Way to the Stars*, and the story of its genesis on the
back of an envelope in an air raid has often been told. The small
collection of poems in which it was first published, *Dispersal Points*,
was reprinted several times during the war, making the distinction
between popular poetry and that designed for a select readership
even more problematic. Pudney noted too in 1976 that the text had
been found on the body of a dead pilot, so that the comfort
inherent in the piece was clearly of a directly functional nature. He
authorized the reprinting of the poem in 1976 for 'another
generation to whom the Hitler war has a period appeal and its air

forces a nostalgic glamour reflected luridly in toys and models', a significant comment in its own right.[92] The poem is brief:

> Do not despair
> For Johnny-head-in-air;
> He sleeps as sound
> As Johnny underground.
>
> Fetch out no shroud
> For Johnny-in-the-cloud;
> And keep your tears
> For him in after years.
>
> Better by far
> For Johnny-the-bright-star,
> To keep your head,
> And see his children fed.

Three balanced stanzas trace Johnny's development. This might be an objectivized version of Yeats's airman: Johnny has his head in the air, in the clouds and then in a spirit world, but already in the first stanza he is also Johnny underground. The simplicity is deceptive, since Johnny-head-in-air is a literary reference, to Heinrich Hoffmann's cautionary tale, as well known in English as in German, and the augmentation of Johnny himself, plus the balance of parallel ideas in each stanza make this into a highly-skilled poem. Most important, it does not offer the response of even carefully cultivated indifference, as when Smith dies, nor the aureole bestowed upon on Icarus as his soul departs *ad astra*. It is entirely pragmatic: Johnny has perhaps reached the stars, but what matters is the social advice, advice found perhaps at its clearest in Kipling's 'Absent Minded Beggar'. The fact of the war remains unquestioned: within it, Johnny will reach for the stars, but his children have to be fed. Heroes or not, it is better to keep your head.

Some of the English poets of the Second World War reject the hero in a far more matter-of-fact way than the earlier poets. J.E. Brookes contrasts in his magnificent 'Thermopylae '41' the British soldiers in Greece with Leonidas and the Spartans. The speaker's comments about the historical events and the heroism of the ancients are neatly and regularly deflated by an Australian colleague:

'A load
of bloody poufdahs!' Thus he laid the ghost
of brave Leonidas.[93]

For all that, there is even in this poem a nostalgia for heroism, and elsewhere far clearer acceptances, especially of the heroic death, may still be found beside more cynical or more pragmatic approaches. The collected poems of Richard Spender, whose memorial to 'RGM' has been cited, is very similar to those produced throughout the First World War, and he, too, fell. The portrait which forms the frontispiece has him in RAF uniform (from a propaganda film), but in his work he echoes not only Brooke but also Binyon, in precise contrast to the sentiments that Denis McHarrie, for example, expresses so firmly:

Oh God! let's have no more of empty words
. . .
The worms don't spare the hero. . .[94]

Spender's quite different attitude is not unusual, and the comforting nature of the sentiments is scarcely deniable:

Now you have sped into the Sun,
And stand ennobled in proud robes of flame.
We can no longer see you,
For the light that clothes you is too fine a fire
For our dull, ordinary eyes;
But every day we shall remember you
In the brave glory of the golden sun.[95]

Even in soldiers' poetry, however, a type of hero familiar in the lyrics of the First World War reappears: the unexpected hero or the rough diamond. The motif is not, admittedly, always taken seriously. Louis Challoner resurrected Stanley Holloway's Sam Small, who once took a prisoner in order to get hold of some rum, and Sam himself is unchanged – 'He'd lived for years in Lancashire, so he wasn't scared o' mines'. But his heroism is intended as a joke, created for a concert-party in 1943.[96] A more serious variation on the poetry of individual heroism which could not have appeared during the First World War is R.F. Palmer's 'The Conchie', printed in Page's first anthology of Second World War songs and ballads. The pattern is similar to the First World War pieces, although the subject is new. The conscientious objector, drafted to the Medical Corps is mocked, and when found to be missing after an engagement is assumed to have deserted, but eventually brings in a wounded man, so that

> Our 'conchie' now wears a VC on his breast,
> We call him a coward no more.
> He still says his prayers e'er [sic] going to rest,
> The pride of the Medical Corps.[97]

Much of the soldiers' poetry proper was, like their songs, more pragmatic in its view of soldiering, designed to provide an ironic outlet for resentment at the situation in which the conscript found himself. Poems reflected and thus defused the implicit problems in situations that could occur. The misbehaviour of the woman at home is a frequent enough theme, but one circumstantial poem that appears to have been widely circulated is the related piece sparked off by the authorization by Sir James Grigg of compassionate leave for fathering children at the end of the war. The words 'for scheduled use' are slightly ominous, however:

> In distant lands the stalwart bands of would-be fathers wait,
> Certificates to join their mates upon affairs of State,
> For para 3 (appendix B) will authorise a chap,
> To reproduce, for scheduled use, the species homo sap.[98]

For the most part, however, the lyrics spoken, sung or chanted, express dissatisfaction with the environment. One of the most frequent lyrics of the Second World War which does appear in a variety of forms in various places has a simplicity of statement that variation cannot obscure. Some versions were sung to tunes like 'So Early in the Morning' or 'Baa, Baa, Black Sheep', but others seem not to have been sung at all. Song or poem, it expresses admirably a classic frustration. The towns mentioned in printed versions vary from Shrimpton Basset to Orkney, but the sentiments are the same, and the purpose remains clear: to get out of the system something imposed by the war situation. A few quotations must suffice, from different versions. Linguistically, the repeated adjective has its own effect of self-irony. In spite of metrical variation, many of the verses are interchangeable in what is clearly an oral piece. A product of the war, it need not actually be linked to the war at all. Halkirk, with one familiar adjective, provides an example:

> This fucking town's a fucking cuss.
> No fucking trams, no fucking bus.
> Nobody cares for fucking us
> In fucking Halkirk.

Another, Australian this time, refers to the siege of Tobruk:

> Air raids all day and bloody night
> Huns strive with all their bloody might
> To give us all a bloody fright
> Oh bloody bloody bloody.

and a close variation restores the adjective:

> The fucking rumours make me smile
> The fucking wogs are fucking vile
> The fucking pommies cramp your style
> In fucking Tobruk.[99]

The general feeling that this lyric encapsulates can be found elsewhere, of course. The anonymous complaint about the diet – 'M and V' (tinned meat and veg.) parallels the complaints about plum and apple in the First World War, and as far as the benefits of enforced foreign travel are concerned, John Warry is fed up with the pyramids of Gizeh in *Return to Oasis*, and Kevin McHale has a single piece in the Oasis collection called 'Com-bloody-parisons' in which the celebrated poplars of Lombardy might be 'dinkum for the Ities' but do not compare with the eucalyptus. He ends his poem with the memorable comment on Italian women:

> I dunno what they're saying
> And I do not bloody care
> I guess a sheila is a sheila
> Any bloody where[100]

Looking forward to the end of the war was especially important for a conscript army. Lyrics on this theme could take the same tone as 'When This Bleeding War is Over', or it could also be sentimental. A poem signed 'LC' in the Rhine Army College's *Goose Girl* magazine early in 1947 dreams of the country and the girl left behind – all the standard ingredients and entirely real:

> In three week's time my service ends
> And I go home to love and friends.

My dreams turn once again to those –
My dearest ones — the life I chose.

The rhyme-scheme and some of the vocabulary is hackneyed:
'beauteous stars illume the night'. But the interesting feature of the
poem is that it contains an element of doubt; has the speaker
changed too much to accept the tranquility of civilian life easily?
The poem's conclusion is somewhat limp, a kind of shrugging 'oh
well, I shall soon find out anyway'. But the essence is in the
question

but have the years
Changed me so much that I may shun
The peace of home. . .?[101]

Indeed, some of the poetry printed by Page in his anthologies of
popular material provides a more cynical answer, as in the chanted
'Won't it be Wonderful Then' (in which not all the rhymes printed
are exactly as in the original). Even more cynical is 'The British
Soldier's Discharge Song', which has the demobbed soldier
'absolutely stranded in the Strand' and commenting

And I confess I was contented, more or less,
When I was stony broke in No Man's Land.[102]

Both soldier and establishment poets expressed religious attitudes to the war. A great deal of Lord Gorell's poetry in the *Wings
of the Morning* collection is religious, usually asking for endurance to
survive the hardships of the wartime period:

Grant me endurance, make my shoulders broad
To bear the burden's weight
In quietude. . . .

wrote Gorell in September 1942, and on VE day in 1945 he
commented simply

Lift up your hearts in thankfulness to God
For mercies given and for darkness fled![103]

Beside longer works like Richard Church's much read sequence
Twentieth Century Psalter,[104] stands, however, a piece with an
interesting history, which appeared in the *People* newspaper in the
first instance. It is called 'A Soldier — His Prayer', and it was

written by Gerald Kersh. It was, however, reprinted as an anonymous work in the *Poems from the Desert* collection in 1944, and a myth had already begun. The text is headed: 'This anonymous poem was blown by the wind into a slit trench at El Agheila during a heavy bombardment'. In the preface to the collection, the then General Montgomery commented:

> The twenty-seventh poem has a unique history. Written on a scrap of paper, it fluttered into the hands of a soldier sheltering in a slit trench, during the battle of El Agheila.[105]

One wonders whether Montgomery contributed the soldier into whose hands the poem fluttered. Even Page, who identifies the real author, embroiders the story a little by having the finder of the piece a soldier in a dug-out who sees a scrap of paper wafting towards him, and then passes the poem to his mates. At all events, as Page points out, the work became very well known, and was even recorded. Its nine quatrains are again rather like a hymn:

> I knew that death is but a door
> I knew what we were fighting for:
> Peace for the kids, our brothers freed,
> A kinder world, a cleaner breed.

It is not difficult to gauge the appeal of the poem. It contains in very simple, and occasionally colloquial vocabulary ('kids'), a philosophy of ordinariness and affirms precisely the self-image a soldier might want to project. Although the prayer is to God for courage, it is clear that the speaker has enough ('I am no coward', 'I'm not afraid') and only rebels against being taken away from his nearest and dearest. For him it is enough to be a simple and honest man, as long as one is not less than that. God is asked merely to maintain the courage that the speaker already has. There is a trust in God 'who stilled the waters at Dunkirk', but the real faith is in being a simple man fighting for simple values. The poem remains consistent in its tone without recourse to a self-conscious demotic.

It must be repeated that no survey of the popular poetry of the Second World War could make the remotest claim to thematic completeness, even one concentrating on material in English. What becomes clear is the continuity of attitudes useful to the conduct of a war, the modified patriotism that can express itself as mockery of Hitler and his fellows on the one hand, or can confirm the conservative historical view of an England still rich in the values for which the soldiers were fighting. The soldiers themselves underscore these values, whilst grumbling about the situation in which they found themselves. Popular material in English during the Second World War had various functions. It continued to vilify the specific enemy leaders, and to remind the reader of verse – by which is meant either the self-conscious purchaser of poetry in book form or the casual reader of occasional verse in newspapers and magazines – of what was being fought against and what was being defended. Poetry was able to provide comfort in the worst moments of attack – as in the case of the Blitz – and reassurance was provided that the country was being led capably.

My Lilli of the Lamplight
Songs of the Second World War

And as the kicks get harder,
They are passed on down to me,
And I am kicked to bleeding hell
To save democracy.

[Anon][1]

Many themes from the poetry of the Second World War are found in a simpler form in the songs. The reduction of political ideas to symbols, which allows for an uncomplicated emotional community, can also bring the sides very close together, as is clear in a comparison between the stirring 'Avanti popolo' [Forward, People!], with its refrain:

> Bandiera rossa, bandiera rossa,
> Bandiera rossa trionfera!

[The red flag will be triumphant!]

and the Fascist counterpart:

> Camicia nera, camicia nera,
> Camicia nera, trionfa gia

[The black shirt has triumphed][2]

The potential audience for a song is usually wider than for a printed poem, and in the Second World War the range of material is very great indeed. With the wider availability of recordings and sound film, too, the role of the individual performer is also important. It would be impossible to come even close to a comprehensive survey. Japanese soldiers, it would appear, were familiar enough with American music to include the name of a country music singer – 'to hell with Roy Acuff' – in their battle-cries[3], but Japanese popular or soldier songs from the war are not familiar in the West, and this is true, too, of many less distant cultures. Nor is it easy to distinguish between songs intended for a

175

home audience and those written for or by soldiers, though a distinction may be made between official and unofficial soldiers' songs. The songs of the Second World War vary in poetic register from settings of works by recognized poets – 'Lili Marleen' is a case in point – to *ad hoc* wit. One of the best-known songs of the Second World War mocks Hitler in a manner which is both witty and memorable, and it deserves to be in more anthologies than those few in which it is found at present.

Probably the best-known of all songs of the Second World War, however, is 'Lili Marleen', which, according to its author, was 'never a war song, but a song in the war'.[4] It has been much discussed, and has attracted myths, but even in recent critical discussion facts about the song are distorted, names are misspelled, dates are confused, and legends confidently reiterated. The song began life as a poem composed in 1915 and published rather later by Hans Leip, who died in 1983 in his ninetieth year. Leip has described how he had been on guard duty in Berlin, prior to being sent to the front, and how he had been in love with two women, Lili and Marleen, who were then fused into one in the poem. The poem is a sombre one: it tells how the speaker is drawn away from his beloved into the barracks and then into war. He wonders what will happen to Lili Marleen if he should fall, and in the final strophe we realize that he *has* died. The reader's attitude to the poem changes with the realization that the whole is in the mouth of a dead soldier, drawn back as a ghost to the mists around the lamp by the memory of the girl. Its context is that of war, and there is an awareness of death:

> Und sollte mir ein Leids geschehn,
> wer wird bei der Laterne stehn
> mit dir, Lili Marleen?

[And if something happens to me, who will stand beneath the lamp with you, Lili Marleen?]

The final strophe develops as a climax the notion of the *revenant*, which Leip himself underlined as the starting point:

> Aus dem stillen Raume,
> Aus der Erde Grund
> hebt mich wie im Traume
> dein verliebter Mund.

Wenn sich die späten Nebel drehn
werd ich bei der Laterne stehn
wie einst, Lili Marleen.

[From the silent emptiness, from the earth's depths I am lifted up by your loving lips. When the late mists drift, I *shall* be there by the lamp, as before, Lili Marleen.]

The song was set to music by Leip himself, and then again later, but it was with a melody by Norbert Schulze, who wrote other military songs, that it became famous. The tune is a march with some echoes of bugle calls, and some of the anecdotes about the song are true. It *was* much admired by all soldiers fighting in North Africa and it was translated into many languages; it also stopped the fighting, at least when it was being broadcast. Eisenhower's would-be visit to Leip after the war (Leip was asleep and Eisenhower did not disturb him) is also well known.[5] The song has a universal applicability, but its artistry is deceptively simple. It centres on the lantern, the light outside the barracks visible in the mists, as the one stable element, which is also quite oblivious of the soldier. But the song is not set in any special war, and the sentiments are those of any soldier. The supernatural aspect is unusual, but there are elements of great familarity: the desire to stay but the need nevertheless to report, the recalled experience, the possibility of death and of the speaker's replacement.

The reception, however, raises a problem. The song became known through the singing of Lale Andersen but it is hardly a woman's song, since the speaker is clearly a man. However, Andersen *became* Lili Marleen as she sang about her, and the audience of soldiers responded with empathy for the ideas, whilst making real the image of the girl by identifying her with the singer. Andersen herself notes this response, and a similar technique was exploited in songs by Vera Lynn. The melody demands the repetition of the final line (and hence the name) in each strophe, so that it is the girl that remains in the mind. Even in German the text was adapted. It was recorded after the war by Marlene Dietrich, for example, with a radical alteration in the last verse, in which a vision of Lili Marleen arises ('hebt sich') from the earth, rather than the dead soldier. The idea of the ghostly return is lost, though not the sense of possible loss, when the statement 'werd ich' ('I shall') is replaced by 'wer wird' – 'Who will?'

Though widely translated, the song was not always fully understood. Leip himself complained that it had been suggested in England that Lili was a prostitute.[6] When the song was, however, translated into English (and recorded by Anne Shelton in the first instance), it underwent changes other than those of the spelling of the name, which now became Lilli Marlene, though the sheet music helpfully supplied 'pronounced "Lily Marlane"' and the hybrid form 'Lili Marlene' eventually took hold. Apparently at the behest of Whitehall, Tommie Connor provided a set of English lyrics and the cover of the English sheet music showed a woman in a perfectly respectable headscarf and coat waiting outside closed barrack gates, which could be those of a prison. The soldier is not dead, though he is remembering the past. The text has lost the crucial final strophe, and any question that Lilli Marlene might meet someone else under the lamp is avoided: what is stressed is the promise of the girl to be faithful. Hans Leip's original is sentimentalized into the common theme of the sweetheart who will still be waiting. The soldier knew she would

> . . .always be
> My Lilli of the lamplight
> My own Lilli Marlene.[7]

The soldier is sent overseas, but Lilli Marlene sustains him. The English version was also recorded by women singers, although it has to be recalled that it *was* sung – with the accompaniment of a mouth-organ – by soldiers as well. John Costello has noted that further sentimental verses were added: in one such (which is based on an Italian adaptation), the soldier is encouraged and warmed by a rose and a lock of hair. The contrast with Leip's poem becomes even stronger.[8]

Both text and melody were quoted and adapted. Jacques Prévert's 'La nouvelle ordre' refers to it, and its elegaic conclusion is used precisely in an elegy in Hamish Henderson's 'Seven Good Germans' – the ironic sense of 'good' meaning 'dead' being appropriate in the context.[9] The tune itself was used for a whole series of quite different words, some of them obscene, some humorous, and many not relating at all to the original text. The collaborating Paris-radio in 1941 attacked Churchill and Roosevelt at the signing of the Atlantic Charter on the Potomac as 'les potes

. . . du Potomac' to the tune, and British soldiers and airmen sang to the same melody:

> They're going to bomb Benghazi
> They're going to bomb BG.

or

> We're going round the corner
> Right round the fucking bend.

or in the context of the Burma plains:

> Of roads that lead to heaven
> And tracks that lead to hell.[10]

In the collection of World War II ballads which he himself published just after the war (with the imprint of the Lili Marleen Club of Glasgow), Hamish Henderson included the original text, though without attribution and with a translation which misreads a reference to the lamp burning every night as if it meant Lili herself – 'every evening she burns with love'. He also printed the Italian version referred to by Costello:

> Dammi una rosa per tenere sul cuor,
> legola col filo dei tuoi capelli d'or. . .[11]

[Give me a rose to carry by my heart, and a strand of your golden hair. . .]

The mists have been replaced by these deliberately sentimentalized motifs. More interesting, however, is the inclusion by Henderson of two German adaptations which mock Hitler's Russian or Italian campaigns, one of which reads:

> In dem Westen Moskaus, vor dem grossen Tor
> Steht die deutsche Wehrmacht, und kommt ja nicht mehr
>   vor.
> Und alle Leute solln es sehn
> Wie Adolf Hitler zu Grunde geht
> Wie einst Napoleon
> Wie einst Napoleon.

[To the west of Moscow, by the great gateway stands the German army and can't get any further. And everyone should see Adolf Hitler collapse, as once did Napoleon, as once did Napoleon.]

Leonhardt prints a variation, as well as a particularly obscene parody. The political German texts could, of course, hardly have been sung too openly by soldiers serving in the German army, but they certainly existed. Henderson includes the best-known set of alternative lyrics to Schulze's tune in English, the 'Ballad of the D-Day Dodgers', but not two further sets of English words to the same melody which merit attention, because both have some link with the sense of the original. The motif of faithless wives or sweethearts avoided so carefully in the English text by Connor is brought to the fore in a version which relates how an English soldier returns to find his place taken by an American, another recurrent motif in the period. The soldier elects to return to battle so that he *will* be killed, so as to forget

> My faithless English sweetheart
> My faithless English rose.

Relating to the original more directly is a version produced in a fighter-bomber squadron in North Africa:

> Half a thousand pounds of
> anti-personnel,
> half-a-dozen rounds of
> the stuff that gives them hell.
> Finish your dive-bomb, zoom away
> and live to fight another day,
> Poor Marlene's boyfriend
> will never see Marlene.[12]

This is war poetry in a quite specific sense and a somewhat unusual one in the modern context. The killing is accepted, as is the comforting hope that the airman will indeed live to fight another day.

In 1949 a last reminder of Lili herself appeared in another set of lyrics by Tommie Connor, again sung by Anne Shelton but with an inferior melody, describing 'The Wedding of Lili Marlene'. There is a reference in the text to 'her old melody' – but there is a nice historical point in that her name now provides a rhyme for 'Alamein'.[13] Leip's song and Schulze's melody, however bridged the gap between the armies in its use of the universal theme of separation, possibly permanent; and it also bridged the gap between the commercial popular song and those actually sung by soldiers. It filled the same role – as Irving Berlin pointed out – as 'Tipperary' in the First World War, only this time the same song was used on both sides.[14] 'Tipperary' and other songs of the First World War were revived and were still included on songsheets sold on VE day in 1945, however.

Percy Scholes produced in 1942 a popular pamphlet on 'God Save the King' in which he noted the effect of the anthem when sung in occupied France as the RAF bombed.[15] The 'Marseillaise', replaced in Vichy France by the personality-based 'Maréchal, nous voilà', which was parodied by the Resistance, gained in patriotic sentiment. Many of the songs of the Soviet Army are comparable with anthems as official expressions of national strength, whilst the Polish national anthem 'Jeszcze Polska nie zginela' [Poland is Not Yet Lost] served then as now as a focus for the expression of national identity and independence in spite of German occupation. Expressly patriotic songs again helped the war effort. Irving Berlin's 'God Bless America' is a straightforward celebration of the nation as such, but was born out of war. Berlin had written it during the First World War, in fact, but he published it only in the Second, and it is interesting that Woodie Guthrie's own celebration of America, 'This Land is Your Land', was composed as an answer to Berlin's piece. They are not so far apart in sentiment, and the dust-bowl folksinger and the New York immigrant were responding to the same threat. The desire to conserve what was seen as good in the pre-war world was in Britain most notably expressed by Ross Parker and Hughie Charles's song 'There'll Always be an England' (with the follow-up line 'and England shall be free'), which dates from the very beginning of the war. It encapsulates not only the affirmation of survival but also the necessity for communal action ('if England means as much to you as England means to me'). The deliberately stirring tune (as with 'God Bless America') is part of the effect, and we may note again that it is England – not Britain – and its country lanes that are hymned. Does the song imply that the strength to win will not be found, say, in the streets of Glasgow?[16]

That British troops marched and sang the advertising 'Song of the Ovaltinies' is interesting in its insistence that the singers were 'happy girls and boys', but this probably does not make it into a war song. But the war as such, and also the national leaders, gave rise to a number of popular humorous songs. Made familiar through radio and recording, they built up civilian morale by deflating the enemy even if they were again sometimes overtaken by history. In England, George Formby invited his audience at the beginning of the war to 'Imagine me on the Maginot Line', and another early song which is still remembered was the somewhat overconfident 'We're Going to Hang Out the Washing on the Siegfried Line' – a joke which apparently occurred to two different song-writers, though only one song has survived. The Carr-Kennedy piece was translated into French ('On ira pendre notre linge sur la ligne Siegfried') and sung at the beginning of the war, and there was an echo of the First World War in Jean Nohain and Pierre Caron's 'Bonjour Tommy' (welcoming him back to France after twenty years; the French version of 'Tipperary' has the phrase). 'Bonjour Tommy' was written as a reply to the voice of Paul Ferdonnet, a French Haw-Haw, broadcasting from Stuttgart, but Tommy's return took a little longer than anticipated.[17]

Popular songs attacked the Germans and their Axis partners (in one case as 'The Jap and the Wop and the Hun') in highly-skilled lyrics such as that broadcast by Noel Coward in July 1943 to an audience some of whom managed to take the title 'Don't Let's be Beastly to the Germans' at face value. The tune of this cabaret song is deliberately and ironically jolly, but the lyric is worthy of close consideration. The tone set by the choice of the word 'beastly' in the title is sustained, and an incidental target in the verse is again Bishop Bell (who is offered to the Germans on a lease-lend basis). But there is a serious underlay, based on the revival of Germany after the First World War. Coward uses an ironic self-effacement whilst quoting the terminology of the Nazis:

> Let's employ with them a sort of
> 'Strength through joy' with them,
> They're better than us at honest manly fun.[18]

The irony in the understatement is even clearer later on:

> Though they've been a little naughty to
> The Czechs and Poles and Dutch,

> But I don't suppose those countries
> Really minded very much. . .

and it is baffling how this could have been misinterpreted, although A.P. Herbert, too, sometimes found himself taken too literally.[19]

As far as Hitler himself was concerned, songs produced from the popular music trade in Britain and America differed. Irving Berlin wrote a song in which Hitler was not actually named, but which has the unequivocal title 'When That Man is Dead and Gone'. It is perfectly clear who that man is, and if the song was written when Americans were still debating their neutrality, there is an added scorn in refusing to name the devil.[20] American patriotic popular music did produce some less well-known lyrics concerned with Hitler, of which two examples may be cited. Huddie Ledbetter (Leadbelly) composed a blues, presumably at the beginning of the war in Europe, called simply 'Mr Hitler' in which some adaptation of history was required by the lyric, Leadbelly claiming that Hitler started out 'in nineteen-thirty-two' so as to provide a rhyme for 'Jew'. At this stage Hitler is blamed, however, only for having driven 'the Jews from their home'. Another verse follows a good formula

> You ain' no iron, you ain' no solid rock

with the rather weak conclusion

> What we American people say, Mr Hitler you is gotta stop.

There is, though, a sixteen-bar chorus (added later?) asserting:

> We gonna tear Hitler down.[21]

A second American lyric curiosity, again illustrating the range of materials available, if not lyric quality – is the work of Sam Liptzin, an American-Yiddish writer, who provided new sets of words for known tunes. 'Mir gedenkn Pearl Harbor' ['We Shall Not Forget Pearl Harbor'] is set to the melody of 'Solidarity Forever' (or 'John Brown's Body'), whilst a Yiddish song tune is used for his new set of lyrics 'Hitler-shvajn' [Hitler the Swine].[22]

Popular songs in English asked 'Who Do You Think You're Kidding Mr Hitler', and Gracie Fields suggested that her celebrated 'Biggest Aspidistra in the World' might serve as a suitable gallows. Another suggested precisely and frequently what might be done 'right in the Fuehrer's face', which upset the BBC, concerned about the vulgarity of the repeated raspberries, although it provided a useful propaganda vehicle for Walt Disney and Donald Duck.[23] Nor did Mussolini fare much better. His failure to take Greece formed the basis in 1941 for a lively song called 'Oh What A Surprise for the Duce', in which his exploits were mocked in sometimes rather fortuitous rhymes. The words 'When Graziani/ lost Sidi Barani' need some historical glossing (General Graziani was defeated at Sidi Barani in North Africa in 1940), as does, perhaps, Mussolini's foreign minister and son-in-law Count Ciano, whose name provides too good a rhyme for 'piano' to be missed, however shaky the context. But it *is* effective to be told of the Duce 'they do say/ he's had no spaghetti for weeks'. The play on *Duce*, pronounced in exaggerated Italian, and the echoed 'do say' is developed when we are told that the white skirts (of the Greek evzones) 'play the deuce with black shirts', this affording an extra pun on Duce and 'deuce' as an avoidance of the term 'devil'. The whole song — which has an infectious waltz melody that is clear on the recording of it by Florence Desmond — remained justifiably well known through the war.[24] That it has not remained so rests upon the fact that there are too many historical allusions to be recognized.

A body of songs directed against the Nazi regime and Hitler in particular came from the German language cabaret in exile, and recent studies have begun to collect these lyrics. Reinhard Hippen has drawn attention to songs which merit inclusion in anthologies of war poetry, although some of them predate the war as anti-Hitler pieces. Erika Mann performed her 'Prinz von Lügenland' [The Prince of the Land of Lies] to music by Eugen Auerbach with the cabaret 'Pfeffermühle' in Zurich in 1935, and the same cabaret in New York included a parody of the 'Lorelei' as a comment on the race laws; beginning with the opening lines of the Heine poem – 'ich weiss nicht, was soll es bedeuten', 'I don't know what it means' – the Lorelei complains that she is under attack because she is in love with a Jew, and where the fatal Lorelei combed her golden hair, the singer complains that her golden hair will be shorn. That song is aimed at Nazi policy rather than aspects of the war as such, insofar as such a distinction can be made. Others were anti-war, however, in a general sense. In 1942 what is supposedly a hymn to Mars criticizes profiteers and statesmen, concluding with the rebellion of humanity against wars:

> Widiwumbumbum, widiwumbumbum
> So leckt uns doch am Mars.[25]

[Tarantara, tarantara, and you can kiss m'ars]

In exile in England, the Lorelei herself again complained in song in 1940 that although she was once sung by everyone in Germany, she is now ascribed to an 'unknown poet', since Heine was a Jew. In New York, the German-Jewish cabarets contributed a poetically noteworthy song such as a bitter comment on Germany and its policies by Victor Berossi, sung in 1943 by Oscar Teller and Victor Schlesinger. An SS man and his blonde wife are obliged by law (of the state, though not, unfortunately, of nature) to have two children per year. The second is born, and the mockery in the verse depends not only upon the situation, but also on Yiddish-isms in the language:

> Und schon nach sechs Monat' ein Bub', wie's gefragt,
> Ganz blond, blaue Augen – dem Adolf gesagt! –
> Und unter der Nase, da sieht man bewegt
> Dass der Bub' schon das Bärtchen von Adolfen tragt.

[And there, as ordered, after six months, is a boy, blond and blue-eyed – Adolf should be so lucky! – and under his nose they see, with emotion, a little Adolf-type toothbrush moustache.]

This new-style German will carry on the tradition, having 'Deutschland über alles' and the 'Horst Wessel Lied' as his entire artistic repertoire (the line 'one Goethe doesn't make you civilized' is striking), and will carry on his favourite pastimes of standing to attention and fighting wars: the indictment of the German people is complete.

One final text, this time from a 1942 Moscow exile, Erich Wienert, is entitled simply 'Der Führer' and does not name Hitler, but refers to 'him, of all people' as a lampoon:

> Diesen Hindenburgumschwänzler
> Diesen tristen Hampelmann
> Diesen faden Temperenzler
> Der's nicht mal mit Weibern kann. . .

[This Hindenburg-bum-licker, this miserable puppet, this tatty
teetotaller who can't even make it with women. . .]

The mockery of Hitler's temperance habits and sexual problems
recurs in other songs designed to encourage the Allies against the
powers of the Axis by direct attack on their leaders.

Sentimentalism typified many commercial songs in America and
in Britain. The lyrics were rarely profound, and an ultimate
reduction is represented by a song like 'I'll Remember You My
Darling' of Hugh Rich and Reg Connelly, the entire thesis of which
is contained in the title. Apart from a reference to being 'across the
sea' and a drawing of a soldier on the sheet cover, there is nothing
to link it with the war, and it may in 1939 have been an
opportunist reworking of something already on the stocks. In
social-historical terms, however, sentiment of a particular type was
demanded by the soldiers, and was supplied to support the effort
on both sides. In her memoir *Vocal Refrain*, Vera Lynn cites
passages from popular music magazines which make this point:
direct sentiment was both demanded and useful. There was
resistance in some British establishment quarters to the provision
of such songs, on the grounds that they might induce homesick
soldiers to desert, but Vera Lynn notes her own counter-view that
the songs also reminded 'the boys of what they were *really* fighting
for'. Many are still known, although they have now acquired an
historical patina. The connection with war is sometimes tenuous
and they are deliberately simplified, but Vera Lynn commented
again on her own 'genuine respect for simple, sentimental lyrics,
which I could sing as if I believed in them because I *did* believe in
them'.[26]

Although she was not the only British singer performing songs of
this type – on record, on radio, and on tour with ENSA in most of
the areas of war – the lyrics associated with Vera Lynn may serve
as models. Their aim was to articulate fairly basic emotions for
those unused to expressing emotion of any sort. The sentiment is
usually that things will, when the war is over, be *precisely* the same
as before the war. There is a difference between these songs and
those of the First World War. Even songs like 'Keep the Home
Fires Burning' implied that it was right and proper for the soldier
to go in the first place, and this was certainly true in songs like
'Your King and Country Want You'. In the songs performed by

and written for Vera Lynn there is simply sadness at the parting and a reassurance that things will be kept. The singer will still be 'Yours' (which was not strictly a war lyric at all), and the departing soldier was assured that 'We'll Meet Again', a song by Ross Parker and Hughie Charles (the same composer and lyricist as of 'There'll Always be an England'). The implicit doubt in the following line ('don't know where, don't know when') was at once countered with an assertive 'But I know we'll meet again. . .' There is not much evidence for what Sheridan Morley has referred to as the 'mindlessly British patriotic idiom of a Vera Lynn'.[27] 'We'll Meet Again' remains one of the best known of the songs in question, but it is again paradoxical that, with its fellow, 'Wish me Luck as You Wave Me Goodbye', it ought properly to be sung by the soldiers themselves. Once more the singer embodies the sweetheart to whom the words are addressed.

A variation on the motif of changelessness looks forward to a satisfactory peace. A celebrated example claims the somewhat unlikely appearance of bluebirds over the white cliffs of Dover – the peace symbol coupled with the national symbol – but more firmly linked with the war at home is 'When They Sound the Last All Clear', which has even appeared in one anthology. The sentiment is as simple as usual: we shall be happy when peace comes. However, the song incorporates many specific points: the lights will go on again, the last siren will have sounded, peace bells (not those for invasion) will ring, and as a personal climax 'you will be mine'.[28] The encouragement is for the fighter, but not to fight. That was accepted anyway as a wearisome necessity.

In America, Tin Pan Alley songs attacked the enemy ('Let's Put the Axe to the Axis', 'You're a Sap, Mr Jap'), commented in sentimental terms on events of the war ('The Last Time I Saw Paris') or on soldiering ('Goodnight, Wherever You Are'). More pragmatic in its thesis was 'Praise the Lord and Pass the Ammunition', and Irving Berlin, once again, produced songs and lyrics about the soldier's situation, most notably in the musical *This is the Army*, the title song of which contained several pointed comments on the changes suffered by the conscripted civilian.

Songs in English were written to encourage and comfort the civilian population, too, and they go beyond the simple entertainment of the popular song in peacetime, their lyrics constituting an ironic and comical war poetry. One song praised the maker of the

'Thingummybob' – a component of an aircraft, recognized as vital but not understood by the layman. Another song reflected, but mocked, the dangers of the times by giving the safety device against bombs a fairly clear sexual innuendo in 'The Deepest Shelter in Town'. The ever-present dangers of the air-raid were made easier by turning George Formby's otherwise simply comical song-character of Mr Wu into an air-raid warden. Other aspects that became the target of comic songs include William Joyce ('Lord Haw-Haw the Humbug of Hamburg'), and the basic fact of shortages ('When Can I Have a Banana Again?'). The lyrics of the last-named song, performed and part-written by the elegant bandleader Harry Roy, are banal, but not in the deliberate sense of the 1923 song 'Yes, We Have No Bananas'. Its unanswerable question focuses the entire problem of shortages onto one not particularly essential item (although the absence of the banana took on a kind of symbolic value and was referred to in poetry), whilst at the same time fulfilling the function of cheering up those facing shortages of all kinds. There were worse privations than the absence of bananas, but these nonsense lyrics made them easier to cope with.[29]

Songs from musicals also underlined aspects of the war effort – Irving Berlin's song 'My British Buddy' needs no more than the title to make its point. Other pieces, though, deserve somewhat closer attention. A song sung by Edith Piaf before and after the German occupation of France asks the simple question

> Où sont-ils mes p'tits copains
> Qui sont partis un matin
> faire la guerre. . .?[30]

[Where are they, all my young mates, who left one one morning to go to war?]

There is no answer, of course, and the song's closest relative is one that has its roots in the Second World War in a novel by Sholokhov, but which was written far later as a 'modern folk ballad' by Pete Seeger. 'Where Have All the Flowers Gone' is a simple indictment of war through the circularity of its theme – the flowers are picked by girls, who marry young men, who become soldiers, who die, and on their graves more flowers grow. It is an anti-war song written in the atomic age, but it belongs in a more general category, and it is of interest in historical terms that the song was translated into German even later, and recorded by Marlene Dietrich in a version which, linked with her remake of 'Lili Marleen' evoked the Second World War more strongly than the protest songs of the 1960s.[31]

Although the propaganda machine of Nazi Germany controlled song lyrics of the war period in the Reich, not only did 'Lili Marleen' enjoy enormous success, but other popular songs, disseminated on record and radio, expressed the longing for return to normality after the fighting, and the desire for home. The lyrics often appear on postcards, which were intended to be sent between the front and home. As in the First World War, the combination of words and image is of some interest. A sentimental lyric by A.L. Wirth with music by Erich Kuntzen, described as a marching song, although the rhythms of the lyrics do not seem especially appropriate for that purpose, is called 'Kleine Mama' [Little Mama], and the card has a picture of a woman reading a letter. Possibly she is the 'Mama' referred to, although this time she hardly looks old enough to be anyone's mama. The four strophes of verse speak first of missing the mother, then of a battle in which the son has acquitted himself well. The soldier then greets the neighbour's daughter, whom he will return to marry, and the last strophe looks forward to the end:

> Einmal ist auch dieser Feldzug aus, kleine Mama!
> Dann kommt Dein Junge zurück nach Haus, kleine Mama!

[The campaign will be over some day, little mama, and then your boy will come back home, little mama!]

In military terms the sentiment is irreproachable, since the implication is of a victory. Somewhat subtler is a postcard-song by Erwin Lehnow (with music by Werner Bochmann), the picture of which shows a group of soldiers writing letters home. The text implies that the mother, who has written a tear-stained letter to her son – a sentimental commonplace – will not live much longer. The idea is, presumably, to encourage the swift completion of the task.

A final example of the genre, again acceptable to the regime, is a jauntier song by Butzl Greiner and Robert H. Bork (who also wrote the music) concerned with the Africa campaign. The specimen from which this version is taken was sent in 1942 by a woman in Germany to a soldier unknown to her, presumably as part of a contact programme: the lyric was therefore indeed used as

189

part of a communication process, although since it must have been enclosed in an evelope (there is no name or address, and the soldier is addressed as 'unknown' by the writer) there is no indication of whether the soldier was serving in Africa. In fact, as with many of the sentimental songs, the lyric is directed from a soldier to a girl. The chorus begins:

> Ich denk an dich, mein deutsches Mädchen!
> Ich trag dich treu in meinem Sinn!

[I'm thinking of you, my German girl, I have you faithfully in my mind!]

If this chorus is somewhat all-purpose, the verse is directly concerned with the war. The campaign will take some time, but it makes clear whose will be the victory:

> Wir kommen wie das Wetter an; Heia!
> und schnappen uns den Englischmann. Heia!
> und sträubt er sich auch noch so sehr
> bald gibt's hier keinen Tommy mehr.
> Dann ist er nicht mehr da, in Afrika!

[We come down like a storm, hurrah! And catch Mr English-man, hurrah! And however much he struggles, there'll soon be no more Tommies, he won't be here any more, in Africa!]

The illustration in this case is of unidentifiable houses with palm trees, the photograph supplied, as in most of these cases, from a central agency in Berlin.

An English-language example of what may be called sentimental patriotism, but which merits analysis as an important war poem, is a rather different work by Noel Coward, his 'London Pride', which he performed first in 1941. The melody is, in its initial part, a variation on the German national anthem, the Hadyn tune used for 'Deutschland über alles'. The lyrics set to it take the flower London Pride as an image of the resilience of London under the Blitz, a point which is made in popular lyric poetry as well, as is the notion that here was a city that had *already* lasted a thousand years (unlike the Reich). There are also quite specific details of the war:

> Ev'ry Blitz your resistance toughening
> From the Ritz to the Anchor and Crown. . .[32]

Blitz was a new word, signifying a bombing raid (rather than its real meaning of 'lightning war, first strike attack') and the rhyme on Ritz as well as the acoustic echo with 'resistance' are skilful. The sense of historic continuity predominates, however: even though the city is darkened, its past still lives and can be felt 'in our shadowed present'.

The small flower – though here the name is significant, and other poets used it – is taken as rallying point, and this idea is itself not uncommon. A French song of 1944 by Maurice Vandair and Henri Bourtayre and sung by Maurice Chevalier celebrated the return of de Gaulle in 'Fleur de Paris', a flower that kept its red white and blue colours and is now

> . . .la fleur du retour,
> Du retour des beaux jours. . .

[The flower of return, of the return of the good days. . .]

In the celebrated Italian partisan song 'Bella ciao', the partisan asks to be buried with a flower on his grave so that it will remind passers-by of the struggle:

> E quest'e il fiore
> del partigiano
> Morto per la libertà. . .[33]

[It is the flower of the partisan, who died for freedom. . .]

A whole range of comic songs in English had the aim of helping the serving soldier to cope, and these, too, were taken to the troops through ENSA concerts. In this case they may be be illustrated through the songs of George Formby, whose persona on film and stage was in itself a studied attack on the efficiency of the Nazi machine: the bumbling innocent portrayed by Formby invariably outmatched the enemy. Fred Karno's army was again a match for militarism. Formby's songs, however, utilized the music hall technique of studied innuendo. Sometimes they were aimed at the German or Italian leaders, but more often they made light of aspects of the war at home or amongst the forces. The songs directed at soldiers have a claim to be part of the study of the war lyric in the Second World War. They derive to a certain extent from actual soldiers' songs with adapted (cleaned-up) words, and they are all very much worm's-eye view in their approach. Set in the various services, they mock, for example, 'Our Sergeant Major', but go no further up the ranks to any general political indictment. Sometimes there *is* direct mockery of Hitler or

Mussolini, but even this is rarely the chief point of the song. Formby's version of a soldiers' set of words placed to the march *El Abenico*, ('You'd Be Far Better Off in a Home') sees Mussolini as 'all puffed up with gas', and the plan is, somewhat predictably, to 'kick him up the Brenner Pass' (a more topical allusion than the usual rhyming slang 'Khyber Pass'). At the centre of the song, however, is the anticipation of the end of army life and the prospect telling the sergeant 'to stick his passes on the wall' (this time not an avoidance, but part of the rhyme-scheme, probably because of the Brenner Pass evasion).[34]

Arguably the best known of Formby's war songs is his version of 'Bless 'em All'. Originally associated with the Air Force, and written by Fred Godfrey, the song was already well known, as was its unspoken but studiedly implicit sub-text in which the word 'bless' is replaced by a more vigorous verb. In the version copyrighted in 1940 by Jimmy Hughes and Frank Lake it is rightly dubbed 'the service song', and 'soldier', 'sailor', or 'airman' are interchangeable.[35] The song is cynical, echoing also the 'never mind' attitude of the earlier war, and the chorus looks forward to returning home. That the song is specifically for other ranks is clear in the attacks on sergeants and indeed corporals, and the refrain

> You'll get no promotion
> This side of the ocean
> So cheer up my lads
> Bless 'em all.

The philosophy of cheerful resignation is again unreflective on the nature of war or its actual leaders, and much in line with texts from the First World War. George Formby's lyrics provided a useful focus for the feelings of many; his songs depend upon the war, and make a positive contribution to coping with it.

Genuinely belligerent material in popular song is relatively rare, although there are some examples, as with an American song performed in 1945 by Perry Como, the point of which is not in fact the war, but rather the slang of the youth of the period. Nevertheless it contains the lines 'It was mighty smoky/ Over Tokyo. . .' and relates how 'a friend of mine/ In a B-29/ Dropped another load for luck. . .' and flew on, laughing as he went.[36] The text predates Hiroshima, the implications of which were, in any case, not grasped for a considerable period of time except by very few.

As in the First World War, the lyric form was used in all contexts, however trivial. Some of the children's rhymes or mnemonic jingles have been noted, and a few have made their way into anthologies.[37] Songs played a part in propaganda or information films, and major figures in the world of entertainment provided what were effectively advertising jingles, which are possibly the most forceful use of any poetic form ever made. Bing Crosby's well-known voice urged people to 'collect today/ For the USA/ 'Cause junk can win the war', whilst a memorable verse in the same mode promoted the eating of 'artichokes/ Until the Nazi party chokes. . .' Both sides utilized the musical film for military purposes.[38] 'Der Fuehrer's Face', in its incarnation as a Disney cartoon, reduced the menace of Hitler to a colourful nightmare in the mind of Donald Duck, and the cartoon of the *Three Caballeros* was aimed at the countries of South America likely to support Hitler.

There is a distinction between official and unofficial songs created for and by soldiers. The Red Army had and has a large repertoire of more or less officially composed pieces designed for singing and marching – a good number have appropriate titles to indicate this combination, such as 'Kogda poyut soldat' [When the Soldier Sings] or 'Poy, soldat' [Sing, Soldier]. Nor are these restricted to the Red Army – most of the fighting forces, including the Wehrmacht, boasted a repertoire of such songs. A fairly typical lyric, in this case one from the Red Army, is:

> Artilleristi, tochni dan prikaz.
> Artilleristi, zovyet otchizna nas.
> Iz tisyach groznikh bataryey
> Za slyezi nashikh materyey,
> Za nashu rodinu, ogon', ogon'.[39]

[Artillerymen, the order! Artillerymen, our country is calling. From a thousand batteries, for our mothers' tears and for our country, fire! fire!]

Interesting material is provided, too, by the songs sung by the Polish forces (represented most readily in those of the army of General Anders in the west). Nationalist and religious lyrics derive in part from earlier periods, but some songs reflect events of the

Second World War in which Polish forces played a major part, such as the battle of Monte Cassino. Many are marching songs, some associated with individual units ('Marsz 1. Brygady' [March of the 1. Brigade]), and sentimental themes also occur, beside songs about war in general. Polish songs concerned with the longing for home took on, however, an additional force after the invasion by Hitler, and some earlier pieces (such as 'Przybyli Ulani' [The Uhlans Were There]) acquired added verses about Hitler just as they had about the Kaiser. In the Second World war itself, writers like Adam Kowalski produced lyrics and music of songs concerned with Poles in Romania, England, and Scotland, a small reflection of the anabasis of the Free Poles. His 'Pieśn Obozowa' [Song in Camp] from 1939/40 is a religious and nationalistic functional piece, moving from a plea to God for strength to fight to a repeated emphasis on the homeland:

> O Boże, skrusz ten miecz, co siekl nasz kraj,
> Do wolnej Polski nam powrócić daj,
> By stał się twierdzę nowej siły
> Nasz dom, nasz dom.[40]

[O Lord, destroy the sword which hacks our land, let us return to a free Poland, so that our house may stand and assert new strength – our home, our home.]

The same tone of understandable patriotic defiance is found in another of his songs, written rather later:

> Nigdy nas, nigdy wróg nie powali
> Będziem się bili o Polskę dalej
> Miesąc rok, uczy pięć lat
> Az do skutku, az udławi się psubrat.

[Never, never shall our enemy defeat us. We shall go on fighting for Poland, be it for a month, a year or even five, to the very end, till the scoundrel falls.]

The same attitude to war is stronger in a song from 1943 by Juliusz Bakowski and Jan Maliński, in which the enemy is not generalized.

> Ryby radują się w Kanale
> Bo mertwy Niemiec nie jest zły. . .

[The fish rejoice in the Channel. A dead German is OK. . .]

One of the best-known Polish war songs celebrates their involvement at Monte Cassino. 'Czerwone Maki na Monte Cassino' [The
Red Poppies of Monte Cassino] is elegaic but triumphant: Polish
blood was spilt, but there is no sense of the betrayal of the
'Chanson de Craonne', for example, and the tone is more
triumphant that McCrae's 'In Flanders Field'. Death was a
marriage in honour

> Czerwone maki na Monte Cassino
> zamiast rosy pily polską krew.
> Po tych makach szedł sołnierz i ginął,
> lecz of śmierci silniejszy był gniew.
> Przeja lata i wieki pzeminą,
> pozostana ślady dawnych dni
> tylko maki na Monte Cassino
> czerwiensze będą, bo z polskiej wzrosły krwi.[41]

[The red poppies on Monte Cassino drank Polish blood with the
dew. The soldier went to the poppies, and he perished, but from
death anger was stronger. Years pass, centuries go by, traces
remain of far-off days, only the poppies on Monte Cassino are
redder, nourished on Polish blood.]

Here as so often the lyrics require the much-sung melody to give
them force – the name Monte Cassino recurs in emphatic position,
for example. The emotional context of the song represents a
different aspect of war lyric, however. It is a poem of battle
honours with nationalist overtones that remind us of the complex-
ities of defining patriotic attitudes at all.

A special situation in the war lyric is represented by the songs,
as well as the poetry of the partisans. Some gained wider currency,
such as the marching songs of the Italian partisans, including
'Bella Ciao' [Farewell My Beauty]. Material in Yiddish, again, has
much of interest, and one song of the Jewish partisans in Eastern
Europe, indeed, is still sung, if out of context. The song 'Dos Kelbl'
[The Calf] is known even in English, under the title 'Donna,
Donna' (which is not a name but an imitation of the Yiddish
refrain, based on the word 'Adonai', 'Lord'). It is not entirely clear
who wrote the English text,[43] but the lyrics are originally by
Yitzkhok Katsenelson, who was born in 1886, lived in Lodz and
later in the Warsaw ghetto, and who was sent to Auschwitz with

195

his wife and children in 1942, where he died in August 1944. The song is defiant, but this is coupled with an idealism that is not entirely realistic. It contrasts the calf, tied up on its way to market, with the bird, flying free, and the implication is that this is a matter of choice:

> ver-zhe heist dikh zayn a kelb?
>
> Bidne kelblekh tut men bindn
> un men shlept zay un men shekht.
> Vers hot fligl, flit aroyf tsu,
> iz bay kaynem nisht kayn knekht.[44]

[Who told you to be a calf. . . Poor Calves are bound, taken and slaughtered. Whoever has wings flies upwards and is a slave to no one.]

The assertiveness of that last line – which contains a reinforced triple negative in Yiddish – is countered, however, by the two-part refrain. The wind is laughing (at man? at the situation?), and the *donay*, 'O Lord', refrain may register a kind of submissive despair at the fact that it is not necessarily possible to change. What remains is at best a warning not to allow oneself to be bound.

Hirsh Glik, the author of several partisan songs in Yiddish, was taken from the Vilno ghetto to a concentration camp, from which he escaped in 1944, and was killed fighting against the Germans at the age of twenty-four. His lyrical song 'Shtil, di nakht is oysgeshtern' [Quiet, the Night is Starry] tells the true story of how, in 1942, a partisan girl with a beautiful face, her hair wreathed with the snow, used her pistol to stop an ammunition car. The act is positive, but the final strophe is realistic: the girl is

> gemutikt fun klayninkn nitsokhn
> far unzer nayem, frayen dor.[45]

[cheered by this tiny victory for our new, free generation.]

Equally well known is Mordecai Gebirtig's song 'S'brent brider', [Burning, Brothers]. Gebirtig, who died in 1942 in Krakow as the ghetto fell, wrote the piece in 1938, though it was sung by the partisans, and the fire became all too real. The message intensifies that implied in Katsenelson's song:

> S'brent, brider, s'brent!
> Di hilf is nor in aykh alleyn gevendt!

Oyb dos shtetl is aikh tayer
nemt di keylim, lesht dos fayer,
lesht mit ayer aygen blut
bavayzt, az ir dos kent!
Shteyt nit, brider, ot asoj mit farleygte hent. . .[46]

[Burning, brothers, it's burning, and help lies in you yourself,
nowhere else! If your homes are dear to you, get hold of buckets
and put out the flames, put them out with your own blood!
Prove you can! Don't stand there with folded hands. . .)

These three songs reflect the situation of the partisans, and each is
designed to lift morale in the most appalling situations; their
lyricism is remarkable. Many similar songs reflect the war as
vividly, however. The collection of songs from the Vilna partisans
– *Dos gezang fun Vilner geto* presented by Shmerke Kaczerginsky –
contains some remarkable illustrations, including 'Bombes'
('Bombs'), welcoming the arrival of support.[47] A work by
Kaczerginsky himself describes the life of the partisan whilst
affirming their resolve, 'Der veg iz shver' [It is a Hard Road],[48]
but probably the best known of the Yiddish partisan lyrics of the
war is again by Hirsh Glik. The death of the young poet caused it
to be echoed in other poems, and it became the rallying hymn of
the United Partisan Organization. After the war it was widely
translated and is still sung at memorial gatherings. The work was
written in 1943 and set to a Russian march tune by Dmitri
Pokrass. It begins

Zog nit kayn mol az du gest den letsten veg[49]

[Never say you are on your last journey]

and this time there is an awareness of the need for violent response.
The inward-looking insistence on the song itself makes its popular
purpose clear:

Dos lid geshribn iz mit blut un nit mit blay
S'iz nit kayn lidl fun a fogl af der fray. . .

[It is a song written in blood and not with lead; it is no song
about a bird flying in the air.]

In contrast to the implicit conditional of Katsenelson's song of the
calf, this is to be

. . .gezungn mit naganes in di hent!

[sung with guns in your hands!]

The very existence of the Yiddish partisan songs is a testimony to
the vigour of the resistance, just like the poetry produced in the
extermination camps themselves. The aim is clear, however:
whatever the general feelings might be about the good or evil of
war as such, in the precise circumstances, this aggressiveness was
vitally necessary. These are real war lyrics, of the kind which do
not negate anti-war poetry, but which emphasize the difference
between the two wars. War is not welcome, but it has to be fought.
It would be possible to refer to the lyrics of many partisan groups.
Italian songs frequently provide reflections of the almost monastic
life of the partisan, rather than of the war as such, although there is
a contrast between the simplicity of the lyrics and actual events, as
in the opening lines of 'Banditi della Acqui':

> Banditi della Acqui in alto il cuore:
> Sui monte di Cefalonia sta il tricolore.

[Bandits of the Acqui Division, firm of heart: The tricolor flies
over the mountains of Cefalonia.]

But four-and-a-half-thousand soldiers were killed after a long
resistance in September 1943, and the song is a brief memorial.[50]
Others are political: the 'Canaglia pezzente', the Tuscan partisan
song of self-mockery as 'rabble' has the refrain 'Viva i soviet, viva
Lenin . . .viva Stalin!', and many looked forward to the time when
the Fascist 'squadristi' would no longer be present.[51] In French,
one partisan song became popular on a wide scale amongst refugee
performers. Anna Marly's 'La marche des partisans' of 1942 was
reworked with Joseph Kessel and Maurice Druon as the 'Chant
des partisans' ('song' rather than 'march', though it remains one)
and it achieves its effect through a simple rallying call. There is one
poetic device of some strength: 'le vol noir des corbeaux', 'the black
flight of the crows' calls the partisans to arms, so that they can pay
back the enemy for the blood and tears already shed.[52] At the end
of the war, we may note a Greek partisan song (collected in the
Cyclades well after the war) which greeted the liberation by the
British and Americans with the words 'I thought they'd never
come. . . . The Americans have come and no one is going to die'.[53]

There were, finally, German songs of resistance sung mainly in

exile, some dating from an earlier period. One of the best known is
the Esser-Langhoff song 'Wir sind die Moorsoldaten' [The Peat-
Moor Soldiers], written in 1933. The song is not strictly a war
lyric, but the assertion that one day the peat-moor soldiers will be
free was applicable to and was sung in camps during the war.
Brecht's texts, too, were used, though again they are not always
strictly war lyrics. The best of the parodies of the 'Horst Wessel
Lied', however, is that by Brecht, used in his *Schwejk im zweiten
Weltkrieg* [Schweyk in the Second World War]. Here the tightly
closed ranks of the SA troops become the tightly closed eyes of the
calves following the butcher. There existed, too, anonymous songs
against Hitler:

> Da heisst es aufmarschieren
> Der Hitler muss krepieren. . .

[We have to march, so Hitler can die like a dog. . .]

Coming from the left opposition, those songs aimed at the worker
audience form an interesting parallel to the worker poetry
promoted by the Nazi regime. One pre-war example adapts a
folksong:

> Herr Hitler reitet schon voran
> auf seinem stolzen schwarzen Rosse.
> Haut ihn, haut ihn, die ihr ihn kennt
> er hat die Arbeiter geschändet.

[Sir Hitler rides out on his bold black horse. Strike him down, he
has shamed the workers' cause.]

Later variations refer to 'Lout Hitler' riding on a 'stolen horse'.[54]

The Nazi use of songs for express patriotism was of course
mocked by exile writers on a large scale. Robert Lucas's BBC
broadcasts to Germany of the witty letters of the reluctant warrior
Private Adolf Hirnschal contain, for example, scenes in which Nazi
songs are contrasted with the reality of the war, as when the
singing of 'Tomorrow the whole world is ours' is interrupted by
news of the Russians having reached the Oder.[55] Private Hirnschal
mentions specific lyrics, as when his colleague Jaksche sings about
the familiar contrast between the soldier and the officers:

> Volksgrenadier, greif an! Greif an!
> Wir müssen an den Feind heran!

Besinn dich nicht! Sprung auf − marsch! Marsch!
Sonst tritt der Leutnant dich in Arsch
Der Oberst will die Schwerter!

[Attack, attack, you grenadiers, we must be at the enemy! Don't pause for thought, leap up, march, march − if you don't, the lieutenant will kick your arse. The colonel wants a medal!]

The construction is neat: at first this sounds like a militaristic piece, culminating in the order to march (as do so many patriotic songs of all forces). But the marching is not for the defence of the fatherland, which would be normal; suddenly 'march' provides a not unfamiliar rhyme for 'arse', and the point of the whole is that the humble grenadier is urged to attack by a kick from a low-ranking officer so that a high-ranking one can get the crossed swords addition to his Knight's Cross.

One of the best-known lyrics of the Second World War uses mockery as a weapon, and is aimed directly at Hitler and his associates. It is not a poem encapsulating the experience of war, but it remains of considerable interest as an enduring historical document and, indeed, as lyric. It is matched, moreover, by a further soldiers' song which applies the same kind of mockery to Mussolini. Both lyrics emasculate the enemy dictators or their armies, and the first is the untitled piece which caused a lively correspondence in the *New Statesman* in the 1970s under the peculiarly British heading 'Hitler's Deficiency':

Hitler
Has only got one ball!
Goering
Has two but very small!
Himmler
Has something similar,
But poor old Goebbels
Has no balls
At all![56]

The word 'similar' has, of course, to be pronounced as a disyllable, and the Propaganda Minister of the Third Reich has to be pronounced 'Go-balls'. The lyric is an oral composition, probably from London, and it is anonymous. Not even a putative author has been suggested for this untitled piece (another feature of oral poetry). It is, however, immensely memorable, brief and comical. It employs outrageous rhyme, somewhat after the manner of the clerihew or the limerick, but it is oral poetry with a quite specific purpose, that of mockery and belittling. Hitler's actual monorchism – the matter of debate in the columns of the *New Statesman* – is an irrelevance, of course, or at best a happy coincidence.

It seems likely that the music came first, Kenneth Alford's tunefully persuasive march 'Colonel Bogey' of 1914, which has had attached to it a variety of different words, mostly unrespectable. The suggestive drop of a minor third with which the piece opens is a precise musical equivalent to the name 'Hitler' in English speech, as with the less specific use of the word 'bollocks' (evoking the response 'and the same to you'.) The description of Hitler may have various folk sources. The ballad of Sam Hall ('and I hates yer, one and all') is one, because it suggested an obvious rhyme:

> Oh my name it is Sam Hall (or Nobby Hall)
> and I've only got one ball. . .

Alan Bold links the song with a bawdy piece called 'No Balls At All', itself a parody of a song about women's clothing called 'Nothing to Wear', of which there was an Air Force version called 'No Bombs At All'.[57] This contributed to the last line, just as 'Sam Hall' probably contributed to the first. Politer versions are also encountered from time to time:

> Hitler
> We're going to finish you

Nevertheless, the better-known text has the essential quality of memorability, it is witty, and it makes a direct attack on the enemy leaders – not, it will be noted, on the enemy in general. It is a poem of Hitler's war as many are of the Kaiser's war. It also has a memorial function, reminding new audiences (largely in school playgrounds) of an historical evil in a neatly adapted past tense:

> Hitler
> He only had one ball. . .

The piece may be compared with another anti-Hitler chant, although the comparison seems at first glance somewhat stretched. Part of an equally traditional and accepted mode, the wartime Maori cursing song (*kaioraora*) appears to have become widely known after it was used at a VC investiture ceremony:

Hitler, frothy-mouth, wooden-head,
He's the man who wanted to fight,
Beaten here, beaten there, all over Russia,
You can wipe him and his works.

The piece goes on to refer to Hitler as a 'cowardly slave' and to Mussolini, whose 'buttocks quake' at the prospect of the Maori battalion reaching Rome.[58] The chant (the Maori *haka* remains a vigorous and succint form of aggressive poetry in any case) may readily be compared with the English song, though the audience was and is far greater for the latter. Both have great value in exorcising fear of the enemy.

Mussolini – or rather the Italian army – received similar treatment in a comical propaganda song. Here the historicity of the matter is less accurate, but the verse is effective. It is again orally transmitted and untitled, but sometimes referred to as 'Abyssinia'. The composer was apparently an RNVR lieutenant, who showed his verses to A.P. Herbert, to whom it was wrongly ascribed and who refers to them as 'clever and decently abusive'.[59] They appear in few collections, though they appeared in the somewhat unlikely context of a collection of rugby songs first published in 1968, something which bears witness to their durability. The version provided in that collection is shorter than two offered by Alan Bold, who notes that they were sung to the tune of 'The British Grenadiers'.[60]

The events described in the song are not quite like the historical invasion of Abyssinia, but the real point is the literary castration this time of Mussolini's army. The Duce sends his organ-grinders to Africa, and that jibe contains not only the notion of the Italian organ-grinder (with monkey) familar in cartoons of the period, but also the sexual innuendo picked up in the next verse, when the returning soldiers have lost their organs and are incapable 'of any kind of grind'. In some versions the Duce then mounts the rostrum with the ashes of the unknown eunuch, but the punchline – and there is some considerable textual variation – is adapted from the earlier parody, 'Christmas Day in the Workhouse/ Harem'. While sometimes referring to the generals, the usual target is the Italian heroes:

> For some real act of gratitude
> This great occasion calls,
> 'What shall we give our heroes?'
> And the heroes answered 'Balls'.

The avoidance-substitution found in 'Christmas Day in the Harem' ('tidings of comfort and joy') is not encountered.

The English-speaking world was not alone in mocking the enemy in verse, and one of the best known but not anthologized French lyrics of the period – the song 'Dans le cul' [Up the Arse] – is described in detail by Simone Berteaut in her biography of her sister, Edith Piaf, noting how the words were fitted to the German anthem:

> Dans le cul, dans le cul
> Ils auront la victoire.
> Ils ont perdu
> Toute espérance de gloire.
> Ils sont foutus
> Et le monde en allégresse,
> Répéte avec joie sans cesse
> Ils l'ont dans le cul,
> Dans le cul!

[Up the arse, up the arse is where they have their victory. They've lost all hope of glory. They are screwed, and the whole world rushes to repeat with delight, it's all up the arse!]

The words are cruder than some, but the situation in which they were composed was perhaps more desperate. That the chanting of these words gave satisfaction, however, is undeniable.[61]

Not only English songs mocked the Italian army. Hitler's claim that Mussolini's invasion of Greece had lost him the war is well documented,[62] but German soldiers' songs express clear views on the Italians. Extremely well known is the song of the 'Avanti-Schritt', the 'Italian Forward March':

> Kennst du den Avanti Schritt?
> Ein Schritt vor und zehn zurück. . .

[Do you know the 'avanti' step? One pace forward, ten paces back. . .]

Henderson also notes a parody of the 'Giovanezza', the anthem of the Italian Fascists, collected in 1944, which is a comical description of the progress of Italian imperialism:

> Oh ihr armen Italiener
> Euer Land wird immer kleener

[Poor old Italians, your country is getting smaller and smaller]

and as in England, Mussolini was mocked as well.[63]

With the allies, the mockery was not restricted to Hitler or Mussolini. The Egyptian anthem 'Salaam al malik' [Salute to the King] drew a large number of English parodies, many of which are simply sexual jokes at the expense of King Farouk and Queen Farida (whose names both alliterate, unfortunately, with a favourite sexual term), but these are of limited interest except perhaps in the linguistic sense; the Arabic phrases interpolated in them are no longer readily understood, and in content they are otherwise unremarkable. Of greater interest are the many adaptations which put new lyrics to popular songs and permitted the soldier stationed in Egypt to let off steam about the situation, as in the imprecatory poems of Tobruk. 'There Is a Tavern in the Town' gave rise to 'Land of Heat and Sweaty Socks', whilst the 1938 nostalgia song 'Thanks For the Memory' was transformed to recall the small but in this case unpleasant aspects of the war in Egypt with heavy irony:

> Thanks for the memory. . .
> Of living in a country where we all got Gyppo guts.
> Oh thank you so much.[64]

Songs looking forward to the end of army life include the ironic 'Kiss me Goodnight, Sergeant Major', and the many variations on 'Bless 'em All'. These are strictly conscript songs, and one of the most striking is a lyric set to the tune of 'Macnamara's Band' (the traditional wordless chorus of which underlines the hopelessness of the situation):

> Oh, the colonel kicks the major,
> And the major has a go.
> He kicks the poor old captain
> Who then kicks the NCO
> And as the kicks get harder,
> They are passed on down to me.

And I am kicked to bleeding hell
To save democracy.[65]

'Chain of command' jokes were and are not uncommon in all armies, though the increasing hardness of the kicks here is a development. The humour lies in the final line, in the sudden intrusion of the concept of democracy (which would be exaggerated in singing with a heavy stress on the last syllable) following the slangy climax of the line before. Most succinct of all, and ironic in the fact that army was in any case a conscript one, was the set of lyrics sung of 'Here's to the Maiden of Bashful Fifteen' which posed the question:

What did you join the army for
You must have been fucking well barmy![66]

Moving to a different style of song and to a request rather than a question for which there was no answer anyway, a blues composed by Memphis Willie B. (who fought in Italy throughout) appeals to Eisenhower and MacArthur not to send him to Japan:

I had so much trouble with the Germans
Don't send me over in Tokyo. . .[67]

Air fighting played a role in the Second World war far beyond that in the First, and Page's anthologies include songs by paratroopers with the comment that 'many of these songs were an attempt to overcome fear by naming it in capital letters'. A primary example of this are the words set to the tune of 'John Brown's Body', of which the chorus (which applies in any case to someone who is dead) is replaced with:

Glory, glory what a hell of a way to die. . .
And he aint going to jump no more. . .[68]

The relationship between the original song and these functional and fear-defying words is of interest, as is the durability of the song, which stays in the general rugby club repertoire as a kind of grotesque. The version cited by Page contains specific phrases linked with the period, however, just as other songs dealt with specific kinds of aircraft:

The lift webs wrapped themselves in knots around each
    skinny bone,

> The canopy became his shroud as he hurtled to the ground,
> And he aint going to jump no more. . .

The relentless rhythm of 'John Brown's Body' is still clearly felt, but there is a poetic grimness in the parachute silk turning into a shroud which is not there in other versions, in which

> He jumped without a parachute from forty thousand feet

and so

> We scraped him off the tarmac like a pot of strawberry jam.

That all too realistic notion is seen too in a parody of the music hall song of the 'Daring Young Man on the Flying Trapeze' – again highly appropriate:

> He jumps through the air with the greatest of ease,
> His feet are together and so are his knees.
> If his chute doesn't open he'll fall like a stone,
> And we'll cart him away on a spoon![69]

In many cases, the Air Force songs mirror those of the other forces. 'The Church's One Foundation', used in the First World War for a 'Fred Karno's Army' and for the RFC, was now used by the RAF as 'We Are the Heavy Bombers', or 'We Are the Air-Sea Rescue'. One RAF version came even closer to the original hymn with 'The Nissen Hut's Foundation'. Similarly words were applied to secular melodies, again including 'Thanks For the Memory' and 'It's Foolish But it's Fun'.[70] A song by C.H. Ward-Jackson for a station concert-party, and included in his anthology of songs for airmen, varies, finally, the worm's-eye view resentment of the war. In this case the lament is not for the situation as such but for the inability to fly. The 'Erk's Lament' (an erk being an aircraftsman and the lowest rank) expresses regret that they are forced to sweep the mess and not the skies. The basis is 'Why Was He Born So Beautiful', and some of the effect rests again on knowledge of the original conclusion ('he's no bloody use to anyone'):

> Why did we join the RAF?
> Why can't we sweep the sky?
> We're browned-off doing ground staff jobs –
> Why can't we learn to fly?[71]

As a counter to this, however, the *Airman's Songbook* contains a song by four members of a coastal squadron, written in 1942, to the tune of 'My Bonnie Lies Over the Ocean':

> A squadron swept over the ocean,
> Their aircraft must airworthy be,
> They're kept in that state by the ground-crews,
> Now who could those fine fellows be?

Another song of actual encouragement, finally, has a political message. Written presumably as a morale-boosting piece in the first instance, allied airmen did sing an English version of the 'Red Airmen's Song', which was included in a collection called *Songs of the People*, in the company of texts such as the 'Internationale', the 'Carmagnole', as well as the less apposite 'Waltzing Matilda'. The lively chorus (in which the music echoes the 'higher' of the text) makes a clear statement of loyalty to a cause. The verse, in English at least, seems to cram too many ideas into too short a space to be effective, however:

> Flying higher, higher and higher,
> Our emblem the Soviet Star,
> And every propellor is roaring
> Red Front! Defending the USSR
>
> But to the workers and the toiling masses,
> A gleam of hope all our propellors whirl,
> We drop them leaflets while we bomb their bosses,
> The first Red Air Force of the world.[72]

The dropping of leaflets and of bombs are more realistic than the distinguishing of the targets.

This chapter began with an analysis of 'Lili Marleen'. Of English variations, however, the best known is a ballad that has appeared many times since its first printing by Hamish Henderson, and it merits a high place in the lyrics of the war as a whole. The song uses the melody only, and the 'Ballad of the D-Day Dodgers', which is known in a number of versions, had its origin in a remark supposedly made by Lady Astor in 1944 to the effect that the soldiers in Italy were D-Day dodgers. She denied making the remark, and there is no evidence for its having been made at all. Neverthless, as a rumour, it provided a focus of discontent for a group of soldiers who felt themselves forgotten or unappreciated. The ballad is ironic throughout, and documents the Italian campaign:

> Naples and Cassino were taken in our stride,
> We didn't go to fight there – we went there for the ride.
> Anzio and Sangro were just names,
> We only went to look for dames –
> The artful D-Day Dodgers, way out in Italy.[73]

Lady Astor may not have made the remarks attributed to her, nor may she have merited the designations afforded her in another strophe, but the lightning conductor effect is clear:

> Dear Lady Astor, you think you know a lot,
> Standing on a platform and talking tommy-rot.
> You, England's sweetheart and its pride
> We think your mouth's too bleeding wide.
> That's from your D-Day Dodgers – in far-off Italy.

Even if accidental, the pun in 'tommy-rot' is appropriate, and better than at least one of the variant versions which has a crude alternative. The last strophe in nearly all versions, however, maintains the ironic mode, but comments on war as such. It does not speculate on whether the fighting in Italy was necessary or not, but states simply the ultimate reality of war:

> Look around the mountains, in the mud and rain –
> You'll find the scattered crosses – (there's some which have no name).
> Heartbreak and toil and suffering gone,
> The boys beneath them slumber on.
> Those are the D-Day Dodgers who'll stay in Italy.

World War Three Blues

The Lyric and August 1945

> *Hiro*
> *Shima*
> *All fall down.*
> Robin Henderson[1]

In an afterword to Wolfgang Borchert's play *Draussen vor der Tür* [The Man Outside], set at the end of the Second World War, Heinrich Boll wrote in 1955

> Stalingrad, Thermopylae, Dien-Bien-Phu. . . What remains is a placename and a little pathos, with which the survivors drink themselves into a stupor, as if it were poor wine. . .[2]

Names from the two world wars function as markers. Those of the First World War are the names of the bloodiest battles: the Somme, Passchendael (with its acoustic overtones of 'passion' in English), Langemarck, Verdun. This is true to an extent of the Second World War too, with Alamein or (in spite of subsequent changes) Stalingrad. However, the best-known names of the Second World War are those associated with atrocities or with the large-scale killing of civilians: Lidice, Oradour, Katyn, Dresden, Coventry, and the two which dominate: Auschwitz and Hiroshima, subsuming Belsen, Treblinka, Dachau, Nagasaki. Furthermore, the tag 'no poetry after Auschwitz' has shown itself to be wrong. There was poetry in Auschwitz, and as a concept it has become in more recent times a poetic metaphor divorced, on the surface at least, from its reality and used by poets with no actual connection with the camps.[3]

Hiroshima, too, soon became a lyric concept found sometimes in the least appropriate contexts, especially in song lyrics ('Jesus Hits Like an Atom Bomb').[4] The last act of the Second World War in August 1945 has made itself felt in all areas of the lyric, translating into poetic form something which is not just an historical event or a general warning, but an indication of the potential of destruction on an even greater scale than had been thought possible. The use of the bare name of Hiroshima might imply something momentary, as indeed it was, as an event of the Second World War. With the sudden death of the city came after-effects, and an awareness that it could happen somewhere else. In European and American literature, Hiroshima is a long way away. What really happened at Hiroshima is not the subject of poetry; realism of the kind used to depict the horrors of the First World War is impossible given the magnitude of the events and of their consequences. Those events were described in John Hersey's account, which appeared in the *New Yorker* in 1946, was widely reprinted, and published in Britain as the Penguin *Hiroshima* in November of the same year. Close to it, with more detail, is Masuji Ibuse's novel *The Black Rain* of 1969,[5] and there has been other Japanese prose material since then. For the most part, though, the name of Hiroshima alone suffices, with the attendant and to an extent formalized details, the mushroom cloud or the light brighter than a thousand suns (Robert Jungck took the title of his well-known book on the subject from the *Bhagavad Gita*), or the deadly rain. Most striking of all tag words of the Second World War is 'the bomb'. In a war in which so many bombs fell, the atomic bomb does not even require an adjective, just the definite article.

Just as the fact of Hiroshima affects everyone, lyric responses to it have been frequent. They have, however, tended towards two moods, which echo the cornerstones of Greek tragedy: the name evokes pity and fear. The pity embraces, however, a feeling of guilt which is more than empathy, and which is bound up with the second element. If the vision of war as an apocalypse is common, the vision now offered is that of *the* apocalypse.

Even with the potential repetition of the events of Hiroshima, guilt and pity for what did happen, and fear in case it happens again are not the only responses found in the lyric. It is to be expected that the very first reflections of the atomic bomb, especially in the popular lyric, were centred positively on the ending of the war. The lyrics of Hiroshima, indeed, predate the dropping of the bomb. Another of the many books on the events of Hiroshima, discussing the USAF group whose B29s were actually to drop the bomb quotes some office doggerel of the period:

Into the air the secret rose
Where they're going, nobody knows. . .

the conclusion of which is, nevertheless, interesting:

But take it from one who is sure of the score,
The 509th is winning the war. . .[6]

That the dropping of the bomb finished a war that was already over in Europe was the dominant emotion in many quarters in the first instance. A body of popular song in America underscored the point, and some of it was used in that valuable source, the 1982 film compilation *The Atomic Café*. Songs asserted the belief that the bomb that struck Hiroshima was the answer to prayers, on the grounds that it would 'stop this awful war'.[7]

In different literary contexts, even those more aware of the implications, perhaps, and certainly not rejoicing in the bomb, did not at once voice fear or pity. C.S. Lewis, writing in the *Spectator* only a few months after, responds really only to the magnitude, and then in the form of 'a metrical experiment'. The poetry, we might say, is in the poetry. In his 'On the Atomic Bomb' he sees the events simply as part of the 'terrible logic of history' and of itself 'no huge advance in the dance of Death', which is inevitable; the reader is told not to look towards an end, but to notice the 'happy orchards' at the side of the road. Not entirely dissimilar is a far more recent work which gives the point an ironic twist. Terry Johnson's 'Optimistic Poem' points out that being hit by the bomb is actually the same as being hit by a bus, except that it happens to everyone else as well. This is, then, the starting point for an ironically positive response: to think about the bomb is to remind yourself that you are still alive. It is the great *memento mori*, and the only responses to that thought have always been either to repent before it is too late or to enjoy yourself because it is later than you think.[8]

The historicity of Hiroshima is soon lost in the lyric, as the event becomes too full of overtones. Nor, of course, is the poetry that of experience, so that problems with other war poetry simply do not arise in this context. It is appropriate to refer to a Japanese view of the events, however. Koichi Kihara's poem 'Revelation' has been translated, and takes as its starting point a fragment of the reality, what is left of a dead woman — her face imprinted on a slip of gauze, the rest of her 'scattered across continents', whilst 'a uranium shroud/darkens the earth'.[9] Beyond Japan, such specific detail is rare, though instances may be found, and not only in contemporary material. David Kerrison was four years old when the bomb fell, and his poem 'The Third Compassion' concentrates on one individual. Statistics, with Hiroshima as with Auschwitz, are less vivid than individual stories, and Kerrison presents us with the image of a child who 'crawled out of the ruins, trying to die'. From this he develops an apocalyptic imagery, beginning, however, with a faint recollection of the traditional response 'for the fallen', remembered at the going down of the sun. For these

> The sun shall rise and set no more[10]

For the dead the statement is all too true, but the sun is more than itself, outshone a thousand times, but equated with the rising sun of the historical flag, which 'melted in the straight red winds'. The compassion in the poem, however, becomes clear in the last strophe. It is not only for the dead, but (in an image which takes us from Trakl in the First World War to Bob Dylan) for the unborn, seen here as a physical casualty. Other poets have used images from the reality of Hiroshima , but in some cases this is countered by the awareness that the fact of the event is enough. Heinz Winfried Sabais begins a poem in 1955 called 'Die Maske von Hiroshima' [The Mask of Hiroshima], which does have allusions to the actual dead, with the words

> Fragt nicht. Der Himmel verschweige diese grausige Sünde[11]

[Don't ask. May the Heavens be silent on this ghastly sin]

Some of the poetry which uses the reality of Hiroshima is indeed striking, even when written well after the event. As a single example we may take a poem by a German, Ingo Hartelt, also a child when the bomb fell. He makes use of the lasting problems rather than of the single event:

> Nach dem Schein der tausend Sonnen
> über Hiroshima
> gebaren etliche Frauen Kinder
> hirnlos
> nichts sehend oder hörend[12]

[After the light brighter than a thousand suns over Hiroshima,
several women gave birth to children who were acephalous,
seeing and hearing nothing.]

But the confronting of the reader with one of the more horrible
aspects is nevertheless developed into an admonitory poetic motif,
as the poet addresses those who *can* see and hear, to use their heads

> damit wir leben können
>
> [so that we can live]

The use of 'we' is clearly different from its propagandistic
inclusiveness in patriotic poems, and the pictures have a more
urgent message even than those of the First World War realistic
poems.

A quite specific guilt manifested itself almost at once, and early
lyrics on the theme sometimes reached large audiences. Hermann
Hagedorn published not long after the war a statement of
approaching fifty pages in a loosely poetic form calling for control
of the great force of the atom by the even greater force of the
human soul. Associated with the Moral Re-Armament movement,
the work – which went into many reprints and sold very widely
indeed – made clear the universal implications of what had
happened. The opening is historical:

> A bomb fell on Hiroshima.
> It wasn't much in size, as bombs go, it wasn't much in
> weight. . .[13]

but it was 'no bomb like other bombs'. Hagedorn describes not
only the actual destruction, the cloud and the black rain, but also
the particles forever flying over Hiroshima as over Almagordo and
the atom-tests. Some of the work is placed in the mouth of 'the
conscience of America', and in these passages Hagedorn tries, not
especially convincingly, to draw a distinction between the bomb on
Hiroshima and those elsewhere, in an attempt to reconcile the
general necessity of a Second World War with its ending. The
implications, incidentally, for other acts of saturation-bombing
with conventional explosives, are interesting:

Lord, we have not forgotten Pearl Harbor.
. . .
We have not forgotten Bataan and Corregidor, the March of
Death, the concentration camps, the calculated humil-
iations, the starving of American prisoners, the massacres
and the torture.
. . .
But we know that more than half of those whom the bomb
obliterated at Hiroshima were women and children, as
innocent of the wrongs committed by Hirohito's arogant
adventurers as our own wives, our own children.

We know that we have dropped other bombs that killed
the innocent by thousands,
But in our hearts we know that this bomb was not like
those.
With the others we merely demolished cities, as we
slaughtered, overturned governments, ended the lives of
nations.
With this bomb we ended an age. . .

The conclusion of this line of thought is the transference of the
awareness of guilt for the atomic bomb to America itself:

The bomb that fell on Hiroshima fell on America too.

The real point is that the event may be repeated. If the bomb
having fallen on America is true in metaphorical terms only, it
could become real; the poem looks ahead to an arms race and to
the cold war, but it accepts the guilt that America was the
progenitor. Throughout the work the actuality of Hiroshima is not
lost from view, and as an event it was still in the recent past, but
there is a warning against making the world into 'one final
Hiroshima'. The historical event has already become universalized:
we remember *the* Somme, and fear *a* Hiroshima.

Hagedorn's moral re-armament is a religious response to the
event. Other lyrical responses, equally widely disseminated, stressed
only the guilt. Indeed, Hiroshima soon gave rise to a scapegoat
myth which was reflected in the lyric. The story arose that the
supposed pilot of the B29 that bombed Nagasaki, a Major Claude
Eatherly had refused a pension, had taken to stealing, and had
been driven mad. The legend took hold, since it allowed for an

empathetic response to the guilt. That every detail of the story was entirely untrue was made clear in a book later by William Bradford Huie, who was himself aware, however, that his book would make very little difference in fact. Eatherly not only became a lyric image, he has remained one even after the exposure of the myth for what it is.[14] The best-known poem about Eatherly came as soon as the false story went into circulation. John Wain's 1958 poem was printed in nine periodicals, including *Encounter*, *The Listener*, and *Poetry*, (another on a similar theme by George Barker appeared in the *New Statesman* in January 1961) and Wain's poem was broadcast on the BBC before being printed in book and anthology form. The poem, 'Major Eatherly', rejects the idea of the pilot as a scapegoat:

> His penitence will not take away our guilt.
> We do not punish him for cries or nightmares
> We punish him for stealing things from stores.

'We' and 'our' are key words: Wain is not writing from an American, but from a global standpoint, and the poem concludes with a broader expression of solidarity with the supposed pilot in his guilt. What we have to say to him, and that only unofficially on a page torn from a notebook, is that we have understood:

> Eatherly, we have your message.

Of course, the fact that the whole is based on myth is immaterial, and the point is that collective responsibility is the only answer. Post-war dramatists have made the point frequently enough, and it is taken to extremes by poets such as Peter Appleton whose poetic voice states simply:

> I am the one behind it all. . .
> I am the one responsible. . .[15]

as part of the great chain that reaches from the taxpayer to the bomb. Poetry from all cultures make the same admission. Iain Crichton Smith writes in Gaelic of the continuing guilt in a poem called 'A' Dol dhachaidh' [Going Home]:

> Ach bidh mi smaontinn (dh'aindeoin sin)
> air ar teine mhor th'air cul ar smuain,
> Nagasaki's Hiroshima. . .

[I shall, however, still think of the great fire in our thoughts, Nagasaki and Hiroshima. . .]

and in another poem he can can say from the relative remoteness of the Western Isles that 'our Hiroshima is still around me'.[16]

The idea of a Hiroshima pilot appeared in others poems, notably in that by Marie Luise Kaschnitz in Germany, who takes in her 'Hiroshima' as a starting point a photograph of the man who

den Tod auf Hiroshima warf,[17]

[cast death onto Hiroshima]

going on to speculate on whether he hanged himself, went mad, spent his time fighting ghosts. But (in the second part of the poem) it becomes clear that none of these things happened. He is alive, photographed in front of his house, the roses are blooming and he is smiling. The poem does not accuse the man, but rather his existence. The rose bushes do not grow so fast that they could become a forest of forgetfulness, and in front of hedge is the unseen photographer. The eyes of the world are on a nameless individual who becomes a symbol for everyone. Kaschnitz's poem has been much discussed, and it appeared in an anthology beside another German piece by Dieter Krusche with the same title. That poem looks at Hiroshima from the point of view of 1968 and describes the city:

Dann gibts da noch
einen Friedenspark
mit Friedensglocke,
Friedensvogel
und ewigem Friedensfeuer.[18]

After the four repetitions of *Frieden-* 'peace' comes the question:

Warum gibts das
in anderen Städten nicht?

[And they also have a peace park with a peace bell and a peace bird and an eternal peace flame. Why don't they have all that in other towns as well?]

Hiroshima is still not like other towns. D.J. Enright took a more bitter view of the monuments in Hiroshima, pointing out that the dead of 1945 would have been grateful for something even as permanent as a coffin.[19]

The extension of the arms race into the so-called cold war and to Korea (during which conflict there was even discussion of dropping the atomic bomb once again), and on to the Cuban missile crisis in 1962, was reflected in lyrics of various sorts. American country and western music produced once again a spate of songs, some alarmingly militaristic. Bill Malone cites in his study of the music titles like 'The Great Atomic Power', 'When That Hell Bomb Falls', and 'The Red That We Want is the Red We've Got in the Old Red White and Blue'. On the other side, a poem from 1956 by Samuel Marshak comments with less aggressiveness on a minister at a peace conference:

> V yevo pyetlitsye — pal'movaya vyetka,
> No on syidyit na bombakh, kak nasyedka. . .[20]

[in his buttonhole a palm-twig, but he is sitting on bombs like a broody hen. . .]

However, as *The Atomic Café* made clear, even the cold war became an image in popular songs, divorced of its reality and made into a description of personal relationships – 'this cold war with you'.

Modified views in which the facts of the historical Hiroshima are merged with a protestation of innocence or a re-apportioning of the guilt may be found in a number of lyrics again from different sources. A German poet, Günter Eich, invokes the idea of Peter Schlemihl, who sold his own shadow:

> Wir haben unsern Schatten verkauft.
> Er hängt an einer Mauer in Hiroshima,
> Ein Geschäft, von dem wir nichts wussten,
> wir streichen die Zinsen ein. . .[21]

[We have all sold our shadow – it is hanging on a wall in Hiroshima. We knew nothing about the deal, but we are still drawing the interest. . .]

Roger Bodart in French visualizes a meeting with the Prince of Darkness in Princeton, dreaming of a mushroom that would devour the works of God – the cloud over Hiroshima soon became an image in its own right. Here, blame is placed upon the scientists, although it will be directed too at the military establishment, at governments and, indeed, at the generation of the Second World War itself. When the 'old master' dies, however, Bodart comments:

> Ce matin-là, l'herbe avait resurgi
> dans la poussière où fut Nagasaki.[22]

[That same morning the grass had sprouted again in the dust that had been Nagasaki.]

There is no logic in blaming Einstein, of course, and more recent verse has taken the whole process back to the discovery of fire.[23] Nevertheless, other poets *have* blamed the scientist, either directly or implicitly. Karl Mickel, from the German Democratic Republic, has a scientist say, in a poem which mixes English and German for a deliberate effect, and recalls Appleton's 'The Responsibility':

> Ich wars! Ich bins! Ich bin der Tod![24]

[It was I! It is I! I am death]

Tom Scott, writing in Scots in a long anti-war poem in 1968, indicts Hiroshima as a cold-blooded scientific experiment. The element of truth in this, of course, is something which has become apparent from books and later comment, and Scott is clear in his indictment of the 'Frankensteinian ghouls' Oppenheimer and Compton, insisting on dropping the bombs in the face of majority protest, and of a hypocrisy which spared Kyoto because it was a religious shrine, but had no doubts about killing a quarter of a million people. However, Scott has to set Oppenheimer, who

> plots a bomb
> Can render the haill earth a barren waste[25]

beside Fleming, curing the ills, and is essentially unable to solve this 'human antisyzygy'. The reader is left, as often in the poetry of the third world war, with a sense of original sin, brought on by someone else, but impossible to shake off. Scott, like Hagedorn, reaches the equally religious solution that man has to rise up – significantly – 'frae Hiroshima's hell'.

Hiroshima produced artistic responses beyond the lyric, of course, in plays like Duras's *Hiroshima mon amour* or Kipphardt's *In der Sache J. Robert Oppenheimer*, in music like Penderecki's *Threnody for the Dead at Hiroshima*, and in painting. Some works retain the name, while other novels and films deal with the idea – that could only have arisen after Hiroshima – of a nuclear war with few survivors,[26] a fear present in the lyric from the beginning. The *Oasis* anthology of soldier poetry ends (as have other anthologies[27]) with a poem of Hiroshima, in this case written just after the dropping of the atomic bomb, and published in a soldiers' magazine. The poem ends in silence – the silence of wondering what can happen next.[28] The fear of a new Hiroshima informs, however, the entire song-lyric of nuclear protest from the 1960s on. In some ways these lyrics are no longer strictly of the Second World War, but many retain links either to the events of the end of the Second World War or, in a curious manner, with the songs of the First World War.

The best-known songs concerned with the nuclear bomb are those associated with the nuclear disarmament movement, which has produced a tradition of original song and contrafactura which has lasted until the present. The simplest forms refer to the atom bomb of Hiroshima or to its successors:

> I'm gonna lay down my atom bombs
> Down by the riverside. . .
>
> Ban, ban, ban, the bloody H-Bomb

The echo of the spiritual in the first of these is of interest. Other songs catalogue man's nuclear achievements beginning with Hiroshima, though one such refers to the men who

> threw a custard pie at Hiroshima.[29]

It is of both historical and poetic interest that a recent collection of anti-nuclear songs adapts soldiers' songs of the First World War, themselves often adaptations:

> When this nuclear war is over. . .
>
> Oh, oh, oh it's a nuclear war. . .

Another is set to the tune of 'Bombed last night. . .'[30]

The fear takes precedence over the guilt for Hiroshima, however, in the poetry of a new generation, and it is here that attacks against those now perceived as guilty are most frequent. Notable in this context is the poetry of Bob Dylan, especially that written and sung between 1962 and 1964, years in which a number of anti-bomb songs appeared. That the flow of such songs is now considerably slower possibly acknowledges the enormity of the task of changing the world with a song. In 'Talking World War III Blues' Dylan dreams that he has survived a nuclear war almost alone. This is a recurrent theme in lyrics as in fiction, and it was not always used in a negative context. One of the songs used in *The Atomic Café* was Bill Haley's 'Thirteen Women', the conceit of which is that the sole survivors of a nuclear explosion are the (male) singer and thirteen women. When Dylan's first-person speaker finds a woman, however, and suggests they 'go play Adam and Eve', the proposition is rejected on the grounds: 'look what happened last time they started'. Many of the images of a post-nuclear-war world conjured up by Dylan are both striking and original, however: driven by the urge to hear a human voice, the speaker rings the telephone clock, which gives the same time 'precisely' for over an hour. The time is precisely wrong, but it is a memorial to the start of the brief third world war. The song returns to the original idea when the speaker realizes that everyone is having similar dreams, and offers a bargain aimed directly at the listener: I'll let you be in my dream if you let me be in yours.[31] In performance, Dylan attributed the statement directly to himself, making the point even more personal. Others of Dylan's songs touch on the possibility of nuclear destruction, and even in a generalized work like 'Blowing in the Wind' it is possible to read an irony that may or may not even have been intentional. He commented on the Cuban missile crisis of 1962 in 'A Hard Rain's A-Gonna Fall', and picked up another theme – that of the fallout shelter – in 'Playboys and Playgirls'. Most savage, however, is a comment in a generally anti-war poem which at the same time criticizes this time the military establishment, the 'Masters of War', who have committed the most dreadful of all acts, by bringing about the

> Fear to bring children
> Into the world. . .[32]

The motif of the unborn children seen in earlier war poems is taken thereby a stage further.

Other protest songs pick upon motifs that go beyond Hiroshima only. Malvina Reynolds's 'What Have They Done to the Rain' is an example, but these lyrics, in their criticism of an unspecified enemy – 'they' – share a common helplessness. They warn of the proximity of 'The Eve of Destruction' or of the dangers of 'Brother

Atom' or 'Old Man Atom', but do not even offer the solution of
Hagedorn's moral re-armament. It may be noted that the
American pronunciation of 'atom' overlaps so strongly with that of
'Adam' that the notion of the beginning of time is sometimes
brought into the lyrics, either as a deliberately developed motif or
as a contrast. Plays on words in phrases like 'Atom and Evil', in a
striking song performed by the Golden Gate Quartet, are not
always visible in print.[33]

Mockery is not directed at Hiroshima, but black humour as a
response to the possibility of a nuclear war soon manifested itself.
In his comments on a play which questions the morality of the
scientist but more so points to collective responsibility in a modern
world, Dürrenmatt's *Die Physiker* [The Physicists], the playwright
himself noted that the situation is too large to be tragic, and that
only comedy is possible. Some of the lyrics of the effects of
Hiroshima reflect this too. A parody that won a competition in
1948 read in full:

> Ring a ring o' geraniums
> A pocket full of uranium.
> Hiro
> Shima
> All fall down.[34]

This is more literary than it seems at first glance, given that the
original nursery rhyme referred to another city-killer, the great
plague of London. In fact another writer, Paul Dehn, had a version
of the same idea with the conclusion

> a fission, a fission
> We all fall down.[35]

but although closer to the 'atishoo' of the original, it is not as
memorable. In the late 1950s Tom Lehrer (who commented on the
morality of the scientist in war in a song about 'Werner von
Braun') produced again some ironic material which was not,
however, misunderstood in the way that verses by Noel Coward or
A.P. Herbert had been. 'We Shall All Go Together When We Go'
contains witty and outrageous rhymes, but the fear behind it all is
quite real. Universal bereavement becomes an inspiring achievement, and the whole is a satire on progress. No one, however, 'will
have the endurance to collect the insurance'; we are assured,

though not reassured, that 'Lloyds of London will be loaded when they go'. The tune, a jolly one, and a variation of sorts on 'She'll Be Coming Round the Mountain' brings to mind the use of that popular lyrical short-circuit (one much sung in the Second World War) in another poem by John Wain, who comments that

> I hope to feel some pity when it comes. . .[36]

Lehrer's recorded presentations of his songs contribute towards the effect of his lyrics, as when he declares 'So long Mom, I'm off to drop the bomb', or sees the Wild West as the place where he can (amongst the stock cactus and thistles) watch the guided missiles and be watched in his turn by the FBI.[37] This is the lyric of desperate protest, implying that if a situation is so bad, all that can be done is to mock it. This is implicit in another American song, the black humour piece 'The Merry Minuet', which catalogues how all races hate each other, and that nature and climate are equally damaging. The only comfort offered is that we should be thankful and indeed proud because we have a mushroom cloud, and before long 'we shall all be blown away'.[38] The forced jollity of the song again contrasts with the blackness of theme.

If this is all laughing to keep from crying, there are not many real alternatives in a world which is largely post-Christian and devoid of religious answers. In one poem, Bernard Kops invented a kind of anti-bomb, a Shalom Bomb, which spreads peace rather than destruction, but this kind of fantasy-optimism is rare. [39] The poetry of the Liverpool group of the 1960s (whose work comes into the some-what unusual category of genuinely popular book-poetry) is general-ly pessimistic. Roger McGough has a poem which is of stylistic interest, beginning in a positive and lively rhythm which recalls once more a nursery rhyme ('the king was in his counting house. . .'):

> The general at the radar screen
> Rubbed his hands with glee,
> And grinning pressed the button,
> And started world war three.[40]

But these rhythms cannot last: at the end they give way to hypermetric questioning:

> The general at the radar screen
> He should have got the sack.
> But that wouldnt bring

WORLD WAR THREE BLUES

Three thousand million seven hundred
and sixty eight people back
would it?

The spelling out of an apparently precise number underlines the point, although this is a theoretical third world war and not an historical second.

The guilt and then the unrelieved fear of a new Hiroshima gives way to a visionary poetry of what will happen *after* the third world war. Bob Dylan's talking blues already considers the point, and more recent material has played with the idea of some survival. Protest songs use the building of fallout shelters as an extra indictment against governments, who will emerge after a holocaust and begin the whole process over again, and this has become a topos.[41] Many poets have envisaged life after the third world war. Men will live under the earth like moles – 'Maulwürfe [Moles] is the title of a poem by Erich Kästner, the German satirist. The poem (subtitled 'Thy Will Be Done') describes the retreat underground to a world where trees and flowers are things from fairy tales; men carry on roughly as before, listen to motets and split atoms, and are buried under neon lights. However, this summary conceals one point: the whole work is set in the past tense, and Kästner's implication is that the mole civilization, too, has gone. The survivors were few in number and emerged into the world only from time to time in protected vehicles to collect cherry blossom before returning to their living graves.[42]

Fallout shelters become motifs in other poems. An Austrian, Herbert Jakob Eisen, takes as his starting point an advertisement for shelters, available to those with money, but questions how well spent it will be. The rich few will wander around lost amongst the millions of corpses after the final destruction.[43] More striking is the awful believability of the narrative in a poem by Peter Porter which is placed at the end of the *Oxford Book of War Poetry* and which has been much anthologized. The poem 'Your Attention Please' sets up the fictionality of a final radio broadcast with a very clear set of circumstances. It is soberly enunciated, and essentially pessimistic; the implicit message is that all man can hope for is the strength not to let the situation arise. Porter's vision is chilling:

If . . . your air becomes
Exhausted, or if any of your family

Is critically injured, administer
The capsules marked Valley Forge
(Red Pocket in No. 1 Survival Kit)
For painless death. . .[44]

The notion of suicide tablets in a survival kit and the exact detail of
the description complement the irony of the use of the name Valley
Forge. For the most part, however, visions of a world after the
third world war are of the silence and the emptiness:

The grey wind carries the grey ashes
No place. There are no places.[45]

Hiroshima was the last act of the Second World War, and in a
sense the last act of the prolonged war that lasted effectively from
1914 to 1945. Iain Crichton Smith, writing in English, links in a
collection of love poems and elegies the century's wars. 'Your
brother', the poem begins, 'clanked his sword for the Boer war',
then later, in France, but now the days of swords are over. The
Second World War and its ending means that there is no room any
more for rooms cluttered with poppies and the relics of empires:

Our skies are clearer and more deadly now,
our hell is all around us in the blue
bubble over Hiroshima, our rooms

more pared to their essentials, the chairs
swaying in a purer breeze, the sun
climbing forever to a shriller place.[46]

This poem appeared in 1972, but the effect of the end of the Second
World War remains, and in this poem it is the effect and not the
guilt that is in the foreground. The ending is both cosmic and, like
many of the poems of Hiroshima, obscure, as indeed it must be,
because a real ending cannot be foreseen. Realism in war poetry is
at an end.

The poetry of the third world war admits less readily than that
associated with the First or the Second World War before
Hiroshima to a categorization of the popular, because the effect
was universal. Even the saturation bombings or the extermination
camps may be presented as things which have happened but must
not happen again. Hiroshima, however, is always possible. The
lyrics of the very end of the war or of the cold war period that

accepted the bomb as a benefit are few – mainly only country music in America, even though many at first welcomed it as ending the war. The later lyric reflections of the final act of the Second World War see it as a disaster. Such (black) humour as is found in the situation is not aggressive but satirical, and its target is those who do not see the full potential. Peter Leher, having established in a brief poem that the bomb has the value of one megatonne, goes on to say that

> 1 Million Dumme sind
> 1 Megadumm.[47]

[1 million idiots equal one mega-idiot]

There is no room for sentiment, and the theme is too large for realism. What remains are guilt, fear, a general or specific anger, blame (directed at military forces, governments, or the scientist). But the first person plural predominates: it is our guilt and our fear. Lyric originality lies either in the force with which the point is made, in aspects of the vision of the end, or in the level of belief that man will not allow another Hiroshima. The directness and indeed the express repetition of P.F. Sloan's statement

> And you tell me
> over and over again, my friend,
> that you don't believe
> we're on the eve of destruction,[48]

or the memorability of Tom Lehrer's ironic

> We shall all go together when we go
> every Hottentot and every Eskimo

are probably more effective than many poems with more pretensions and smaller circulations. The theme is too serious for aesthetics. Popular lyrics and poems in small magazines alike point to a lesson of futility, and ultimately to the fact that we have even come to get used to the fear of annihilation.[49]

It is appropriate to end with a poem that seems not to be a poem at all and which makes its point in the form of a paradox. It is by a well-known Austrian poet, who has 'popularized' his poetry by readings that are, in effect, peformances. Ernst Jandl's 'Fragment' is almost an anti-poem. It has very little about it to mark it out as poem: the heading might be a title, or it may be a description. What does identify it as a poem is its place in a collection of poems; it is a poem because we take it to be one, and it depends on an audience for effect. More important, the situation it shows has not happened. It exists only as a fiction, and in its fictionality its title and audience are not of the present.

None of the classical tenets of poetry applies to Jandl's poem, which has no rhyme and no metrical pattern. Indeed, the six lines contain only eight complete words (plus another five that can be guessed) and no complete syntactic units:

> wenn die rett
> es wird bal
> übermor
> bis die atombo
> ja herr pfarr[50]
>
> [if the resc
> it will soo
> tomorr
> until the atom-bo
> yes indeed, Rever]

The form, indeed, seems to indicate a fragment of spoken (telephonic?) conversation, though in its fictionality it has perhaps been transcribed. Possibly there is a slight optimism in that fragments like this are usually of ancient civilizations published like this by later scholars, and sometimes incomplete and unintelligible, like Etruscan or Linear A. The title here applied to it is uncomprehendingly neutral. But for our time, it warns that the later scholar might have nothing more of our civilization than this. For all that, we are quite able to reconstruct the missing parts, and this makes clear to us that the world could not be reconstructed. The atomic bomb that destroyed Hiroshima has here been applied to the world and to the lyric. Within the fiction of the piece (which cannot be seen as a poem in any real terms), our world has gone.

The trumpeter has sounded the last call, that which in the final verse of the Edwardian song merges with the last trump itself:

> Lucky for you if you hear it at all.

Notes

CHAPTER 1: GOOD WAR POETRY?

1 See his *Soldiers and Soldiering*, London: Cape, 1953, p.141 (reprinting a lecture of 1948).

2 See Dominic Hibberd, *Poetry of the First World War. A Casebook*, London: Macmillan, 1981, pp.69–75.

3 In Dominic Hibberd and John Onions, *Poetry of the Great War*, London: Macmillan, 1986, p.83, and other anthologies.

4 *Lyrik des expressionistischen Jahrzehnts*, Munich: dtv, 1962, p.133. John Ferguson's study of *The Arts in Britain in World War I*, London: Stainer & Bell, 1980, p.44, makes the same point with different illustrations.

5 As many critics have commented. See Michael Hamburger, *The Truth of Poetry*, Harmondsworth: Penguin, 1972, p.164.

6 Hibberd and Onions, *Great War*, p.79. In Rickword's poem a soldier is reading Donne to a dead man.

7 *Ibid.*, p.156.

8 Holger M. Klein, 'Tambimuttu's *Poetry in Wartime*', *Forum for Modern Language Studies*, 21 (1985), pp.1–18, with reference to many anthologies in the notes (although more remain).

9 Francis Hope, 'Tommy's Tunes' in: Ian Hamilton, *The Modern Poet*, London: Macdonald, 1968, p.139.

10 Denys Thompson, *The Uses of Poetry*, Cambridge: CUP, 1978, p.132.

11 Hamburger, *Truth of Poetry*, p.192.

12 Catherine W. Reilly, *English Poetry of the First World War. A Bibliography*, London: Prior, 1978, and *English Poetry of the Second World War. A Biobibliography*, London: Mansell, 1986. The value of these two works cannot be overestimated.

13 Theodor Plievier, *Des Kaisers Kulis* (1929), Munich: dtv, 1984, p.79f. Erich Maria Remarque, *Im Westen nichts Neues* (1929), ed. Brian Murdoch, London: Methuen, 1984, p.69 (in slightly different form).

14 See Randall Jarrell, *Poetry and the Age*, London: Faber, 1955, pp.154–61 on anthologies and on bad poets.

15 Jon Silkin, *The Penguin Book of First World War Poetry*, Harmondsworth: Penguin, 1979, see p.72.

16 Gavin Ewart, 'Both Sides of the Trenches', the *Observer* 12 August 1979, p.37.
17 The anthologies by Hibberd and Onions, and that by Silkin have been noted already. The others mentioned here are Brian Gardner, *Up the Line to Death*, London: Methuen, 1964; I.M. Parsons, *Men Who March Away*, London: Chatto & Windus, 1965; Maurice Hussey, *Poetry of the First World War*, London: Longmans, 1967. The last-named (a text used in schools, incidentally) is particularly broad, and includes works by Alfred Austin and even Newbolt's 'Vitaï lampada'. There is a brief but valuable discussion of some of the points at issue in Matthew Parris's review in the *Sunday Times* of 7 August 1988, p.G5, of Martin Stephen, *Never Such Innocence*, London: Buchan & Enright, 1988, one of the many 'anniversary' anthologies. See also Robert Giddings, *The War Poets*, London: Bloomsbury, 1988.
18 Most countries have produced 'national' anthologies of war poetry, of course. Nevertheless, the Hibberd and Onions anthology has a wider range than most others, using as illustrations postcards and posters. Equally valuable, though shorter, is the anthology by Anne Harvey (see note 19) which covers both wars. Tim Cross edited *The Lost Voices of World War I*, London: Bloomsbury, 1988.
19 Ian Hamilton, *The Poetry of War, 1939–1945*, London: Ross, 1965; Brian Gardner, *The Terrible Rain*, London: Methuen, 1966, paperback 1977; Charles Hamblett, *I Burn for England*, London: Frewin, 1966; Anne Harvey, *In Time of War*, London and Glasgow: Blackie, 1987. The last-named is the most extensive in material covered, including children's rhymes as well as songs for both wars.
20 Jon Stallworthy, *The Oxford Book of War Poetry*, Oxford: OUP, 1984; Philip Larkin, *The Oxford Book of Twentieth Century English Verse*, Oxford: OUP, 1973.
21 Wolfgang Deppe, Christopher Middleton and Herbert Schonherr, *Ohne Hass und Fahne*, Hamburg: Rowohlt, 1959. See the detailed review by Michael Hamburger, in *Encounter*, 85 (15/4, October, 1960), pp.53–8.
22 Catherine W. Reilly, *Scars Upon My Heart*, London: Virago, 1981, and *Chaos of the Night*, London: Virago, 1984; Martin Page, *Kiss Me Goodnight Sergeant Major*, London: Panther, 1975, and *For Gawdsake Don't Take Me!*, London; Panther, 1977. Page's two anthologies were originally published in 1973 and 1976, but the paperbacks have appeared in different editions. I cite the editions noted as they have easily identifiable titles. Rudolf Walther Leonhardt's *Lieder aus dem Krieg* (which also includes a few French and English songs) appeared as a book in 1979 (Munich: Goldmann), having been a series in the weekly *Zeit* in 1977.
23 Victor Selwyn, *Return to Oasis*, London: Editions Poetry, 1980, and *Poems of the Second World War. The Oasis Selection*, London: Dent, 1985. *Oasis* itself was the title of a collection made during the Second World War, hence the titles. The short title *Oasis* will here refer to the second, fuller, anthology, which overlaps a little with the first.
24 See notes to chapter 4 for Nazi anthologies; Hans Werner Richter's

Deine Söhne, Europa, has been reprinted, Munich: dtv, 1985.

25 M.S. Windsor and J. Turral, *Lyra Historica*, Oxford: Clarendon [1911] was still in print in the 1920s, alongside the various Oxford books of verse. On the whole *Lyra Heroica* type of anthology, see J.H. Grainger, *Patriotisms*, London: RKP, 1986, pp.65–85, with reference to what he calls 'public poets'. Others referred to are: Arthur Burrell, *A Book of Heroic and Patriotic Verse*, London: Dent [1912]; Christopher Stone, *War Songs*, Oxford: Clarendon, 1908. The once well-known but now forgotten 'Private of the Buffs' is discussed by Grainger, p.66.

26 V.H. Collins, *Poems of War and Battle*, Oxford: Clarendon, 1914. Two other works by Collins, *Poems of Action* and a simpler version, *Stories in Verse*, published by the Clarendon press in 1914 and 1917 respectively also remained in print long after the war.

27 *Songs and Sonnets for England in War Time*, London: Bodley Head, 1914. As an example of a single-poet collection from the First World War – and note the date – see William Dunbar Birrell, *War and Patriotic Poems*, Dundee: Thomson, 1918, and as examples from the beginning of the Second World War, see Cumberland Clark's *The British Empire at War* and *The War Poems of a Patriot*, Bournemouth: Henbest, both 1940. Note, too, the concept of the 'local production'. The German text is *Der Kampf. Neue Gedichte zum heiligen Krieg*, Jena: Diederichs, 1914.

28 See Cate Haste, *Keep the Home Fires Burning*, London: Allen Lane, 1977, p.28.

29 H.B. Elliot, *Lest We Forget*, London: Jarrold, 1915; *King Albert's Book*, London: Daily Telegraph [1915]; George Goodchild, *The Blinded Soldiers and Sailors Gift Book*, London: Jarrold [1915], with the verse by Nesbit on p.153f. ('Prayer in Time of War'). Reilly, *Scars Upon My Heart*, p.79f., has two similar verses by Nesbit. The three anthologies mentioned – there were plenty of others – contain virtually no poems by serving soldiers.

30 *Soldier Poets. Songs of the Fighting Men*, London: Erskine Macdonald, 1916 and (Second Series) 1917, issued in many reprints and editions, including a 'Trench Edition'. These collections – which are discussed sporadically in secondary literature and which contain work by some poets well known later (Grenfell, Sorley) and represented all ranks – played a part in continuing the tradition of poetry in the trenches. Erskine Macdonald's lists at the end of the volumes are of bibliographic interest, and the Second Series includes part of a leading article from the *Daily Telegraph* of 12 June 1917, which concludes that the poetry has given 'yet another proof of the virile quantities of our race'. For trench magazines, see Patrick Beaver, *The Wipers Times*, London: Peter Davies, 1973, and collections like that by Frederick Treves and George Goodchild, *Made in the Trenches*, London: Allen & Unwin, 1916 (with a Bairnsfather frontispiece). Bruce Bairnsfather's 'Old Bill' and other cartoons were published in collected numbers by *The Bystander* as *Fragments from France* from 1916, and his sketches are not so dissimilar from the official war sketches of artists like Muirhead Bone, and often rather more informative: see C.E. Montague, *The Front*

Line, London: Hodder & Stoughton, 1917. There were, of course, also German and French trench magazines.

31 *Mr Punch's History of the Great War*, London: Cassell, 1919. The editor of Punch, Sir Owen Seaman, published a collection of verses of his own, *War-Time*, London: Constable, 2nd edn. 1916, which was reprinted more than once, and of course contemporary issues of *Punch* (as of *Kladderadatsch* and other national equivalents) are interesting sources of contemporary war verse.

32 Bertram Lloyd, *Poems Written During the Great War*, London: Allen & Unwin, 1918, p.2.

33 J. Bruce Glasier, *The Minstrelsy of Peace*, Manchester and London: National Labour Press [1918].

34 Pamela Glenconner's *Edward Wyndham Tennant*, which appeared in 1919 (London: Bodley Head), includes every scrap of verse from Tennant's fourth year onward. As a fortuitous example of a larger anthology, the Royal Artillery produced a *War Commemoration Book* with some poetry in 1920. A. St John Adcock's *For Remembrance* appeared in 1918 (London: Hodder & Stoughton) and Frederic W. Ziv's anthology *The Valiant Muse* in 1936 (reprinted Freeport: Books for Libraries, 1971).

35 George Herbert Clarke, *A Treasury of War Poetry*, London: Hodder and Stoughton [1919].

36 Vernon Scannell, *Not Without Glory*, London: Woburn, 1976, p.9.

37 The example of Ronald Barnes, Lord Gorell is an interesting one. *The Times* referred to his work as 'clearly in the great tradition of English poetry', and others critics spoke of his 'true English patriotism'. He is now all but forgotten outside the pages of the *DNB*, though his work might bear reconsideration. See Lord Gorell, *Poems 1904–1936* and *Wings of the Morning* London: Murray, 1937 and 1947. Patriotism differs from blood-and-soil nationalism, and so does bias from propaganda.

38 Hibberd, *Poetry . . . Casebook*, p.31.

39 All these collections are listed in the notes to chapter 3.

40 See Klein, 'Tambimuttu', for details of his and other anthologies. He does not include Harold Nicolson, *England*, London: Macmillan/English Association, 1944, or the Readers Union *Fear No More*, Cambridge: CUP, 1941.

41 *An Anthology of War Poetry*, Harmondsworth: Penguin, 1942 (with the usual request on the title page to leave the book at a Post Office for sending to soldiers).

42 A P. Wavell's *Other Men's Flowers* first appeared in 1944 (London: Cape) and has been in print pretty well ever since. The poem is on p.89.

43 These cases are discussed in chapter 5.

44 *Other Men's Flowers*, p.75.

45 Ibid., p.426.

46 Guy Chapman, *Vain Glory*, London: Cassell, 1937; Peter Vansittart, *Voices from the Great War*, London: Cape, 1981. For a slightly different approach for the Second World War, see Ronald Blythe, *Writing in a War*, Harmondsworth: Penguin, rev. edn. 1982, with English material

only. Nazi material was presented to the English-speaking public in texts like N. Gangulee,*The Mind and Face of Nazi Germany*, London: Murray, 1942.

47 Playtext: *Oh What a Lovely War*, by Charles Chilton and the Theatre Workshop, London: Methuen, 1965; Susan Briggs, *Keep Smiling Through*, London: Weidenfeld & Nicolson, 1975. Anne Harvey's anthology has songs from both wars. French and German sources are noted in chapter 3.

48 Marquess of Crewe, *War and English Poetry*, Oxford: English Association, 1917; C.F.E. Spurgeon, *Poetry in the Light of War*, Oxford: English Association, 1917; Alfred Noyes, *The Edge of the Abyss*, London: Murray, 1944, p.18.

49 For some comments on Kipling's reputation see Edmund Wilson, *The Wound and the Bow*, London: Methuen, rev. edn. 1961, pp.94–161. See Roger Lancelyn Green's casebook *Kipling. The Critical Heritage*, London: RKP, 1971. For a wartime view see Edward Shanks, *Rudyard Kipling*, New York: Doubleday Doran, 1940, and Coulson Kernahan, *Nothing Quite Like Kipling Had Happened Before*, London: Epworth, 1944, and note that Kipling was translated into French during the war: *Poèmes*, trans. Jules Castier, Paris: Laffont, 1949. Andre Maurois commented that the French have no Kipling (Green, *Kipling*, p.382), and Ivor Gurney read Kipling and Noyes in the trenches: *War Letters*, London: Hogarth, 1984, pp.38, 103, 159. Of *Soldier Poets*, too, Gurney noted 'little of value but much of interest', p.159.

50 I.A. Richards, *Science and Poetry*, London: Kegan Paul, 1926, p.43

51 For Reilly, see above, note 12. Martin van Wyk Smith, *Drummer Hodge*, Oxford: Clarendon, 1978; Paul Fussell, *The Great War and Modern Memory*, London: OUP, 1975. There are, of course, a great many social-historical studies of the war and its effect on the different nationalities, as well as comparative literary studies such as Robert Wohl's *The Generation of 1914*, London: Weidenfeld and Nicolson, 1980 and J.M. Cohen, *Poetry of this Age*, London: Hutchinson, rev. edn. 1966.

52 Edmund Wilson, *Patriotic Gore*, London: Deutsch, 1962. See also Willard A. and Porter W. Heaps, *The Singing Sixties*, Norman: University of Oklahoma Press, 1960.

53 See for example David Craig and Michael Egan, *Extreme Situations*, London: Macmillan, 1979, pp.253–75

54 Steve Mason, *Johnny's Song*, Toronto: Bantam, 1987.

55 'Saigon Bride' is by Nina Dushek and Joan Baez, 1967; 'Nineteen' by Paul Hardcastle, 1985, and 'Camouflage' by Stan Ridgeway, 1986.

56 See the anthology edited by Daryl Hine, *Against the War* (*Poetry*, 120/1, September 1972). For songs, see Tony Palmer, *All You Need is Love*, London: Futura, 1977, pp.193f. and 201f.; and Samuel Charters, *The Legacy of the Blues* London: Calder & Boyars, 1975, p.105f.

57 Susannah Yorke and Bill Bachle, *The Big One*, London: Methuen, 1984, p.40. The letter is in *The Second Cuckoo*, ed. Kenneth Gregory, London: Unwin, 1983, p.288f. Lisa Appignanesi, *Cabaret*, London: Methuen, new edn. 1984, p.187, cites a satirical text linking the Falklands with

the Dunkirk Spirit, Vera Lynn, and the Blitz.

58 There is a wealth of material on the literature of the Holocaust. As a few examples, see: Ruth Rubin, *Voices of a People*, New York: Yoseloff, 1963; Laurence Langer, *The Holocaust and the Literary Imagination*, New Haven: Yale UP, 1975; Alvin Rosenfeld, *A Double Dying*, Bloomington and London: Indiana UP, 1980.

59 Patrick Bridgwater, 'German Poetry and the First World War', *European Studies Review*, 1 (1971), p.160f.

60 'We're Glad You've Got a Gun', 1915: see chapter 3, note 11.

61 Adrian Henri, Roger McGough, and Brian Patten, *The Mersey Sound*, Harmondsworth: Penguin, 1967, p.73. There are echoes of the First World War Song 'I Want to Go Home', too.

62 *Mersey Sound*, p.89f.

63 Glenconner, *Tennant*, p.131f.

64 James Simmons, *Judy Garland and the Cold War*, Belfast: Blackstaff, 1976, p.30.

65 The song is by Steve Harris of the group Iron Maiden and is used on their 1985 *Live After Death* album. Other references to the Second World War in popular culture include those in the important 1979 film *Pink Floyd The Wall*, where the mixture of music, lyric, and the images by Gerald Scarfe merit consideration. The First World War is referred to in songs such as that by Sting on his 1985 album *The Dream of the Blue Turtles*, 'Children's Crusade'; the children are the betrayed dead.

CHAPTER 2: WE HATE AS ONE

1 The card is undated, and there is no further identification of the author.

2 Wilfred Owen, *War Poems and Others*, ed. Dominic Hibberd, London: Chatto & Windus, 1973, p.137, has Owen's preface.

3 *Women and Children First*, London: Gollancz, 1978, p.63. There were also wartime nursery rhymes. A series of French postcards show a mother and child playing with toy soldiers whilst the father is in camp: 'Maman m'a dit qu'il est tres beau/ De combattre pour son drapeau'. ('Mama has told me that it is fine to fight for the flag').

4 A few random examples include Coningsby Dawson, *The Glory of the Trenches*, London: Bodley Head, 1918; Patrick MacGill, *The Diggers*, London, Herbert Jenkins, 1919; A. Corbett-Smith, *The Marne – and After*, London: Cassell, 1917. Sometimes poems are tucked away in texts: Gustav Hester, *Als Mariner im Krieg*, Berlin: Rowohlt, 1929, ends with a citation from a poem originally written on a wall at the end of the war.

5 Cited in John Ferguson's anthology, *War and the Creative Arts*, London: Macmillan, 1972, p.151f.

6 *War-Time*, p.7f.

7 Elliott, *Lest We Forget*, p.36 (Frank Danby).

8 Alfred Noyes, *A Salute from the Fleet*, London: Methuen, 1915, p.165.
9 John Black, *The Flag of the Free*, West Hartlepool: Garbutt, 1917, p.8. The nicely-produced shilling volume gave profits to the Red Cross.
10 John Mason, *The Valley of Dreams*, London: Erskine Macdonald, 1918, p.8.
11 In Albrecht Janssen and Felix Heuler, *Als der Weltbrand lohte*, Würzburg: Kabitzsch, 1915, p.85.
12 *Der Kampf*, p.10f. Richard Schaukal's poem cites both national anthems.
13 In Thomas Anz and Joseph Vogl, *Die Dichter und der Krieg*, Munich: Hanser, 1982, p.15.
14 *Sir Edward Elgar*, London and Glasgow: Blackie, 1938, p.160.
15 *King Albert's Book* (with Elgar's music), pp.84–91.
16 Owen, 'Strange Meeting', *War Poems*, p.103: Charles Hamilton Sorley, *Marlborough and Other Poems*, Cambridge: CUP, 4th edn, 1919, p.73.
17 *Gedichte*, ed. Johannes Klein, Dusseldorf and Cologne: Diederichs, 1965, I, p.63f.
18 Cited in John Ellis *Eye-Deep in Hell*, London: Croom Helm, 1976, p.168
19 *Lest We Forget*, p.136 ('Night Outposts').
20 Nick Russel, *Poets by Appointment*, Poole: Blandford, 1981, p.168 (October 1918).
21 Anz and Vogl, *Dichter*, p.28f.
22 Janssen and Heuler, *Weltbrand*, p.254, by Heinrich Molenaar, from a 1914 collection called 'Sonnets in Armour'.
23 See Fussell, *Great War*, pp.114–35.
24 *Der Kampf*, p.94f., by Ernst Otto Berger.
25 See Janssen and Heuler, *Weltbrand*, p.181f.; *Der Kampf*, p.82 for German examples.
26 *The Moonraker*, 2 (October 1917), p.11 (signed S.S.) – the magazine of the Wiltshire regiment in Salonika.
27 Cited in S.R. Gibbons and P. Morican, *World War One*, London: Longmans, 1965, p.46.
28 Janssen and Heuler, *Weltbrand*, p.251.
29 *Punch* printed many cartoons on the subject, and also claimed that Lissauer's work was not original: *Mr Punch's History*, p.16.
30 Hall Caine, *The Drama of 365 Days*, London: Heinemann, 1915, pp.81f.; James W. Gerard, *My Four Years in Germany*, London: Hodder & Stoughton, 1917, pp.215–27 (the chapter is called 'Hate'). The poem itself is available in Anz and Vogl, *Dichter*, p.185f. Vesper's 'Liebe oder Hass?' (originally in Julius Bab's series, *Der deutsche Krieg im deutschen Gedicht*, No. 4 in 1914) is on p.187. Lissauer is translated in part in Vansittart, *Voices*, p.188. See Wilhelm J. Schwarz, *War and the Mind of Germany I*, Berne and Frankfurt/M.: Lang, 1975, p.27.
31 *Mr Punch's History*, p.195 (January, 1918).
32 Clarke, *Treasury*, p.94 (Cone's poem is called 'A Chant of Love for England').
33 Printed London: Knight, probably in 1915.
34 Elliott, *Lest We Forget*, p.123. One of very many similar in the

collection, this is by Douglas Spens Steuart, who wrote poetry about peace at the end of the Second World War.

35 Birrell, *War and Patriotic Poems*, p.13.

36 *A Subaltern's Musings*, London: Long, 1918, pp.41 and 40. The poems are dated 1915 and 1916. Mann fell at Arras in 1917. A piece by one George C. Guthrie published after the war (*In Days of Peace, In Times of War*, Ardrossan: Arthur Guthrie, 1928) celebrates the killing of two Belgian children who had warned of the attack on Liege as 'The Massacre of the Innocents', linking them with Horatius holding the bridge.

37 *Ballads of Battle*, London: Murray, 1916, p.56.

38 Fussell, *Great War*, p.118f. John Oxenham, *The Vision Splendid*, London: Methuen, 1917, pp.48–53. Examples could be multiplied for the use of the motif: thus George Guthrie's 'Goth of Golgatha', *Days*, p.66.

39 The pastiche of *Alice* (the poem is on p.8) was published by *The Car Illustrated*, London, 1914, and has excellent quasi-Tenniel illustrations. 'The Rubaiyat of William Hohenzollern' is not signed. Beaver, *Wipers Times*, p.193.

40 Violet Jacob, *More Songs of Angus*, London: Country Life, 1918, p.17f.

41 Rudolf Herzog, *Ritter, Tod und Teufel*, Leipzig: Quelle & Meyer, 1915, p.15. The second poem is on p.68. Another poem in the collection bears witness to Herzog's ecumenical approach when he invokes the aid of Joan of Arc against the British.

42 Janssen and Heuler, *Weltbrand*, p.163 (Eduard Heyck).

43 *Ibid.*, p.20 (A.R. Lindenthal).

44 Seaman's piece is in *War-Time*, p.29. For Begbie, see Hibberd and Onions, *Great War*, p.37f. The notes p.190 refer to the records, songs, postcards, and badges of this piece. But see E.A. Mackintosh's 'Recruiting' in Hussey, *Poetry*, p.90f.

45 *More Songs by the Fighting Men*, (*Soldier Poets* II), p.99.

46 Guthrie (the book was printed presumably by a relative), *Days*, pp.56–63. Given than he wrote about the Boer War and Queen Victoria, Guthrie probably did not fight. The Australian poem is in Dennis's *Backblock Ballads*, Sydney: Angus & Robertson, 1918, p.147–50. More recruiting poems are in M. R. Fenton-Livingstone, *The Silent Navy*, Glasgow: Livingstone, 1918.

47 Willi Warstat, *Das Erlebnis unserer jungen Kriegsfreiwilligen*, Gotha: Perthes, 1916, p.3.

48 *War and Patriotic Poems*, p.28. Few of the individual poems are dated, but some are on historical incidents. One on the death of Edith Cavell, entitled 'Von Bissing' affords the man who signed her death warrant a somewhat undeserved memorial.

49 On the idea in popular culture, see Stuart Sillars's wide-ranging study *Art and Survival in First World War Britain*, London: Macmillan, 1987, p.71. Wilkinson is in Ziv, *Valiant Muse*, p.114; Vernède's piece is cited and discussed by Hilda Spear, *Remembering, We Forget*, London: David-Poynter, 1979, p.25. Burton and others are in a section of Hibberd and Onions, *Great War*, pp.56–61.

50 See J.A. Nicklin, 'From Whitechapel', *ibid.*, p.38.
51 Coldstreamer, *Ballads of the Boer War* appeared in 1902 (London: Grant Richards), by which time Kipling's collection was in its fourteenth edition; Robert W. Service, *Rhymes of a Red Cross Man*, London: Fisher Unwin, 1916 (and many reprints).
52 *Ritter, Tod und Teufel*, p.46f.
53 *Ballads of Battle*, p.38.
54 Cited from Treves and Goodchild, *Trenches*, pp.31–6.
55 Brian Brooke, *Poems*, London: Bodley Head, 1918, p.178. The introduction to the volume by M.P. Willcocks creates a picture of an enthusiastic warrior; his brother earned the VC and his own death at Mametz in 1918 was mentioned in despatches. The music hall pieces are in Michael Marshall, *The Book of Comic and Dramatic Monologues*, London: Elm Tree/EMI, 1981, pp.104–7. Dennis, *Backblock Ballads*, pp.29–33
56 See Sybil Bristowe's piece in *Scars Upon My Heart*, p.13.
57 Brooke, *Poems*, p.177.
58 Dorias's poem is in Otto Doderer, *Das Landserbuch*, Oldenburg: Stalling, 1940, p.128f. Steffen's is in *Im Schützengraben*, n.p., 1916, p.79., poems from the magazine of the 54th infantry division.
59 (Drawing and poem): *Fragments from France* I (1916), p.4.
60 Beaver, *Wipers Times*, p.289.
61 I have been unable to identify 'Rochan' (who is not in Reilly's bibliography). My copy contains an autograph letter (signed 'Rochan') with an address in Weybridge.
62 Owen Rutter, *The Song of Tiadatha*, London: Fisher Unwin, 1920, pp.80–8.
63 *Soldier Poets*, pp.90–2
64 R.A. Hopwood, *The Old Way*, London: Murray, 1917, pp.37–41.
65 *Der Kampf*, p.92 (Otto König).
66 *Volk im Kriege*, Jena: Diederichs, 1934, p.26 (Reinhold Braun, 'Fliegerkampf' ['Dogfight']).
67 Gilbert Frankau, *The City of Fear*, London: Chatto & Windus, 1917, p.39 ('Eyes in the Air').
68 The author is unidentified, but it is a poetic curiosity that the most celebrated photograph of Wilfred Owen is that taken during his spell at Witley Camp. Many other camps had similar cards: one from Rugely Camp ends 'BUT WE'RE NOT DOWNHEARTED YET'.
69 Janssen and Heuler, *Weltbrand*, p.141f., amongst many similar pieces. Lee's are in his *Ballads of Battle*, pp.77 and 21, as is his 'The Green Grass', p.22, with the unanswerable question of the fallen as they speak to one another: 'why are we dead?'
70 *Ballads of Battle*, p.78. A similar point (noting how hate is greater at home) is made by James Norman Hall in: Lloyd, *Poems Written in the Great War*, pp.49–52.
71 Robert de la Vaissière, *Anthologie poétique du XXe siècle*, Paris: Cres, 1923, I, p.52f.
72 *High Altars*, London: Methuen, 1918.

73 *The King's High Way*, London: Methuen, 1916, p.76.
74 *Wide Horizons*, London: Methuen, 1940, p.52.
75 Poems are all cited from the 1929 memorial edition, London: Hodder & Stoughton, which was reprinted often. See pp.25, 91, 118, 116, 169.
76 James R. Monk and Cedric Lawson, *Words that Won the War*, Princeton: UP, 1939, p.188f.
77 Vladimir Markov and Merrill Sparks, *Modern Russian Poetry*, London: MacGibbon & Kee, 1966, p.238f.
78 Nikolai Os'makov, *Russkaya proletarskaya poeziya*, Moscow: Akademiya Nauka, 1968, p.236.
79 Wilfred Wilson Gibson, *Battle*, London: Elkin Mathews, 1916, p.15; W.D. Cocker, *Poems*, Glasgow: Brown & Ferguson, 1932, repr. 1960 p.169; John Squire, *Selected Poems*, London, Moxon, 1948, p.22.
80 *Tides*, London: Sidgwick & Jackson, 1917, p.34.
81 *The Old Stalker*, Edinburgh and London: Moray, 1936, p.85f.
82 William Noel Hodgson, *Verse and Prose in Peace and War*, London: Murray, 3rd edn 1917, repr. 1920; Robert W. Sterling, *The Poems*, London: OUP, 1916; Rupert Brooke, *1914 and Other Poems*, London: Sidgwick & Jackson, 1915; Laurence Binyon, *For the Fallen and Other Poems*, London: Hodder & Stoughton, [1917].
83 Russel, *Poets by Appointment*, p.170.
84 In J.L.L. D'Artrey, *Anthologie internationale*, Paris: France Universelle, 1927, pp.284–6.
85 See Gerhard Schaub, 'Totentanz 1916', *Trierer Beiträge*, 15 (October 1985), pp.29–52 with illustrations of postcards and other material on the dance of death.
86 Erich Mühsam in his own journal *Kain*, 5 (1918/9) No. 1, p.2 ('Rebellenlied', [Rebel Song] − typical of others).
87 Marshall, *Monologues*, p.109f. Soldier poets also criticised those who did not do much else than give concerts. See H. Rippon-Seymour, *Songs from the Somme*, London: Long, 1918, p.31.
88 *Jutland*, London: Benn, 1930. The text covers about 200 pages, with times of events in the margins, and a bibliography.
89 *The Horoscope*, London: Hamish Hamilton, 1934. A fictional life in verse with a treatment of the war to which justice cannot really be done here is George Dickson's *Peter Rae*, London: Allen & Unwin, 1925.
90 Published by the *Forfar Herald* in 1929, the work presents the war in (mostly) ababcc stanzas, and a few passages of prose.
91 Beaver, *Wipers Times*, p.325.

CHAPTER 3: WHEN THIS BLEEDING WAR IS OVER

1 Reinhard Olt, *Krieg und Sprache*, Giessen: Schmitz, 1980–1, II, p.132. The song is entitled 'Malheur la guerre', and there are other more obscene strophes. John Brophy and Eric Partridge, *Songs and Slang of the British Soldier*, London: Scholartis, 1930, p.25.
2 The film of *Oh What a Lovely War* was produced in 1969 by Richard

Attenborough. On music hall patriotism, see van Wyk Smith, *Drummer Hodge*, pp.76–80; John M. MacKenzie, *Propaganda and Empire*, Manchester: UP, 1984, pp.40–66 and especially Penny Summerfield's essay in MacKenzie's *Imperialism and Popular Culture*, Manchester: UP, 1986, pp.15–48.

3 Elliott, *Lest We Forget*, p.137. See Percy Scholes, *'God Save the King'*, London: OUP, 1942, p.51f.

4 *Songs of the Irish Republic*, Cork: CFN, 1966, p.29.

5 Otto Biba, *'Gott erhalte!'*, Vienna and Munich: Doblinger, 1982, p.16. There is, however, a reworking of the song in Janssen and Heuler, *Weltbrand*, p.177, by Selma Wichtrich linking the two emperors.

6 Text in Olt, *Krieg und Sprache*, II, p.85f. See Scholes, *'King'*, p.55f.

7 *British War Songs Album*, London: Sheard, [1914]. The Anglo-American company was taken over by Darewski. Texts cited are on pp.2f., 36f., and 28f.

8 Ellis, *Eye-Deep in Hell*, p.195 has a picture, and there is a contemporary recording of the song on the Saydisc compilation *Keep the Home Fires Burning* (1986).

9 Probably the most imitated and parodied national song; there is a text in Olt, *Krieg und Sprache*, II, p.54f. See John Stuart Blackie, *War Songs of the Germans*, Edinburgh: Edmonston & Douglas, 1870, p.151f.

10 Plievier, *Des Kaisers Kulis*, p.123.

11 Ascherberg, Hopwood and Crewe, 1915. The song is by Leonard Cooke and Arthur de Blong.

12 Michael R. Turner and Antony Miall, *The Edwardian Song Book*, London: Methuen, 1982, pp.63–9 (Boosey).

13 Ascherberg, Hopwood and Crewe, 1915.

14 'When the Great Day Comes', Ascherberg, Hopwood and Crewe, 1915.

15 Ascherberg, Hopwood and Crewe, 1914.

16 Francis and Day's *36th Album*, London, 1917, p.55. The other songs cited are on pp.13f., and 45.

17 Giles Brandreth, *I Scream for Ice Cream*, London: Eyre Methuen, 1974, p.63.

18 Feldman's *23rd Song Album*, London, [1918], pp.31–3. 'Ten Days Leave' is by William Hargreaves.

19 Herman Darewski, 1918.

20 See John Ferguson, *The Arts in Britain in World War I*, London: Stainer & Bell, 1980, see plates 46–7.

21 S. Louis Giraud, *Songs that Won the War*, Lane/Daily Express, 1930. The text is on pp.31–3, copyright 1914 (Francis, Day and Hunter) by Charles Knight and Kenneth Lyle. 'Goodbyee' is sometimes mistaken for a song of the beginning of the war: the copyright (also Francis, Day and Hunter) for B.P. Weston and Bert Lee's song is 1917.

22 See Denys Thompson, *The Uses of Poetry*, Cambridge; CUP, 1978, p.118 and also John Press, *Poets of World War I*, Windsor: Profile, 1983, p.54. Thompson misdates 'Tipperary', for which he claims 'instant popularity'. That he speaks of 'Sassoon's war' is revealing. Many of the accounts of the war refer to that song and to the singing of others. See

as a few examples: R.H. Mottram, *The Spanish Farm Trilogy*, Harmondsworth, Penguin, 1979 (originally 1927), p.83 and *Ten Years Ago*, London: Chatto & Windus, 1928, p.5f.; Henry Williamson, *The Patriot's Progress*, London: Bles, 1930, pp.42–7; Richard Aldington, *Death of a Hero*, London: Chatto & Windus, 1929, p.287; Robert Graves, *Goodbye to All That*, Harmondsworth: Penguin, 1960 originally 1929), p.93; Edmund Blunden, *Undertones of War*, Harmondsworth: Penguin, 1982 (originally 1928), p.128f.

23 *Fragments from France*, I (introduction).

24 Turner and Miall, *Songbook*, pp.34–9. The recording described is on the Saydisc *Keep the Home Fires Burning*.

25 Pierre Saka, *La chanson Française*, Paris: Nathan, 1980, p.116 discusses 'La Madelon' ('Quand Madelon. . . .'). The song of Verdun is on p.117. Both are sung on a recording by Luc Barney, *Ceux de 14–18*, Barclay (Belgium), 1962.

26 Dieter Struss, *Das War 1914*, Munich: Heyne, 1982, p.152. Olt, *Krieg und Sprache*, II, p.30, has this strophe with some parody verses cited below. The song about Emmich is in Struss, p.152, and Olt, II, p.183, has other songs about Belgium, which contrast with those in *King Albert's Book*.

27 Harry Lauder, *Roamin' in the Gloamin'*, London: Hutchinson [1928], p.180f. He cites on p.198 an American poem in his own honour, telling how he 'sang about the laddies that so well had fought and won'.

28 Ian Whitcomb, *After the Ball*, London: Allen Lane, 1972, has an interesting chapter on 'Alleymen versus the Allemands', pp.56–71. On that song see p.58. It is referred to in a German novel of 1930, Edlef Köppen's *Heeresbericht*, Reinbek bei Hamburg: Rowohlt, 1979, p.27 (citing a newspaper of 1915). Page, *Kiss me Goodnight*, locates it in the north of England in the Second World War, p.121, as does Harvey, *Time of War*, p.67.

29 Heap and Heap, *The Singing Sixties*, p.5.

30 Michael Freedland, *Irving Berlin*, London and New York: W.H. Allen, 1974, pp. 70–8.

31 *A Minstrel in France*, London: Melrose, 1918. See p.260. He sang the song referred to later in his memoirs, as above, note 27.

32 The cards are not dated, but the style is like that depicted in Ellis, as above, note 8.

33 R.F. Nettleingham, *Tommy's Tunes*, London: Erskine Macdonald, 1917, p.23. On p.14 Nettleingham states that the tune was rarely sung except in its parody version. However, see Peter Honri, *Working the Halls*, London: Futura, 1974, p.151.

34 Saka, *Chanson*, p.114; Nettleingham, *Tommy's Tunes*, p.30.

35 Brophy and Partridge, *Songs and Slang*, p.48, with a comment on the rarity of such themes. But it was well known: it is in Giraud, *Songs that Won the War*, p.91f.

36 John A. and Alan B. Lomax, *Folk Song USA*, New York: Duell, Sloan, & Pierce, 1947, p.111.

37 Nettleingham, *Tommy's Tunes*, p.37.

38 Olt, *Krieg und Sprache*, II, p.116. See also I, p.121f.
39 *Ibid.*, II, p.70f. See also II, p.124f.
40 Vansittart, *Voices*, p.x.
41 Nettleingham, *Tommy's Tunes*, pp.42–5; Brophy and Partridge, *Songs and Slang*, p.26; Giraud, *Songs That Won the War*, p.91; C.H. Ward-Jackson, *Airman's Songbook*, London: Sylvan, 1945, p.13.
42 Vansittart, *Voices*, p.207.
43 Olt, *Krieg und Sprache*, II, p.194. The units vary.
44 Brophy and Partridge, *Songs and Slang*, p.47; see also pp.46, 62, 86 for similar themes. Giraud, *Songs That Won the War*, p.90 has 'Kaiser'.
45 Saka, *Chanson*, p.117, citing Blaise Cendrars.
46 Wolfgang Steinitz, *Deutsche Volkslieder demokratischen Charakters aus 6. Jahrhunderten*, ed. H. Strohbach, Berlin: deb, 1973, p.201f.
47 Vansittart, *Voices*, p.72.
48 Olt, *Krieg and Sprache*, II, p.56f, with other cynical songs in II, p.91.
49 Lomax and Lomax, *Folk Song*, p.111.
50 Brophy and Partridge, *Songs and Slang*, p.81. Ward-Jackson, *Airman's Songbook*, and Nettleingham, *Tommy's Tunes*, both mention the exclusion of outright obscenities.
51 Brophy and Partridge, *Songs and Slang*, p.49 (with the name as Armenteers, as sung); Giraud, *Songs That Won the War*, p.66; Lomax and Lomax, *Folk Song*, p.112.
52 Janheinz Jahn and Alfons Michael Dauer, *Blues und Work Songs*, Frankfurt/M.: Fischer, 1964, p.101f. See Samuel Charters, *The Poetry of the Blues*, New York: Oak, 1963, p.77f.
53 Nettleingham, *Tommy's Tunes*, p.21 opens with the work; Brophy and Partridge, *Songs and Slang*, p.63. Most of the other collections include the song, and other revivalist hymns were similarly adapted. This was particularly well known: see its use in the last issue of the trench newspaper *The Better Times*, in Beaver, *Wipers Times*, p.319, marking the actual end of the war. On the text, see Palmer, *All You Need Is Love*, p.199 (misquoting the hymn title), and Pat Hodgson, *Talking About War*, Hove: Wayland, 1979, p.60.
54 Heap and Heap, *Singing Sixties*, pp.10, 104, pp.222–6.
55 There is no author and no indication of date or place.
56 Nettleingham, *Tommy's Tunes*, p.24; Brophy and Partridge, *Songs and Slang*, p.84; Giraud, *Songs That Won the War*, pp.96 and 50.
57 *Tommy's Tunes*, p.56 notes the Dixie variations.
58 Steinitz, *Volkslieder*, p.219.
59 Olt, *Krieg und Sprache*, II, pp.8–16. See I, pp.137–41 on the text.
60 *Ibid.* II, p.140f. See Steinitz, *Volkslieder*, p.221f.
61 Giraud, *Songs that Won the War*, p.81.
62 Saka, *Chanson*, p.117f. (only the chorus, as sung in *Oh What a Lovely War*). See F. Vernillat, 'La chanson politique et la vie des Français II', *Vie et langage*, 262, January 1974, pp.79–93, esp. p.88.
63 Cited from Zygmunt Andrzejowski, *Skarbiec pieśni Polskiej*, Glasgow: Książnica Polska, 1945, p.155f., a text and translation in Josepha K. Contoski, *Treasured Polish Songs*, Minneapolis: Polish Club Inc., 1953,

p.88. The extra verse is in the collection by Bronislaw Rutkowski, *Spiewamy piosenki*, Krakow: Polskie wydawnictwo muzyczne, 1948, p.40, and Marta Jasińska, *Sto pieśni i piosenek Polskich*, Warsaw: COK, 1975, p.27f. The song is on the recording *Polskie pieśni żolnierskie i ludowe*, Warsaw, Muza, 1962.

64 Giraud, *Songs That Won the War*, pp.49 and 96. See Beaver, *Wipers Times*, p.64 for a version headed 'Minor Worries'.

65 Cited in Robert Lucas, *Teure Amalia, vielgeliebtes Weib!*, Frankfurt/M.: Fischer, 1984, p.53 (originally 1945), with the last verse of the 'Argonnerwald' song.

66 The song is often cited. On the point see Sir Ian Hamilton and Erich Maria Remarque, 'The End of War', *Life and Letters*, 3, 1929, pp.399–411.

67 James N. Healey, *Ballads from the Pubs of Ireland*, Cork: Mercier, 1965, 2nd edn, 1966, p.110f.

68 Olt, *Krieg und Sprache*, II, p.30; Steinitz, *Volkslieder*, p.220.

69 All cited from Steinitz, *Volkslieder*, pp.221, 222, 224, 217.

70 For example, there are some relevant songs in Vaclav Chlumecký-Enšperger, *Špevník robotníckych pieśní*, Prague, 1921, repr. Matica Slovenská, 1977.

71 Discussed and cited by Whitcomb, *After the Ball*, p.70.

CHAPTER 4: TOMORROW THE WHOLE WORLD

1 In Ernst Loewy, *Literatur unterm Hakenkreuz*, Frankfurt/M.: Fischer, 1969, p.229f. 'We never wanted war, we grumbled at our enemies when they brought war, and what we wanted was work and peace, but these were not granted to us! We experienced struggle, victory, withdrawal and victory and mortal danger. Now we want war!' The end of the poem is, in fact, somewhat ambiguous, but the message is clear. Von Scholz (1874–1969) was sympathetic to the ideas of Nazism: see Loewy, p.307.

2 Thomas Rothschild, *Von grossen und von kleinen Zeiten*, Frankfurt/M.: Fischer, 1981, p.15.

3 Helmut Lamprecht, *Deutschland, Deutschland*, Bremen: Schunemann, 1969 is, together with Loewy (note 1 above) and Wulf (note 15 below) a major modern source of this material. Lamprecht states in p.xxi that his book has a specifically documentary purpose. See also Wolfgang Gast, *Politische Lyrik*, Stuttgart: Reclam, 1973; Karlheinz Fingerhut and Norbert Hopster, *Politische Lyrik*, Frankfurt/M.: Diesterweg, 1981 and the appendix to Albrecht Schöne, *Über politische Lyrik im 20. Jahrhundert*, Göttingen: Vandenhoek & Ruprecht, 3ed edn, 1972.

4 Schöne, *Lyrik*, p.40f. and p.74 with (post-war) examples.

5 Karl Eckhardt and Adolf Lüllwitz, *Fröhlicher Anfang*, Frankfurt/M.: Diesterweg, 1940, p.49. A fortuitous but entirely typical illustration, the title means 'Happy Beginning' and the brown cover has a six-year-old giving a Nazi salute; Hitler is on the frontispiece, with a small girl. The marching song of the Hitler Youth is discussed by Günter Hartung,

Literatur und Ästhetik des deutschen Faschismus, Berlin (GDR): Akademie, 1984, p.230f., and the text can be heard on the Inter Nationes presentation *Der Nationalsozialismus*, Bonn: Inter Nationes, 4th edn, 1984, cassette, and text on p.273. The song was well known abroad: see Gangulee, *Nazi Germany*, p.41. On the reaction in the Third Reich, see the fascinating paper by Detlev Peukert in Richard Bessel, *Life in the Third Reich*, Oxford: OUP, 1987, pp.25–40 as well as his book (with examples of songs): Detlev J. K. Peukert, *Inside Nazi Germany*, trans. Richard Deveson, London: Batsford, 1987, pp.145–74.

6 Erwin Guido Kolbenheyer (1878–1962) was one of many writers in this medium: *Deutsches Bekenntnis/ Unser Leben. Dichtungen fur Sprechchöre*, Munich: Langen & Müller, 1933, was an early example, soon produced in a cheap edition. There are many descriptions of poetry used in this way, including Edgar Mowrer, *Germany Puts the Clock Back*. Harmondsworth: Penguin, rev. edn, 1938, p.200f.

7 See for example Joseph Wulf, *Theater und Film im Dritten Reich*, Gutersloh: Mohn, 1964, p.328, and his *Musik im Dritten Reich*, Gutersloh: Mohn, 1963, pp.206–310. On German film: Julian Petley, *Capital and Culture. German Cinema 1933–1945*, London: BFI, 1979; David Welch, *Propaganda and the German Cinema 1933–1945*, Oxford: Clarendon, 1983. On Italian film: Marcia Landy, *Fascism in Film. The Italian Commercial Cinema 1931–1943*, Princeton: University Press, 1986.

8 Both examples are taken from a fascinating catalogue of an exhibition of aerial propaganda, 1914–68: *The Falling Leaf*, Oxford: Museum of Modern Art, 1978. See the cover and pp.12 and 16f.

9 In English see Ronald Taylor, *Literature and Society in Germany 1918–1945*, Brighton: Harvester, 1980, pp.181–263; and J.M. Ritchie, *German Literature under National Socialism*, London: Croom Helm, 1983. In German see Hartung, *Ästhetik*; Ingrid Girscher-Wöldt, *Theorie der modernen politischen Lyrik*, Berlin: Spiess, 1971; and Renate and Reinhard Meurer, *Texte des Nationalsozialismus*, Munich: Oldenbourg, 1982. Linguistically less acessible but extremely valuable is Hubert Orłowski, *Literatura w III Rzeszy*, Poznań: Wydanictwo Poznańskie, 1979 (in Polish with a German summary and illustrations).

10 J.A.C. Brown, *Techniques of Persuasion*, Harmondsworth: Penguin, 1963, pp.20–8.

11 Orłowski, *Literatura*, pp.63–98.

12 Taken from a 1934 anthology, *Das deutsche Herz*, ed. Rudolf Mirbt, Berlin: Ullstein, l934, p.266.

13 On Mussolini, see writings as early as Margherita G. Sarfatti, *The Life of Benito Mussolini*, trans. Frederic Whyte, London: Thornton Butterworth, 1925, and later G.T. Garratt, *Mussolini's Roman Empire*, Harmondsworth: Penguin, 1938. On Pétain, see Françoise Renaudot, *Les Français et l'occupation*, Paris: Laffont, 1975, p.40 and H.R. Kedward, *Occupied France. Collaboration and Resistance*, Oxford: Blackwell, 1985, p.19. Works on Hitler are legion: see Alan Bullock, *Hitler. A Study in Tyranny*, Harmondsworth: Penguin, 1962, and more recently Ian Kershaw, *The 'Hitler Myth': Image and Reality in the Third Reich*, Oxford:

Clarendon, 1987.

14 Cited in Gangulee, *Nazi Germany*, p.117.

15 Text in Joseph Wulf, *Literatur und Dichtung im Dritten Reich*, Reinbek bei Hamburg: Rowohlt, 1966, p.350f. (the paperback edition is cited for convenience). Also in Lamprecht, *Deutschland*, p.392, and discussed in Hartung, *Ästhetik*, p.242f. Menzel died in 1945.

16 Loewy, *Hakenkreuz*, p.249. Schuhmann after the war noted that he had been very young at the time of writing this and other lyrics; see his correspondence with Albrecht Schöne included as an appendix to Schöne, *Lyrik*.

17 Filippo Fichera, *Il Duce e il Fascismo nei canti dialettali d'Italia*, Milan: Convivio Letterario, 1937, p.309. The song is described as a 'canto fervidissimo' and is by one Ambrogio Reggiori.

18 *Ibid.*, p.63.

19 *Ibid.*, p.80.

20 *Ibid.*, p.441.

21 Saka, *Chanson*, p.217.

22 W.D. Halls, *The Youth of Vichy France*, Oxford: Clarendon, 1981, p.295f. See p.14 on the Pétain cult.

23 Pétain's age *was* stressed abroad, of course: see Philip Guedalla, *The Two Marshals*, London: Hodder & Stoughton, 1943.

24 Lamprecht, *Deutschland*, p.379. On Anacker see Orłowski, *Literatura*, pp.353–60. On Hitler as a speaker, see Loewy, *Hakenkreuz*, p.243f. and Wulf, *Literatur*, p.121, for additional poems.

25 *Ewiges Deutschland* (see below, note 38), p.83. See also Lamprecht, *Deutschland*, p.381 for similar material.

26 Loewy, *Hakenkreuz*, p.262. On Weinheber, see p.313, and Ritchie, *Literature*, p.25f.

27 *Ewiges Deutschland* (see below, note 38), p.85.

28 Wulf, *Literatur*, p.417. Fosterberg's poem is on p.123, but Rudolf Hess made the same point, Gangulee, *Nazi Germany*, p.1, beginning a section of extracts on the 'Führer-Saviour'. See also Schöne, *Lyrik*, p.61, where there is an adaptation of another Christmas carol.

29 Wulf, *Literatur*, p.344.

30 *Volk im Kriege*. The cover in red, black, and white has a border motif which suggests the swastika without actually showing one. The afterword is on p.68 and there is (as in many English anthologies, too), a list of poets who fell in 1914–18. Bröger's poem is on p.66 (see Loewy, *Hakenkreuz*, p.292 on this poet, whose dates are 1886–1944); Trakl is on p.59; Reinhold Braun – who is not known – is on p.26 and Lersch (on whom see Loewy p.303) on p.3; Johst (1890–1978) is on p.10, and on the poet see Orłowski, *Literatura*, pp.337–5. For comments on Lersch and Bröger, see Lamprecht, *Deutschland*, p.616.

31 The motif is an old one (there is an example in one of the *Wunderhorn* poems set by Mahler). See also the poem by Peter Huchel in *Seventeen Modern German Poets*, ed. Siegbert Prawer, London: OUP, 1971, p.79 ('Soldatenfriedhof' [Military Cemetery]). The speaker there is haunted by the memory of the dead.

NOTES

32 Böhme, *Rufe*, pp.35, 43 and 223 are especially relevant. Other collections also bear examination: *Das kleine Gedichtbuch*, edited by Kurt Matthies, with a 1933 copyright but apparently first published in 1934, was, in terms of poetry books, a best seller, quickly running to 60,000 copies. It contains work by a number of poets later favoured by the Reich, but almost immediately after publication a revised edition appeared with a number of additional poems including Gerhard Schuhmann's sonnet 'Das neue Reich' [The New Reich], which concludes with a declaration of hate against those who are against the new Reich. The expanded edition, Munich: Langen & Müller, 1934, has Schuhmann's poem on p.11. On the poet see Loewy, p.307f.

33 Doderer, *Landserbuch*, title page.

34 Oskar Wöhrle, *Kamrad im grauen Heer. Ein Soldatenbrevier*, Munich: Beck, 1940. Wöhrle was born in 1890 and wrote poetry in the First World War; he died in 1946. Texts cited from pp.11, 25 and 73.

35 See Dieter Struss, *Das war 1943*, Munich: Heyne, 1983, p.163.

36 Achim von Winterfeld, *So oder so ist das Leben*, Leipzig: Boreas, 1943, p.112. The poet was born in 1884.

37 Ogden Nash, *I'm a Stranger Here Myself*, New York: Universal Library, 1962, p.35f. 'Fellow Creatures II. The Japanese'. The poems predate American involvement and voice the hope that the perpetual motion of German-French aggression stays in Europe.

38 *Ewiges Deutschland. Ein deutsches Hausbuch* (Weihnachtsgabe des Winterhilfswerkes des Deutschen Volkes), Brunswick: Westermann, 1939. Besides a preface by Goebbels is an opening section from *Mein Kampf* on reading with a purpose. The book is illustrated, has a calendar and a printed ex-libris with eagle, snake, and swastika. Although again a fortuitous example of the way in which Nazi verse was disseminated, it is typical. Most Nazi poets are represented, Finkh on p.256. See Loewy, *Hakenkreuz*, p.296, on this poet.

39 Albert Soergel, *Kristall der Zeit*, Leipzig and Zurich: Grethlein, 1929; Mirbt, *Das deutsche Herz* (above, note 12).

40 Fritz Stein, *Chorliederbuch für die Wehrmacht*, Leipzig: Peters, 1940, rev. edn, 1944.

41 See Ritchie, *Literature*, p.76, with a text in the same form in *Ewiges Deutschland*, p.70; Lamprecht, *Deutschland*, p.339 reverses the order of the strophes, which appear to have been written at different times (see p.620). The music was by Hans Gansser. See Hartung, *Ästhetik*, pp.199–215.

42 Inter Nationes, *Nationalsozialismus*, p.70. Hartung, *Ästhetik*, notes the use of the phrase 'Deutschland Erwache! Juda [or Rotfront] verrecke!' [Awake Germany! Perish the Jews/ The Reds] as a chant, p.211.

43 Lamprecht, *Deutschland*, p.389. Also in Gast, *Lyrik*, p.30 and in Schöne, *Lyrik*, p.60, with comments on its perversion of Christianity on p.17.

44 Text in Leonhardt, *Lieder*, p.65 with notes; Lamprecht, *Deutschland*, p.390f. with notes on p.629; Loewy, *Hakenkreuz*, pp.253f. and 286 on the poet, who was born in 1914; the work is discussed by Hartung, *Ästhetik*, pp.248–50, and by Ritchie, *Literature*, pp.89–91.

45 Gangulee, *Nazi Germany*, p.40, cites the line without the author. Of special interest are some comments by W.J. Brown, General Secretary of the Civil Service in one of the National Book Association War Pamphlets, *Where's it Going to End?*, London: Hutchinson, n.d., p.15, where the two lines are set against a hymn by Whittier.

46 Loewy, *Hakenkreuz*, p.133.

47 Lamprecht, *Deutschland*, pp.387.

48 *Ibid.*, p.354. The placard of the *Anschluss* is reproduced in the exhibition catalogue *Fragen an die deutsche Geschichte* produced by the Bundestag, 12 edn, Bonn, 1987, p.319.

49 Loewy, *Hakenkreuz*, p.204.

50 Lamprecht, *Deutschland*, p.349, has the text. See Wulf, *Literatur*, pp.344–7 for later references, including one by Baldur von Schirach which has the line 'Horst Wessel fiel, und Deutschland steht auf' ('Horst Wessel fell and Germany rises up'), which is in Mirbt, *Das deutsche Herz*, p.270f., and which is cited also by Taylor, *Literature*, p.261, who refers to the Horst Wessel novel of Hans Ewers; see also Ritchie, *Literature*, pp.79–81, with comments on Brecht's response. The song is sung on the Inter Nationes cassettes: see *Nationalsozialismus*, p.324.

51 *Ästhetik*, p.223f.

52 *Literature*, p.81.

53 *Ibid.*, p.75. It is also referred to in Wulf, *Musik*, p.244.

54 Gangulee, *Nazi Germany*, p.67.

55 'Deutschland über alles' mentions German borders as extending 'from the Meuse [in Belgium] to the Memel [in the USSR], and from the Adige [in Italy] to the Belt [Scandinavia]'.

56 Texts are in Lamprecht, *Deutschland*, pp.395 (Weinheber), 396 (Nordhausen), 397f. (Moder) and in Loewy, *Hakenkreuz*, p.219 (Miegel).

57 *Literature*, p.90f., referring to Hartung, *Ästhetik*.

58 Inter Nationes, *Nationalsozialismus*, p.181. The songs discussed in this section are nearly all on the cassettes which accompany the presentation.

59 *Ibid.*, pp.151, 155. A song 'Bomben auf Engelland' by Wilhelm Stöppler (with a tune by Norbert Schultze, composer of that for 'Lilli Marleen') was used in a wartime film; Leonhardt, *Lieder*, p.67.

60 *Münchener Feldpost*, No. 14 (December, 1942), unpag. Once more a typical production, the periodical was subtitled *Heimatblätter für die Frontsoldaten des Gaues München-Oberbayern* [Local Paper for Serving Soldiers of the Munich–Upper Bavaria Region].

61 Inter Nationes, *Nationalsozialismus*, p.185.

62 Leonhardt, *Lieder*, p.64.

63 Text and commentary in Leonhardt, *Lieder*, p.66, with notes on the composition of the melody in 1939 and the radio dissemination of the tune. *Volk im Kriege*, p.15 has the text, with the slightly different sung version in the Inter Nationes *Nationalsozialismus* book, p.163, and on cassette.

64 *Ibid.*, p.147.
65 Some interesting examples from Vichy France may be found in Pascal Ory's study of a Nazi comic published in Vichy France, *Le petit Nazi illustré:* 'Le Téméraire' *(1943–44)*, Paris: Albatros, 1979, who notes on p.48 a bloodthirsty adaptation of the Breton folk song 'Tan, Tan' [Fire, Fire].

CHAPTER 5: THERE IS NO NEED FOR ALARM

1 Written in 1941; Marshall, *Monologues*, p.144.
2 See Ian Higgins's introduction to his *Anthology of Second World War French Poetry*, London: Methuen, 1982, p.11.
3 A.P. Herbert, *Siren Song*, London: Methuen, 1940, p.v.
4 Some of the posters are reproduced in Harvey, *Time of War*. See Hodgson, *Talking About War*, p.62.
5 Briggs, *Keep Smiling Through*, p.23; Harvey, *Time of War*, p.118.
6 *Fear No More* has the subtitle 'A Book of Poems for the Present Time by Living English Poets'. See pp.viii and 88. It is dedicated to Masefield.
7 *Poets in Battledress* by Robin Benn, Dennis Birch, Robert Smith, Alan White, London: Fortune [1942], p.4. The *Modern Reading Library* was published by John Bale and Staples in London, and included an anthology of wartime material from the Oxford magazine *Kingdom Come*. On the whereabouts of war poets, see for example R.N. Currey, *Poets of the 1939–1945 War*, London: British Council/Longmans, 1960, rev. edn, 1967 p.7f; Robert Hewison, *Under Siege*, London: Quartet, 1979, pp.95–116; Angus Calder, *The People's War*, London: Granada, 1971, pp.599–604.
8 *Poems from the Desert*, London: Harrap, 1944; *Poems from Italy*, London: Harrap, 1945, with a foreword by Lieut.-Gen. Oliver Leese, and Sassoon's introduction on pp.10–12. See Currey, *Poets*, p.39f.
9 *British Way and Purpose*, Directorate of Army Education, London, 1944, p.14.
10 Marshall, *Monologues*, p.144.
11 Marshall, *Monologues*, p.144.
12 See the poem 'Southern Counties' by A.P. Herbert in justification of this in his collection *Light the Lights*, London. Methuen, 1945, p.59.
13 Gardner, *Terrible Rain*, p.45–7.
14 Dorothy L. Sayers, *Those Mysterious English*, London: Macmillan, 1941, p.9f.
15 See Calder, *The People's War* p.130.
16 Alfred Noyes, *Shadows on the Down*, London: Hutchinson [1945], p.12.
17 Herbert, *Light the Lights*, p.13. Fay Kershaw's poem appeared in the new verse supplement of the *Poetry Review*, *Poetry of Today*, 2, 1947, No.76, p.58. There are no biographical details.
18 *Return to Oasis*, p.196.
19 Cited from a schoolbook published in the 1960s (although the text makes it clear that the poem is concerned with the Second World

War): *Rodnaya Ryech'*, ed. E.E. Solov'yova, Moscow: Uchpedgiz, 1961, p.277. The work opens with a similarly military patriotic poem by Isakovskiy praising the Soviet homeland and this closes the book. A similar piece by the same poet may be found in *Den' Russkoi poezii* 1958, p.43.

20 Higgins, *Anthology*, p.61.

21 Aragon, *Le crève-coeur*, London: Horizon/La France Libre, 1942 (and later, expanded editions, with a French text published in 1946); Charles Morgan, *Ode to France*, London: Macmillan [1942]; *Poems for France*, ed. Nancy Cunard, London: La France Libre, 1944.

22 A. Boguslawski, *Mist Before the Dawn*, London: Allen & Unwin, 1942, p.26.

23 The quotation is from a piece by Mauriac entitled 'Poets of the resistance', originally broadcast, and published in a translation by Roy Campbell in the anthology *Poèsie 39–45* edited by Pierre Seghers, London: Editions Poetry, 1947, p.73. See also the earlier and comparable paper 'Poètes Français d'aujourd'hui', in the exile journal *La France Libre* 3, No. 17 (1942), pp.423–8 by Denise V. Ayme, and containing the long 'Hymne de la liberté' of Pierre Emmanuel.

24 Hewison, *Under Siege*, p.98. See Lord Vansittart, *Lessons of My Life*, London: Hutchinson, [1943], p.212f. on Vierordt and on Lissauer, and in general on the Germans. In wartime production, the work ran to well over ten thousand copies. On Vansittart in general, see Norman Rose, *Vansittart*, London: Heinemann, 1978. Vansittart is probably best remembered in this context for works like *The Black Record* of 1942. The question of collective guilt was debated throughout the war: see for opposing views Richard Baxter, *Hitler's Darkest Secret*, London: Quality, 1941, p.xii; and Victor Gollancz's *What Buchenwald Really Means*, London: Gollancz, 1945.

25 *Siren Song*, p.20. See p.1f.

26 A.P. Herbert, *Less Nonsense*, London: Methuen, 1944, p.17.

27 *Ibid.*, p.52.

28 *Light the Lights*, pp.6 and 10.

29 *Ibid.*, p.27f.

30 *Light the Lights*, p.59.

31 *Ibid.*, p.62.

32 Page, *Kiss me Goodnight*, p.108f.

33 *Targets*, London: Cape 1943, p.96f.

34 *Targets*, pp.100–120.

35 See Rubin, *Voices of a People*, pp.423–61. See my paper 'Transformations of the Holocaust', *Comparative Literature Studies*, 11 (1974), p.125.

36 The collection *Di festung* from 1945 is available in the collected Jubilee edition of Sutzkever's work, Abraham Sutzkever, *Poetishe verk*, Tel Aviv: Yuvelkomitet (Jubilee Committee), 1963. See I, p.299. For details, see Heather Valencia, 'The Poetry of Abraham Sutzkever', *Lines Review*, 102 (September 1987), pp.4–22.

37 Richter, *Deine Söhne, Europa*, p.93 (Vitalis, 'Deutsches Soldatenlied', [German Soldier's Song]).

38 Bertolt Brecht, *Gedichte* V, Frankfurt/M.: Suhrkamp, 1964, p.42. See the neat translation in Brecht, *Poems*, ed. John Willett, Ralph Manheim, with Erich Fried, London: Eyre Methuen, 1976, p.239. 'So small a toothbrush for so big a mouth'. Much of Brecht's material, often songs in plays, has been widely discussed. See, however, his curious poem on Churchill, *Gedichte* VI, Frankfurt/M.: Suhrkamp, 1964, p.96 and p.19. The sense remains unclear. See the translated *Poems*, p.592.

39 All the examples are from *Orient*, ed. Wolfgang Yourgran and Arnold Zweig, reprint edn, Albert Walter, Hildesheim: Gerstenberg, 1982. There is an excellent introduction. Poems cited are from III, 32/3 (11 November 1942), p.24; 36 (11 December 1942), p.18; 37 (18 December 1942), p.19; IV, 4/5 (29 January 1943), p.29; III, 34/5 (4 December 1942), pp.25–8.

40 See the poem 'This is Bushido', which has echoes of 'This is the happy warrior: this is he'. *Light the Lights*, p.3.

41 *Targets*, p.19f and *Shadows on the Down*, p.69. Many people mocked the nonsensical racial incongruities of the Axis. Irving Berlin had a song called 'Aryans under the Skin' and the American ambassador, Joseph Grew, commented more solemnly in his *Report from Tokyo*, London: Hammond & Hammond, 1943, p.79.

42 A P. Herbert, *ATI*, London: Ornum, 1944, p.26.

43 *ATI*, p.15, with a drawing of Hitler as a rat.

44 *Less Nonsense*, p.25.

45 *Light the Lights*, p.23.

46 *Light the Lights*, p.33.

47 *Light the Lights*, p.13.

48 *Siren Song*, p.21.

49 *Less Nonsense*, p.31, and see 'The Roarer' in *Siren Song*, p.3f. More direct still were the leaflets dropped on the audience at the London Palladium as a publicity device, which informed the reader that 'When not smuggling stocks and bonds,/ Little Goebbels chases blondes;/ Naughty naughty little Goebbels,/ adding to your Fuehrer's troebbels.' See Ian Bevan, *Top of the Bill*, London: Muller, 1952, p.121.

50 *Siren Song*, pp.27–9. The Lord Chamberlain banned a song referring to Hitler's moustache in a Cambridge revue in 1938: Robert Hewison, *Footlights*, London: Methuen, 1983, p.85; the rules had changed by 1939.

51 The comment is by G.S. F[raser] in the *Penguin Companion to Literature* I, Harmondsworth: Penguin, 1971, p.393. Other critics have been more sympathetic: see Derek Stanford, 'The Poetic Achievement of Alfred Noyes', *English* 12 (1958), pp.6–8.

52 Alfred Noyes, *Shadows on the Down*, (London: Hutchinson, [1945]), pp.109–27. It had been published in New York in 1941.

53 *Targets*, p.26f. The same collection contains the poem 'Strange Bedfellows', on the Anglo-Soviet pact, p.31f. The two pacts concluded by Stalin and Hitler's attack were commented upon by several of the popular poets. Texts like the MP D.N. Pritt's *The USSR, Our Ally,*

London: Muller, 1941, makes interesting reading. See A.P. Herbert, *A.P.H.*, London: Heinemann, 1970, p.59.

54 *Siren Song*, p.45.

55 *Less Nonsense*, p.12f., dated October 1942.

56 *Siren Song*, p.62. Herbert gave up the use of 'Wop' after Mussolini's first fall in 1943; Calder, *The People's War*, p.564.

57 *Selected Poems and Epigrams*, London: Heinemann, 1945, p.124.

58 Saggitarius, *Targets*, pp.95 and 42. See Herbert, *Less Nonsense*, p.36.

59 See Guedalla, *The Two Marshals*, p.361 and Cunard, *Poems for France*, pp.22–5. Saggitarius, *Targets*, p.87 and Herbert, *Siren Song*, p.64, both attack Pétain, and see also Pierre Seghers, *La résistance et ses poètes*, Paris: Seghers, 13. edn, 1974, p.105.

60 Cunard, *Poems for France*, p.25.

61 James Dyrenforth and Max Kester, *Adolf in Blunderland*, London: Muller, 1939, is an example.

62 By A.Z. Ngani, in *The Penguin Book of South African Verse*, ed. Jack Cope and Uys Krige, Harmondsworth: Penguin, 1968, p.286f.

63 *ATI*, p.9. Herbert commented to Churchill in a poem after the election defeat in 1945 that he had won for the people 'the right to throw you down', *Full Enjoyment*, London: Methuen, 1952, p.9.

64 Saggitarius, *Targets*, p.39 and 90; Herbert, *ATI*, p.24 (*Light the Lights*, p.60). See also *Siren Song*, p.44; *Light the Lights*, pp.27 and 58; *Less Nonsense*, p.65, *ATI*, p.17.

65 *Targets*, p.99.

66 *Mist Before the Dawn*, p.23.

67 Cecil Roberts, *A Man Arose*, London: Hodder & Stoughton, 1941.

68 Cited from the second edition, 1952, which contains a foreword not present in the 1941 edition: the text is the same.

69 *New York Times*, May 12 1944. See the collected volume of *New York Times Film Reviews* for 1939–48, p.2000f.

70 Alice Duer Miller, *The White Cliffs*, London: Methuen, 1941. The 23rd edition appeared in 1944. See Briggs, *Keep Smiling Through*, p.10f.

71 Douglas's poem is in Hamilton, *Poetry of War*, p.127.

72 Francis Brett Young, *The Island*, London: Heinemann, 1944; see pp.263–5, 426f.

73 A.P. Herbert, *Mild and Bitter*, London: Methuen, 1936, rpr. 1941, p.225f.

74 Herbert, *Less Nonsense*, p.2.

75 *Oasis*, p.145. Lord Beaverbrook's speech of July 1940 referred to pots and pans being turned into Hurricanes and Spitfires. See Briggs, *Keep Smiling Through*, p.185.

76 *England*, ed. Nicolson, p.127f.

77 *Ibid.*, p.272, under the heading 'Epilogue'. The poem originally appeared in *The Ballad of St Barbara* in 1922. See *The Collected Poems of G.K. Chesterton*, London: Methuen, 1933, p.79f.

78 *Poets in Battledress*, p.11f.

79 Reilly, *Chaos of the Night*, p.54.

80 See E.L. Woodward in *The Character of England*, ed. E. Barker, Oxford:

Clarendon, 1947, p.546f. Barker, p.566, links the Battle of Maldon with the Blitz, an historical long view found often (in poets like Lord Gorell, for instance). In 1948 the *Daily Graphic* produced two volumes of prose and verse by Arthur Bryant and Edward Shanks on *Trafalgar and Alamein* and on *Dunkirk/ The Great Miracle*, both widely distributed to libraries and schools. The first title speaks for itself; the second links Dunkirk with 'the England of Nelson and Alfred' (p.15). Edward Shanks's poem-cycle of Dunkirk (pp.25–31) compares Hitler's Stukas with the Roman invasion and with Genghis Khan. Shanks's war poetry is not unimpressive, but the historical parallels are extreme.

81 *Ibid.*, pp.34, 77, 27, 75.
82 London: Cape, 1941.
83 London: Heinemann [1940].
84 Paula von Preradovic, *Ritter, Tod und Teufel*, Innsbruck: Oesterreich-ischer Verlagsanstalt, 1946, pp.38 and 40. See Leonard Forster's, *German Poetry 1944–1948*, Cambridge: Bowes & Bowes, 2nd edn, 1950. Kuckhoff is in Richter, *Deine Söhne, Europa*, p.46f. and of course examples could be multiplied. Gustav Zürcher's *Trümmerlyrik*, Kronberg/T.: Scriptor, 1977, pp.93–100 has some moving examples.
85 See Noel Coward's *Collected Verse*, London: Methuen, 1984, p.137; and *Oasis*, p.251. Herbert's pieces are discussed in detail below.
86 Jarrell's poem is in Hamilton, *Poetry of War*, p.141, Clapham's is in Hamblett, *I Burn for England*, p.62 (first published in 1945).
87 Herbert, *ATI*, pp.8 and 12.
88 *Air Force Poetry*, London: Bodley Head, 1944. Rostrevor Hamilton's poem is in his *Selected Poems*, p.146, Scarfe's in his own *Forty Poems and Ballads*, London: Fortune, [1941], p.20; and Waller's in Hamblett, *I Burn for England*, p.356. See also the poem 'Ad Astra' by Molly Corbally, in *Return to Oasis*, p.24, and *Oasis*, p.247.
89 *Herzeloyde in Paradise*, Oxford: Blackwell, 1953, p.25.
90 Richard Spender, *The Collected Poems*, London: Sidgwick & Jackson, 1944, p.10. The edition was in its fourth reprint by 1946.
91 See Fredrick Alderson, 'John and "Johnny". John Pudney 1909–1977', *London Magazine*, 21 (1981/2), pp.79–87.
92 The text is from the reprint issued shortly before Pudney's death: *For Johnny. Poems of World War II*, London: Shepheard & Walwyn, 1976, p.17, with many other relevant pieces. It appeared originally in *Dispersal Point*, London: Bodley Head, 1942 (reprinted in 1942, 1943, and 1944), p.24 and also in *Air Force Poetry*. After the war it was included in Pudney's *Selected Poems*, most notably in the text of that name published by the British Publishers Guild as a cheap paperback Guild Book, p.37. Few anthologies of war poetry omit it: Hamilton, Gardner, Hamblett, Harvey, and Stallworthy all include it, as does Blythe, *Writing in a War* ('the most popular epitaph of its period', p.388) and the *Oasis* collection, p.256. *The Way to the Stars* (subtitled 'Johnny in the Clouds') was filmed in 1945 and released after the end of the war.
93 *Oasis*, pp.178–81. See the BBC2 Open Space notes *War Poets of '39* (22

July 1987) for an interview with Brookes.

94 Denis McHarrie's 'Luck' is in *Return to Oasis*, p.172, and is used as a motto for the later *Oasis* collection, p.xxx.

95 See above, note 90.

96 *Return to Oasis*, p.147f.

97 Page, *Kiss me Goodnight*, p.99–101.

98 *Return to Oasis*, p.201, *Oasis*, p.136.

99 See Page, *Kiss me Goodnight*, pp.52 and 93, *Return to Oasis*, p.200. Other places thus treated range from Rekjavik to Mersa Matruh.

100 *Oasis*, p.214.

101 *The Goose Girl Magazine* 2/3 (April 1947) p.38f.

102 *Kiss me Goodnight*, p.224f.

103 Gorell, *Wings of the Morning* pp.16f. and 69.

104 Richard Church, *Twentieth Century Psalter*, London: Dent, 1943. Extracts appeared in a variety of newspapers and journals, and the work was reprinted.

105 I cite the text from the *Poems from the Desert* collection, p.45f. Martin Page has a text with slightly different punctuation in *For Gawdsake Don't Take Me*, pp.56–9, as well as an introductory history of the piece, pointing out that many people tried to claim authorship (and royalties).

CHAPTER 6: MY LILLI OF THE LAMPLIGHT

1 For the full text and details, see below, note 65.

2 The texts are taken from: *The Big Red Songbook*, ed. Mal Collins, Dave Harker, and Geoff White, London: Pluto, 1981, pp.13 and 77; Pier Paolo Pasolini, *La poesia popolare Italiana*, Milan: Garzanti, 1960, p.241.

3 At Okinawa, Japanese soldiers were reputed to have shouted 'To hell with Roosevelt ... Babe Ruth ... Roy Acuff'. Acuff had sung the patriotic song 'Great Speckled Bird'. See Palmer, *All You Need is Love*, p.186; and Whitcomb, *After the Ball*, p.199.

4 Cited from Hans Leip's 'Richtigstellende Bemerkungen zu Lili, zu Marleen und zum Lied "Lili Marleen"' ('Corrective Comments on Lili, on Marleen, and on the song "Lili Marleen"') in: *Das Hans-Leip-Buch*, ed. Joachim Jessen and Detlef Lerch, Frankfurt/M.: Ullstein, 1985, p.78. Leip's comments first appeared in the *Jahrbuch der Freien Akademie der Künste in Hamburg* in 1973/4. There are detailed comments on the song in John Costello, *Love, Sex and War, 1939–1945*, London: Pan, 1986, pp.106–9 (inaccuracies with names and dates and a misreading of the text); and in Page, *Kiss Me Goodnight* p.101f. (every name incorrect). The text is cited from the *Hans-Leip-Buch*, p.76f. It is in Leonhardt, *Lieder*, p.157f, and is appended to Lale Andersen's *Leben mit einem Lied* (originally *Der Himmel hat viele Farben*), Munich: dtv, 1974, p.267. See her comments on p.172.

5 *Das Hans-Leip-Buch* p.80. See Costello, *Love*, p.108f.

6 *Das Hans-Leip-Buch*, p.79.

7 (Peter Maurice Music, 1944). See Calder, *The People's War*, p.428.

Marlene Dietrich also recorded it during the war for the American Office of Strategic Services as propaganda: see Sheridan Morley, *Marlene Dietrich*, London: Sphere, 1978, p.65.

8 *Love*, p.108. 'My love for you renews my might/ I'm warm again, my pack is light. . .' Lale Andersen sang this version in English after the war.

9 Jacques Prévert, *Paroles*, Paris: NRF, 1949, p.207f (and translated by Lawrence Ferlinghetti, *Selections from 'Paroles'*, Penguin: Harmondsworth, 1965, pp.76–9. Hamish Henderson, *Elegies for the Dead in Cyrenaica*, Edinburgh: EUSPB, n.d. [1977?], originally London: Lehmann, 1948, p.35–7.

10 Saka, *Chanson*, p.216 ('The buddies of the Potomac') has the French song. Of the two English pieces, Costello, *Love*, p.106, cites the first, but there is a full text in Ward-Jackson, *Airman's Songbook*, p.181. The others are in Page, *Kiss me Goodnight*, pp.217 and 202. See Calder, *The People's War*, p.428.

11 Hamish Henderson, *Ballads of World War II*, (Glasgow: The Lili Marleen Club, n.d. [1950?]), p.33f. (See pp.31–6 for all texts.) See Leonhardt, *Lieder*, pp.151–75 for a variety of versions and comments.

12 Both are in Page, *Kiss me Goodnight*, pp.147 and 103f.

13 Box and Cox, London, 1949.

14 Freedland, *Irving Berlin*, p.183. See also Briggs, *Keep Smiling Through*, p.200.

15 Scholes, *'God Save the King'*, p.59.

16 The song was published in 1939 at the very beginning of the war. Unofficial versions included the addition later by colonial forces of 'while Australia will be there' to the title. See Page, *Kiss me Goodnight*, p.120f.

17 Saka, *Chanson*, p.211f. As an aside on the Siegfried Line, a nice visual joke was achieved in the printing of the words on novelty underwear: Briggs, *Keep Smiling Through*, p.46. Simone Berteaut comments on the popularity of that song in France at the beginning of the war: *Piaf*, Harmondsworth: Penguin 1973, p.157.

18 The text is in Charles Castle, *Noel*, London: Allen, 1972, pp.180–2, with comments on the misunderstanding. The broadcast was to the Forces.

19 Herbert, *Less Nonsense*, p.34.

20 Freedland, *Irving Berlin*, p.187.

21 *Leadbelly*, ed. John A. Lomax and Alan Lomax, New York: Folkways, 1959, p.62.

22 Sam Liptsin, *Krig un zig*, New York: Amalgamated Branch 82, 1942, pp.79f. and 78f. The book, by a popular Yiddish writer, has the title 'War and Victory'.

23 See Heaps, *Singing Sixties*, p.5.

24 Chappell Music, 1942.

25 Reinhard Hippen, *Satire gegen Hitler*, Zurich: pendo, 1986. All texts cited are from this valuable source-book, pp.46, 104, 106, 121, 158, 162, 166. The Wienert piece is printed with the music. The cartoons in the

volume are also of some interest, and the series, when complete, will provide a great amount of material.

26 Vera Lynn, *Vocal Refrain*, London: Wyndham, 1976, pp.83 and 80. 'I'll Remember You' (not sung by Vera Lynn) was published by Campbell, Connelly.

27 Morley, *Dietrich*, p.64. The injunction to 'keep smiling through' is surely not 'mindless patriotism'?

28 The text of 'When They Sound the Last All Clear' is included in part in Harvey, *Time of War*, p.130.

29 See Heaps, *Singing Sixties*, p.4f; Whitcomb, *After the Ball*, p.198; Myra Schneider's poem 'Drawing a Banana' is in Harvey, *Time of War*, p.96.

30 Berteaut, *Piaf*, p.158. When the song was banned, Piaf complained that it could be about any lost friend.

31 The text is in *Modern Folk Ballads*, ed. Charles Causley, London: Studio Vista, 1966, p.40f. The German text was sung by Joan Baez, for example.

32 The text is in *Sir Noel Coward: His Words and Music*, ed. Lee Snider, New York: Chappell, n.d. [song copyright 1941], pp.120–124.

33 Maurice Vandair and Henri Bourtayre, 'Fleur de Paris', performed by Maurice Chevalier was a great success in late 1944: Saka, *Chanson*, p.224. 'Bella Ciao' is probably the best known of the Italian partisan songs. There is a text and music in *Liederbuch*, Bad Soden: Student fur Europa, 1974, No. 51.

34 Most of the songs in question are in *George Formby Complete*, ed. Andrew Bailey and Peter Foss, London and New York: Wise, n.d. See p.144 for 'Our Sergeant Major' and p.162 for 'Maginot Line'. The collection, by no means complete, omits both 'Bless 'em All' and 'You'd Be Far Better Off in a Home' (which is published by Cavendish Music).

35 *Airman's Songbook*, p.xi f. has comments, and the text is on pp.17–19. Godfrey wrote the piece in about 1916 but it was not published until the late 1930s 'in a completely clean pinafore'. On Godfrey, see Brendan Ryan, 'Songsmiths to George Formby: Henry Gifford and Fred E. Cliffe', *Call Boy*, 24/2 (Summer 1987), 13.

36 'Dig You Later' (Adamson and McHugh) has a 1945 copyright.

37 Especially Harvey, *Time of War*, with children's rhymes and others cited on p.109.

38 George Formby's films, for example, made him one of the best-known wartime figures in the USSR; see Jack Winstanley on the 25th anniversary of Formby's death, the *Guardian*, 8 March 1986, p.11.

39 *Dusha soldata*, ed. A. Tishchenko, Moscow: Vsyesoyuznoye izdatel'stvo sovyetskiy kompozitor, 1983. The 'Pyesnya Artilleristov' is on p.58f., by V. Gusev and T. Khrennikov, and there are numerous similar examples. See also *Ya lyublyu tyebya, zhizn'!*, ed. W. Steinitz, Berlin: Volk und Wissen, 1965, p.39f.

40 All songs from *Skarbiec pieśni Polskiej*, ed. Andrzejowski, pp.176f., 177, 178f.

41 Jasińska, *Sto pieśni*, p.32f.

42 The 'Ballad of Monte Cassino' is sung with other World War Two

NOTES

songs on the recording *Polskie pieśni* (see chapter 3, note 63).

43 There is a text in English in *The Joan Baez Songbook*, ed. Elie Siegmeister, New York: Ryerson, 1964, pp.167–9, attributing it to Arthur Kevess and Teddi Schwartz; the same text on a recording (Fontana TFL 6002) of 1960 is ascribed on the sleeve-notes by Maynard Solomon to Sholom Secunda and Aaron Zeitlin. The recent Student für Europa *Liederbuch*, No. 62, assigns both the English text and the music to Secunda.

44 Text cited from the *Liederbuch* which has the original and a German translation. Also in Lin Jaldati and Eberhard Rebling, *'s brent, briderlech, 's brent*, Berlin: Rutten and Loening, 1985, p.150f. (the collection includes other songs discussed). On Katsenelson and the other Yiddish writers see for example Sol Liptzin, *The Maturing of Yiddish Literature*, New York: David, 1970, p.269f.

45 Cited from Shmerke Kaczerginski, *Dos gezang fun Vilner geto* Paris: Farband fun di Vilner in Frankraykh, 1947, p.47, which has detailed notes on the historical background (in Yiddish). Once again the durability of the song is shown by its inclusion in the student songbook *Liedercircus*, Cologne: Bund, 2nd edn, 1985, No. 41 (with German translation and some notes).

46 Cited from Eleanor Gordon Mlotek, *Mir trogn a gezang!*, New York: Workmen's Circle, 3rd edn, 1982, p.231f. The collection contains other material by Gebirtig. This song has several variant titles. It is included, too, in Elisabeth Janda and Max M. Sprecher *Jiddische Lieder*, Frankfurt/M.: Fischer, 1970, pp.178–81.

47 Kaczerginski, *Gezang*, p.46.

48 *Ibid.*, p.50.

49 *Gezang*, p.52 (with notes). Mlotek, *Mir trogn. . .*, p.190f.; Janda and Sprecher, *Lieder*, pp.182–5.

50 Pasolini, *Poesia*, p.244.

51 Henderson, *Ballads*, pp.38 and 41–2.

52 Saka, *Chanson*, p.220. The song was performed by Germaine Sablon and later by Yves Montand, on which see Leonhardt, *Lieder*, p.193f.

53 Ellen Frye, *The Marble Threshing Floor. A Collection of Greek Folksongs*, Austin and London: U. Texas Press, 1973, p.238f.

54 There is an English version of the 'Moorsoldaten' in *The Big Red Songbook*, p.56, which illustrates the words with pictures taken rather later in (probably) Dachau, and gives no author. The other German songs are all cited from Steinitz, *Volkslieder*, pp.323–33.

55 Lucas, *Teure Amalia*, pp.164 and 175. The song is on p.175.

56 See the *New Statesman*, for 23 February 1973, p.270 and for 2 March 1973, p.306, summarized by Martin Page in *Kiss Me Goodnight*, pp.38–41. The text is on p.42. Brophy and Partridge, *Songs and Slang*, p.6, note the addition of coarse words in the First World War to the tune. The text is included in Leonhardt's *Lieder*, p.180.

57 *The Bawdy Beautiful*, ed. Alan Bold, London: Sphere, 1979, p.152.

58 *The Penguin Book of Oral Poetry*, ed. Ruth Finnegan, London: Allen Lane, 1978, p.311.

59 Herbert, *A.P.H.*, p.64f.

60 There are two texts in Bold, *Bawdy Beautiful*, p.108f., and another slightly different version (indicating again the durability of the lyrics out of context) in *More Rugby Songs*, London: Sphere, 1968, p.18. Given what actually happened to Abyssinia, the text is not very accurate as an historical document.

61 Berteaut, *Piaf*, p.194.

62 A.J.P. Taylor, *The War Lords*, Harmondsworth: Penguin, 1978, pp.29 and 31.

63 Henderson, *Ballads*, pp.27 and 39f.

64 Page, *Kiss Me Goodnight*, pp.69–99 contains a good number of relevant pieces. Besides Farouk and Farida, some of the more apocryphal characters of these songs have retained a certain notoriety, such as Dirty Gertie from Bizerte.

65 Page, *Kiss me Goodnight*, p.47.

66 Page, *Gawdsake*, p.16.

67 Charters, *Poetry of the Blues*, p.78f. cites the entire text, and notes that this was one of many.

68 Page, *Kiss me Goodnight*, p.166.

69 Page, *Kiss Me Goodnight*, p.163.

70 The *Airman's Songbook* contains most of these songs. The introduction to that text distinguishes, incidentally, between prescriptive song books and collections of genuine compositions by men in the services. The distinction between the two types is perhaps not as clear as implied, however, and the actual singing of 'Bless 'em All', 'Die Wacht am Rhein', the 'Marseillaise' and the 'Horst Wessel Lied' by groups of soldiers could all unify.

71 *Airman's Songbook*, pp.129/171f.

72 *Songs of the People*, Cambridge: University Labour Federation, n.d. [Wartime], p.1.

73 Henderson *Ballads*, p.9f. has a text which is reprinted in, for example, Finnegan, *Oral Poetry*, p.376f., and *The Rebel Ceilidh Songbook*, ed. William Kellock, Bo'ness: Rebels Literary Society, n.d. [Postwar], p.9f. Another version is in Page, *Kiss Me Goodnight*, p.193f. (see also Leonhardt, *Lieder*, p.187f., with slightly odd notes), and there is an alternative version with a different last verse (which is less effective) in *Oasis*, p.237f.

CHAPTER 7: WORLD WAR THREE BLUES

1 Arnold Silcock, *Verse and Worse*, London: Faber, 1952, p.88. Originally in the *Observer*, Christmas, 1948.

2 *Hierzulande*, Munich: dtv, 1963, p.137.

3 See Murdoch, 'Transformations of the Holocaust'.

4 Bill Malone, *Country Music USA*, Austin and London: U. Texas Press/ American Folklore Society, 1968, p.229.

5 John Hersey, *Hiroshima*, Harmondsworth: Penguin, 1946; Masuji Ibuse, *The Black Rain*, tr. John Bester, London: Secker & Warburg, 1971; Robert Jungk, *Brighter Than a Thousand Suns*, Harmondsworth: Penguin, 1960.

6 Fletcher Knebel and Charles Bailey, *No High Ground*, London: Weidenfeld & Nicolson, 1960, p.94.

7 *The Atomic Café* was directed by Kevin Rafferty, Jayne Loader and Pierce Rafferty in 1982, utilizing a great amount of archive material. See the British Film Institute *Monthly Film Bulletin*, 49 (1982), p.289 for details and a list of songs.

8 C.S. Lewis *Poems*, ed. Walter Hooper, London: Bles, 1964, p.64f., originally in the *Spectator*, 28 December 1945. Johnson's poem is in Susannah Yorke and Bill Bachle, *The Big One*, London: Methuen, 1984, pp.71–3.

9 *Japanese Poetry Now*, trans. Thomas Fitzsimmons, London: Rapp & Whiting, 1972, p.33f. Kihara was born in 1922.

10 In Michael Horovitz, *Children of Albion*, Harmondsworth: Penguin, 1969, pp.164–6.

11 In Willi Fehse, *Deutsche Lyrik der Gegenwart*, Stuttgart: Reclam, 5th edn, 1975, p.189f.

12 In Friedrich G. Kürbisch, *Anklage und Botschaft*, Hanover: Dietz, 1969, p.330. The poem is entitled 'Bitte' [Plea].

13 *The Bomb That Fell On America*, London: Blandford [1947]. The many editions of this text and its impact are discussed in Jungk, *Suns*, p.220. Citations are from pp.7–9 and 30. Unlike later protest poetry, this does not apportion blame, but asks for maturity for the children (who would protest again in the 1960s).

14 Willian Bradford Huie, *The Hiroshima Pilot*, London: World, 1966, with discussions of Wain's poem on p.9f. See also Malcolm Muggeridge, 'The Passion of St Eatherly,' in his *Tread Softly, For You Tread On My Jokes*, London: Fontana, 1968, pp.219–26, with further comments on the wide dissemination of the poem. 'A Song About Major Eatherly' is collected in Wain's *Weep Before God*, London: Macmillan, 1961, pp.40–5. It also appeared in anthologies such as Elizabeth Jennings's *An Anthology of Modern Verse*, London: Methuen, 1961, pp.270–6.

15 'The Responsibility' appeared in a widely-used school anthology, frequently reprinted after 1957: Raymond O'Malley and Denys Thompson, *Rhyme and Reason*, London: Hart-Davis, rev. edn, 1974, p.58. In Ferguson's anthology, *War and the Creative Arts* it is the sole poem on Hiroshima, p.319.

16 The first poem is in Gaelic and English in Domhnall Macamhlaigh (Donald Macaulay), *Nua-bhardachd Ghaidhlig*, Edinburgh: Southside, 1976, pp.174–8, and in English in Iain Crichton Smith's *Hamlet in Autumn*, Edinburgh: Macdonald, 1972, p.40. The second is in Macaulay's collection, p.180–2.

17 In Hilde Domin, *Nachkrieg und Unfrieden*, Neuwied and Berlin: Luchterhand, 1970, p.39. There is a discussion of the poem with reference to others (though not Wain's, and without reference to Huie)

255

by Reinhold Grimm, 'Ein Menschenalter danach: über das zweistrophige Gedicht "Hiroshima" von Marie Luise Kaschnitz', *Monatshefte*, 71 (1979), pp.5–18.

18 Again called 'Hiroshima', in Domin, *Nachkrieg*, p.107.

19 'The Monuments of Hiroshima', originally in Enright's *Bread Rather Than Blossoms*, London: Secker & Warburg, 1956, and in D.J. Enright, Dannie Abse, and Michael Longley, *Penguin Modern Poets 25*, ed. Anthony Thwaite, Harmondsworth: Penguin, 1975, p.75. See the comments by W. Walshe, *D.J. Enright*, Cambridge: CUP, 1974, p.75.

20 Vladimir Markov and Merrill Spark, *Modern Russian Poetry*, London: MacGibbon & Kee, 1966, p.732f.

21 'Geometrische Ort' [Geometrical Place], in Heinz Piontek, *Deutsche Gedichte seit 1960*, Stuttgart: Reclam, 1972, p.22f.

22 In Pierre Seghers, *Le livre d'or de la poésie Française I*, Verviers: Gerard, 1969, p.99f.

23 Bachle and Yorke, *Big One*: see centre fold-out by Gerald Scarfe.

24 Karl Mickel, *Odysseus in Ithaka*, Leipzig: Reclam, 1976, p.85f. The poem is called 'Cities Consumed'.

25 Tom Scott, *At the Shrine O the Unkent Sodger*, Preston: Akros, 1968. See pp.12f. and 20.

26 On the films, see Jay Hyams, *War Movies*, New York: Smith, 1984, pp.175–7, with reference to *Year Zero* (1962), *Dr Strangelove* (1964), *The War Game* (1965), *Wargames* and *The Day After* (1983), and such oddities as *The Bed-Sitting Room* (1969).

27 Stallworthy's *Oxford Book of War Poetry* ends, like Gardner's *Terrible Rain*, with a poem about the atomic bomb (see below). Gardner, of course, takes his title from the Edith Sitwell poem. The bombers depicted on one of the paperback editions are B29s.

28 *Oasis*, p.352 concludes with a poem by Edward Lowbury called 'August 10th 1945 – the Day After' published in December 1945. Hamblett's anthology *I Burn For England* has a poem by Cyril Hughes (p.175) which also ends with the silence: Hughes's piece is once more called simply 'Hiroshima', demonstrating again the self-sufficiency of the name from an early stage.

29 See Peter Lewis, *The Fifties*, London: Heinemann, 1978, p.100. The catalogue of nuclear development ('Bugger Off Boys') is in *The Anti-Nuclear Songbook*, Nottingham: Mushroom, 1982, p.35, and another poem referring to Hiroshima, 'Protest and Remember', adapts a hymn tune, p.12. The more general nuclear preoccupations of such collections push Hiroshima back to the beginning of nuclear history. The explosion of a power station at Chernobyl in the Soviet Union in 1986 was referred to in the media as 'the greatest nuclear disaster ever', making some ask whether Hiroshima had been forgotten.

30 *The Celebrated Sheffield Street Band Songbook*, Sheffield: Street Band, 1984, contains all of these.

31 All in Bob Dylan, *Writings and Drawings*, London: Panther, 1974, pp.72–4, 57, 66f., 256f. See Wilfred Mellers, *A Darker Shade of Pale*, London: Faber, 1984, pp.122–6. The 'Blues' and other relevant pieces,

including those sung by Bill Haley and Tom Lehrer, are cited in Nicholas Humphrey and Robert Jay Lifton, *In a Dark Time*, London: Faber, 1984.

32 Dylan, *Writings*, p.60f.

33 While songs like that by Malvina Reynolds depend upon simple questioning (and even in Dylan's 'Blowing in the Wind' the answer is not a real one), other songs go beyond this to adopt a speculative approach, almost a sung equivalent of Hagedorn's work. Dylan's talking blues and others, like, 'Talking Atom Bomb Blues' combine discursive quasi-speech and narrative with repeated chorus-like comments. The idea of singing away the dangers (it is there in Scott's *Unkent Sodger* poem in fact) is expressed in fairly naive terms by Ian Dury in a song included in Yorke and Bachle's *Big One* anthology, p.62f.

34 See above, note 1.

35 In D.J. Enright, *The Oxford Book of Death*, Oxford: OUP, 1983, p.279.

36 Lehrer's extremely well-known song is cited by Lewis, *Fifties*, p.104. Wain's is in his *A Word Carved on a Sill*, London: RKP, 1956, p.20f.

37 See *The Tom Lehrer Songbook*, London: Elek, 1954.

38 The copyright control song was recorded by, among others, the Kingston Trio.

39 In *Children of Albion*, p.173, Rolf Hochhuth dismisses God, though in a twentieth-century theological term, as 'Deus absconditus', in a poem about the atomic bomb: *Die Berliner Antigone*, Reinbek bei Hamburg: Rowohlt, 1975, p.44.

40 *Mersey Sound*, p.71f. The poem is called 'Icarus Allsorts'. See also McGough's 'At Lunchtime', p.69f., which builds another idea on the possibility of instant total destruction.

41 See the various poems in the Sheffield Street Band collection (above, note 30).

42 Collected in Eric Singer, *Bankelbuch*, Frankfurt/M.: Fischer, 1966, pp.47–9.

43 *Noch ist es still*, Vienna: Bergland, 1966, p.27. The text begins with a framed-off advertisement for a shelter as part of the poem.

44 The position in Stallworthy's *Oxford Book* is significant, p.339f., but the poem has also appeared in much-reprinted school anthologies such as Ted Hughes's *Here Today*, London: Hutchinson, 1963, p.120f., for which an accompanying cassette was also issued.

45 Nancy Sullivan, 'After the Bomb' in her *Telling It*, Boston: Godwine, 1975, p.39.

46 *Love Poems and Elegies*, London: Gollancz, 1972, p.19. See Reilly, *Chaos of the Night*, p.122 for a poem by Margaret Wainwright addressed to a woman living under various stages of war and in the peacetime of the atomic bomb.

47 In W. Weyrauch and J. Poezen, *Lyrik aus dieser Zeit 4. 1967/8*, Munich and Esslingen: Bechtle, 1967, p.115.

48 On P.F. Sloan's 'Eve of Destruction' see Arnold Shaw, *The Rock Revolution*, London: Collier-Macmillan, 1969, p.55. The text of the 1965

song is also in the Student für Europa *Liederbuch*, No. 66.

49 See P.D. Aichinger, *The American Soldier in Fiction*, Ames: Iowa State UP, 1975, p.95, with reference to Faulkner's Nobel Prize speech in 1950.

50 *Laut und Luise*, Stuttgart: Reclam, 1976, p.41. See B. Murdoch and M. Read, 'An Approach to the Poetry of Ernst Jandl', *New German Studies*, 5 (1977), pp.125–55.

Bibliography

This bibliography divides primary and secondary material, but there are areas of overlap when a lyric is cited from a secondary study or from a contemporary prose source. It is primarily of works used, and makes no claims to comprehensiveness. See for example the bibliographies by C.W. Reilly for a full range of primary First and Second World War verse in English. No general reference works, and only a few histories of the wars are listed. Anthologies are arranged by editor or compiler. Periodicals listed for themselves are treated as individual works. The (few) recordings, music sheets, and postcards used as sole sources are not included here, but are, with the films, listed in the index.

I. Primary sources

A. *Anthologies*

Amis, Kingsley and Cochrane, James, *The Great British Songbook*, London: Faber, 1986

Andrzejowski, Zygmunt, *Skarbiec pieśni Polskiej*, Glasgow: Książnica Polska, 1945

Anti-Nuclear Songbook, The, Nottingham: Mushroom, 1982

Anz, Thomas and Vogl, Joseph, *Die Dichter und der Krieg. Deutsche Lyrik 1914–1918*, Munich and Vienna: Hanser, 1982

Auden, W.H. and Garrett, John, *The Poet's Tongue*, London: Bell, 1935

Bab, Julius, *1914. Der deutsche Krieg im deutschen Gedicht*, Berlin, Morawe & Scheffelt, n.d. [1915–9], 12 numbers, mostly 48pp

Blackie, John Stuart, *War Songs of the Germans*, Edinburgh: Edmonston & Douglas, 1870

Blythe, Ronald, *Writing in a War*, Harmondsworth: Penguin, rev. edn, 1982

Böhme, Herbert, *Rufe in das Reich. Die heldische Dichtung von Langemarck bis zur Gegenwart*, Berlin: Junge Generation, 1934

Bold, Alan, *The Martial Muse. Seven Centuries of War Poetry*, Exeter: Wheaton, 1978

Bold, Alan, *The Bawdy Beautiful*, London: Sphere, 1979

Brereton, Frederick [= Frederick Thomson Smith], *An Anthology of War Poems*, London: Collins, 1930

Bridges, Robert, *The Spirit of Man*, London: Longmans Green, 1916 (and many reprints down to the Second World War)

British War Song Album, London: Sheard [1914]

Brophy, John and Partridge, Eric, *Songs and Slang of the British Soldier: 1914–1918*, London: Scholartis, 1930 [revised as: *The Long Trail*, London: Deutsch, 1965 (various editions)]

Burrell, Arthur, *A Book of Heroic and Patriotic Verse*, London: Dent [1912]

Causley, Charles, *Modern Folk Ballads*, London: Studio Vista, 1966

Chapman, Guy, *Vain Glory*, London: Cassell, 1937

Chlumecký-Enšperger, Vaclav, *Špevník robotníckych piešní*, rev. reprint of 1921 edn, Prague: Matica Slovenská, 1977

Clarke, George Herbert, *A Treasury of War Poetry. British and American Poetry of the World War, 1914–1919*, London: Hodder & Stoughton [1919]

Collins, Mal, Harker, Dave, and White, Geoff, *Big Red Songbook*, London: Pluto, 1981

Collins, V.H., *Poems of War and Battle*, Oxford: Clarendon, 1914

Collins, V.H., *Poems of Action*, Oxford: Clarendon, 1914, and many later editions

Collins, V.H., *Stories in Verse*, Oxford: Clarendon, 1917

Contoski, Josepha K., *Treasured Polish Songs*, Minneapolis: Polish Club Inc., 1953

Cope, Jack and Krige, Uys, *The Penguin Book of South African Verse*, Harmondsworth: Penguin, 1968

Cross, Tim, *The Lost Voices of World War I*, London: Bloomsbury, 1988

Cunard, Nancy, *Poems for France*, London: La France Libre, 1944

Cunningham, Valentine, *The Penguin Book of Spanish Civil War Verse*, Harmondsworth: Penguin 1980

D'Artrey, J.L.L., *Anthologie internationale. Quinze ans de poèsie Française à travers le monde*, Paris: France universelle, 1927

Den' Russkoy poezii 1958, Moscow: Sovyetskaya Rossiya, 1958

Deppe, Wolfgang G., Middleton, Christopher, and Schonherr, Herbert, *Ohne Hass und Fahne*, Hamburg: Rowohlt, 1959

Doderer, Otto, *Das Landserbuch. Heiteres und Besinnliches aus den Feldzeitungen des Weltkrieges*, Oldenburg i. O and Berlin: Stalling, 1940

Domin, Hilde, *Nachkrieg und Unfrieden*, Neuwied and Berlin: Luchterhand, 1970

D'Oyley, Elizabeth, *Modern Poetry*, London: Arnold, 1930

BIBLIOGRAPHY

Eberlein, Gotthard and Knolle, Theodor, *Volksliederbuch für die deutsche Jugend*, Jena: Diederichs, 1926
Elliot, H.B., *Lest We Forget. A War Anthology*, London: Jarrold, 1915
Enright, D.J., *The Oxford Book of Death*, Oxford: OUP, 1983
Ewiges Deutschland. Ein deutsches Hausbuch, Brunswick: Westermann, 1939

Fear No More, Cambridge: CUP and Readers Union, 1941
Fehse, Willi, *Deutsche Lyrik der Gegenwart*, Stuttgart: Reclam, 5th edn, 1975
Feldman's 23rd Song Album, London: Feldman [1918]
Ferguson, John, *War and the Creative Arts. An Anthology*, London: Macmillan/Open University, 1972
Fingerhut, Karlheinz and Hopster, Norbert, *Politische Lyrik*, Frankfurt/M.: Diesterweg, 1981
Finnegan, Ruth, *The Penguin Book of Oral Poetry*, London: Allen Lane, 1978
Fouchet, Max-Pol, *les poètes de la Revue Fontaine*, Paris: Garnier, 1978
Francis and Day's 36th Album, London: Francis and Day, 1916
Frye, Ellen, *The Marble Threshing Floor. A Collection of Greek Folksongs*, Austin and London: U. Texas Press, 1973

Gangulee, N., *The Mind and Face of Nazi Germany*, London: Murray, 1942
Gardner, Brian, *Up the Line to Death. The War Poets 1914–1918*, London: Methuen, 1964
Gardner, Brian, *The Terrible Rain. The War Poets 1939–1945*, London: Methuen, 1966; paperback, 1977
Gast, Wolfgang, *Politische Lyrik. Deutsche Zeitgedichte des 19. und 20. Jahrhunderts*, Stuttgart: Reclam, 1973
Georgian Poetry, London: The Poetry Bookshop, 1912–22 (esp. vols II, 1913–15, III, 1916–17 and IV, 1918–19)
Giddings, Robert, *The War Poets*, London: Bloomsbury, 1988
Giraud, S. Louis, *Songs That Won The War*, London: Lane/ Daily Express, 1930.
Glasier, J. Bruce, *The Minstrelsy of Peace*, Manchester and London: National Labour Press [1918]
Goodchild, George, *The Blinded Soldiers and Sailors Gift Book*, London: Jarrold [1915]

Hamblett, Charles, *I Burn For England. An Anthology of the Poetry of World War II*, London: Frewin, 1966
Hamilton, Ian, *The Poetry of War, 1939–45*, London: Ross, 1965
Harvey, Ann, *In Time of War*, London and Glasgow: Blackie, 1987
Healey, James N., *Ballads from the Pubs of Ireland*, Cork: Mercier, 1966
Heath-Stubbs, John and Wright, David, *The Faber Book of Twentieth Century Verse*, London: Faber, rev. edn, 1965
Henderson, Hamish (Seumas Mor Maceanruig), *Ballads of World War II. First Collection*, Glasgow: Lili Marleen Club [1950?]
Hibberd, Dominic and Onions, John, *Poetry of the Great War*, London: Macmillan, 1986

261

Higgins, Ian, *An Anthology of Second World War French Poetry*, London: Methuen, 1982

Hine, Daryl, *Against the War*, Poetry 120/i (September 1972)

Hippen, Reinhard, *Satire gegen Hitler*, Zurich: pendo, 1986

Hofmannsthal, Hugo von, *Oesterreichischer Almanach auf das Jahr 1916*, Leipzig: Insel, 1916

Horovitz, Michael, *Children of Albion. Poetry of the Underground in Britain*, Harmondsworth: Penguin, 1969

Hughes, Ted, *Here Today*, London: Hutchinson, 1963

Humphrey, Nicholas and Lifton, Robert Jay, *In a Dark Time*, London: Faber, 1984

Hussey, Maurice, *Poetry of the First World War*, London: Longman, 1967, corr. repr. 1971

Im Schützengraben. Eine Sammlung von Gedichten aus der Feldzeitung der 54. Inf.-Div., n.p.: Im Schützengraben, 1916

Jahn, Janheinz and Dauer, Alfons Michael, *Blues und Work Songs*, Frankfurt/M.: Fischer, 1964

Jaldati, Lin and Rebling, Eberhard, *'s brent, briderlech, 's brent. Jiddische Lieder*, Nachdichtung Karl Kahlau, Berlin: Rutten & Loening, 1985

Janda, Elsbeth and Sprecher, Max M., *Jiddische Lieder*, Frankfurt/M.: Fischer, 1970

Janssen, Albrecht and Heuler, Felix, *Als der Weltbrand lohte. Das Echo des grossen Krieges im Lied I*, Würzburg: Kabitzsch, 1915

Japanese Poetry Now, trans. Thomas Fitzsimmons, London: Rapp & Whiting, 1972

Jasińska, Marta, *Sto pieśni i piosenek Polskich*, Warsaw: COK, 1975

Jenkinson, Editha, *The Malory Verse Book*, London: Erskine Macdonald, 1919

Jennings, Elizabeth, *An Anthology of Modern Verse 1940–1960*, London: Methuen, 1961

Kaczerginski, Schmerke, *Dos gezang fun Vilner geto*, Paris: Farband fun di Vilner in Frankraykh, 1947

Kampf, Der. Neue Gedichte zum heiligen Krieg, Jena: Diederichs. 1914

Kellock, William, *The Rebel Ceilidh Songbook*, Bo'ness: Rebels Literary Society, n.d.

King Albert's Book, London: Daily Telegraph [1915]

Kürbisch, Friedrich G., *Anklage und Botschaft*, Hanover: Dietz, 1969

Lamprecht, Helmut, *Deutschland, Deutschland*, Bremen: Schunemann, 1969

Larkin, Philip, *The Oxford Book of Twentieth Century English Verse*, Oxford: OUP, 1973

Ledward, Patricia and Strang, Colin, *Poems of This War*, Cambridge: CUP, 1942; reprinted as *Retrospect 1939–1942*, London: Falcon, 1947

Leonhardt, Rudolf Walter, *Lieder aus dem Krieg*, Munich: Goldmann, 1979

Lewis, C. Day, and Lehmann, John, *The Chatto Book of Modern Poetry. 1915–1955*, London: Chatto & Windus, 1956

Leydi, Roberto, *Canti Soziali Italiani I*, Milan: Avanti, 1963

Liederbaum, Liederbuch, Liedercircus, Liederkarren, Liederkiste, Liederkorb: see Student für Europa

Lloyd, Bertram, *Poems Written During the Great War*, London: Allen & Unwin, 1918

Loewy, Ernst, *Literatur unterm Hakenkreuz. Das Dritte Reich und seine Dichtung. Eine Dokumentation*, Frankfurt/M.: Fischer, 1969

Lomax, John A. and Lomax, Alan B., *Folk Song USA*, New York: Duell, Sloan, & Pearce, 1947

Lyrik des expressionistischen Jahrzehnts, Munich: dtv, 1962

Macamhlaigh, Domhnall [Donald Macaulay], *Nua-bhardachd Ghailhig — Modern Scottish Gaelic Poems*, Edinburgh: Southside, 1976

Markov, Vladimir and Sparks, Merrill, *Modern Russian Poetry*, London: MacGibbon and Kee, 1966

Marshall, Michael, *The Book of Comic and Dramatic Monologues*, London: Elm Tree/EMI, 1981

Matthies, Kurt, *Das kleine Gedichtbuch. Lyrik von Heute*, Munich: Langen & Müller, 1934 [copyright 1933, also for expanded edition]

Mersey Sound, The: see Henri, Adrian under individual poets

Mirbt, Rudolf, *Das deutsche Herz. Ein Volksbuch deutscher Gedichte*, Berlin: Ullstein, 1934

Mlotek, Eleanor Gordon, *Mir trogn a gezang!*, New York: Workmen's Circle, 3rd edn, 1982

Modern Muse, The, London: OUP/English Association, 1934

Monro, Harold, *Twentieth Century Poetry*, London: Chatto & Windus, 1929

More Rugby Songs, London: Sphere, 1968

More Songs of the Fighting Men, see: *Soldier Poets*

Nettleingham, F.T., *Tommy's Tunes*, London: Erskine Macdonald, 1917

Nettleingham, F.T., *More Tommy's Tunes*, London: Erskine Macdonald, 1918

Newbolt, Sir Henry, *The Tide of Time in English Poetry*, London: Nelson, 1925

Nicolson, Harold, *England. An Anthology*, London: Macmillan/English Association, 1944

Oasis collections: see Selwyn, Victor

Olt, Reinhard, *Krieg und Sprache. Untersuchungen zu deutschen Soldatenliedern des ersten Weltkriegs*, Giessen: Schmitz, 1980–1

O'Malley, Raymond and Thompson, Denys, *Rhyme and Reason*, London: Hart-Davis, rev. edn, 1974

Page, Martin, *Kiss Me Goodnight, Sergeant-Major. The Songs and Ballads of World War II*, London: Panther, 1975 [originally with subtitle as title,

1973, reprinted 1982 as *The Bawdy Songs and Ballads of World War II*]

Page, Martin, *For Gawdsake Don't Take Me! The Songs, Ballads, Verses and Monologues of the Call-Up Years, 1939–1963*, London: Panther, 1977 [originally 1976]

Parsons, I.M., *Men Who March Away. Poetry of the First World War*, London: Chatto & Windus, 1965

Pasolini, Pier Paolo, *La poesia popolare Italiana* Milan: Garzanti, 1960

Piontek, Heinz, *Deutsche Gedichte seit 1960*, Stuttgart: Reclam 1972

Pocock, Guy, *Modern Poetry*, London: Dent, n.d.

Poems from the Desert, London: Harrap, 1944

Poems from Italy, London: Harrap, 1945

Poems of Today, London: English Association, 1915, 1922, 1938, 1951

Poets in Battledress, London: Fortuna [1942]

Pouzol, Henri, *La poèsie concentrationnaire*, Paris: Seghers, 1975

Prawer, Siegbert, *Seventeen Modern German Poets*, London: OUP, 1971

Pudney, John and Treece, Henry, *Air Force Poetry*, London: Bodley Head, 1944

Reilly, Catherine W., *Scars Upon My Heart. Women's Poetry and Verse of the First World War*, London: Virago, 1981

Reilly, Catherine W., *Chaos of the Night. Women's Poetry and Verse of The Second World War*, London: Virago, 1984

Reeves, James, *Georgian Poetry*, Harmondsworth: Penguin, 1962

Richter, Hans Werner, *Deine Söhne, Europa. Gedichte deutscher Kriegsgefangener*, Munich: dtv, 1985 [originally 1947]

Ridler, Anne, *A Little Book of Modern Verse*, London: Faber, 1941

Roberts, Denys Kilham, *The Century's Poetry II. Bridges to the Present Day*, Harmondsworth: Penguin, 1938

Romano, Tito and Solza, Giorgio, *Canti della Resistenza Italiana*, Milan: Avanti, n.d.

Rothschild, Thomas, *Von grossen und von kleinen Zeiten. Politische Lyrik von den Bauernkriegen bis zur Gegenwart*, Frankfurt/M.: Fischer, 1981

Royal Artillery War Commemoration Book, London: Bell, 1920

Russel, Nick, *Poets by Appointment. Britain's Laureates*, Poole: Blandford, 1981

Rutkowski, Bronislaw, *Spiewamy piosenki*, Krakow: Polskie wydawnictwo muzyczne, 1948

Saka, Pierre, *La chanson Française*, Paris: Nathan, 1980 (with cassettes)

Seghers, Pierre, *Poésie 39–45*, London: Editions Poetry, 1947

Seghers, Pierre, *Le livre d'or de la poésie Française I*, Verviers: Gerard, 1969

Selwyn, Victor, *Return to Oasis*, London: Editions Poetry, 1980

Selwyn, Victor, *Poems of the Second World War. The Oasis Selection*, London: Dent, 1985 [= *Oasis*]

Sergeant, Howard, *These Years*, Leeds: Arnold, 194?

Shaw, Martin and Coleman, Henry, *National Anthems of the World*, London: Blandford, 1960

Sheffield Street Band Song Book, The Celebrated, Sheffield: Sheffield Street Band, 1984

Siegmeister, Elie, *The Joan Baez Songbook*, New York: Ryerson, 1964

Silber, Irwin, *Songs of the Civil War*, New York: Columbia UP, 1960

Silcock, Arnold, *Verse and Worse*, London: Faber, 1952

Silkin, Jon, *Living Voices*, London: Vista, 1960

Silkin, Jon, *The Penguin Book of First World War Poetry*, Harmondsworth: Penguin, 1979; 2nd edn, 1980

Singer, Eric, *Bänkelbuch. Deutsche Chansons*, Frankfurt/M.: Fischer, 1966

Skelton, Robin, *Poetry of the Thirties*, Harmondsworth: Penguin, 1964

Skelton, Robin, *Poetry of the Forties*, Harmondsworth: Penguin, 1968

Soergel, Albert, *Kristall der Zeit. Eine Auslese aus der deutschen Lyrik der letzten fünfzig Jahre*, Leipzig and Zurich: Grethlein, 1929

Soldier Poets. Songs of the Fighting Men, London: Erskine Macdonald, 1916

Soldier Poets, Second Series. More Songs of the Fighting Men, London: Erskine Macdonald, 1917

Solov'yova, E.E. and others, *Rodnaya ryech' IV*, Moscow: Uchyebno-pedagogichyeskoe izdatel'stvo, 1961

Songs and Sonnets for England in War Time, London: Bodley Head, 1914

Songs of the Irish Republic, Cork: CFN, 1966

Songs of the People, Cambridge: University Labour Federation, n.d.

Squire, John, *Selections from Modern Poets*, London: Secker, 1921, 1924 and 1932

Stallworthy, Jon, *The Oxford Book of War Poetry*, Oxford: OUP, 1984

Stein, Fritz, *Chorliederbuch für die Wehrmacht*, Leipzig: Peters, 1940, rev. edn, 1944

Steinitz, Wolfgang, *Ya lyublyu tyebya, zhizn'! Russisches Liederbuch*, Berlin: Volk und Wissen, 1965

Steinitz, Wolfgang, *Deutsche Volkslieder demokratischen Charakters aus sechs Jahrhunderten*, abridged edn, Hermann Strobach, Berlin: deb, 1973; full edn, Berlin: Akademie, 1972

Stephen, Martin, *Never Such Innocence. A New Anthology of Great War Verse*, London: Buchan & Enright, 1988 [reviewed by Matthew Parris, *Sunday Times*, 7 August, 1988].

Stone, Christopher, *War Songs*, Oxford: Clarendon, 1908

Student für Europa, Student für Berlin, *Liederbaum*, 1984; *Liederbuch*, 8th edn, 1980; *Liedercircus*, 2nd edn, 1985; *Liederkarren*, 3rd edn, 1981; *Liederkiste*, 5th edn, 1984; *Liederkorb*, 1983. Places of publication: Bad Soden/T.: Verlag Student für Europa *or* Cologne: Bund.

Symons, Julian, *An Anthology of War Poetry*, Harmondsworth: Penguin, 1942

Tambimuttu, M.J., *Poetry in Wartime*, London: Faber, 1942

Theatre Workshop/Charles Chilton, *Oh What a Lovely War*, London: Methuen, 1965

Tishchenko, A., *Dusha soldata*, Moscow: Vsyesoyuznoye izdatel'stvo sovyetskiy kompozitor, 1983

Treves, Frederick and Goodchild, George, *Made in the Trenches*, London: Allen & Unwin, 1916

Turner, Michael R. and Miall, Antony, *The Edwardian Song Book*, London: Methuen, 1982

Twelve Poets, London: Selwyn & Blount, 1918

Vaissière, Robert de la, *Anthologie poétique du XXe siècle*, Paris: Cres, 1923
Vansittart, Peter, *Voices from the Great War*, London: Cape, 1981
Volk im Kriege. Gedichte, Jena: Diederichs, 1934

Ward-Jackson, C.H. and Lucas, Leighton, *Airman's Songbook*, London: Sylvan, 1945
Wavell, A.P., *Other Men's Flowers*, London: Cape, 1944 (many reprints; memorial edn, 1952 also with numerous reprints)
Weyrauch, W. and Poezen, J., *Lyrik aus dieser Zeit 4. 1967/8*, Munich and Esslingen: Bechtle, 1967
Windsor, M.S. and Turral, J. *Lyra Historica. Poems of British History AD 61 – 1910*, Oxford: Clarendon [1911]
Wollmann, Maurice, *Poems of Twenty Years. An Anthology 1918–1938*, London: Macmillan, 1938
Yeats, W.B., *The Oxford Book of Modern Verse*, Oxford: OUP, 1936
Yorke, Susannah and Bachle, Bill, *The Big One*, London: Methuen, 1984

Ziv, Frederic W., *The Valiant Muse. An Anthology of Poems by Poets Killed in the World War*, Freeport, NY: Books for Libraries Press, 1971 [originally 1936]

B. Individual authors

Adcock, St John, *Collected Poems*, London: Hodder & Stoughton, 1929
Aragon, Louis, *Le crève-coeur*, London: Horizon/La France Libre, 1942

Binyon, Laurence, *For the Fallen and Other Poems*, London: Hodder & Stoughton [1917]
Birrell, William Dunbar, *War and Patriotic Poems*, Dundee: Thomson, 1918
Black, John, *The Flag of the Free*, West Hartlepool: Garbutt, 1917
Boguslawski, Antoni, *Mist Before the Dawn*, trans. L.E. Gielgud, London: Allen & Unwin, 1942
Brecht, Bertolt, *Gedichte V-VI*, Frankfurt/M.: Suhrkamp, 1964
Brecht, Bertolt, *Poems*, ed. John Willett, Ralph Manheim with Erich Fried, London: Eyre Methuen, 1976
Brooke, Brian, *Poems*, London: Bodley Head, 1918
Brooke, Rupert, *1914 and Other Poems*, London: Sidgwick & Jackson, 1915; also *Collected Poems*, New York: Dodd, Mead, 1915, reprint 1980

Chesterton, G.K., *The Collected Poems*, London: Methuen, 1933
Church, Richard, *Twentieth Century Psalter*, London: Dent, 1943
Clark, Cumberland, *The British Empire at War*, Bournemouth: Henbest Publicity, 1940
Clark, Cumberland, *The War Poems of a Patriot*, Bournemouth: Henbest Publicity, 1940

BIBLIOGRAPHY

Cocker, W.D., *Poems*, Glasgow: Brown, Son and Ferguson, 1932, repr. 1960

Coldstreamer [H. Graham], *Ballads of the Boer War. Selected from the Haversack of Sergeant J. Smith*, London: Grant Richards, 1902

Coward, Noel, *Collected Verse*, London: Methuen, 1984

Coward, Noel, *His Words and Music*, ed. Lee Snider, New York: Chappell, n.d.

Dane, Clemence [Winifred Ashton], *Trafalgar Day 1940*, London: Heinemann, 1940

Dennis, C.J., *Backblock Ballads*, Sydney: Angus and Robertson, 1919

Dickson, Gordon, *Peter Rae*, London: Allen & Unwin, 1925

Duncan, Robert, *Passages 22–27 of the War*, n.p.: Oyez, 1966

Drinkwater, John, *Tides*, London: Sidgwick & Jackson, 1917

Dylan, Bob, *Writings and Drawings*, London: Panther, 1974

Dyrenforth, James and Kester, Max, *Adolf in Blunderland*, London: Muller, 3rd edn, 1939

Eisen, Herbert Jakob, *Noch ist es still*, Vienna: Bergland, 1966

Enright, D.J., *Bread Rather Than Blossoms*, London: Secker & Warburg, 1956

Enright, D.J., *Daughters of Earth*, London: Chatto & Windus, 1972

Enright, D.J., Abse, Dannie, and Longley, Michael, *Penguin Modern Poets 25*, ed. Anthony Thwaite, Harmondsworth: Penguin, 1975

Fenton-Livingstone, M.R., *The Silent Navy*, Glasgow: Livingstone, 1918

Formby, George, *George Formby Complete*, ed. Andrew Bailey and Peter Foss, London and New York: Wise, n.d.

Frankau, Gilbert, *The City of Fear*, London: Chatto & Windus, 1917

Frankau, Gilbert, *The Judgement of Valhalla*, London: Chatto & Windus, 1918

Gibson, Wilfred Wilson, *Friends*, London: Elkin Mathews, 1916

Gibson, Wilfred Wilson, *Battle*, London: Elkin Mathews, 1916

The Goose Girl. Magazine of the College of the Rhine Army, 1946–7

Gorell, Lord [Ronald Barnes Gorell], *Poems. 1904–36*, London: Murray, 1937

Gorell, Lord, *Wings of the Morning*, London: Murray, 1947

Guthrie, George, C., *In Days of Peace In Times of War*, Ardrossan: Arthur Guthrie, 1928

Hagedorn, Hermann, *The Bomb That Fell on America*, London: Blandford [1947]

Håkanson, Bjorn, 'Poems', *Micromegas*, 4/i [1969], pp.44f. (Swedish issue)

Hall, John, Douglas, Keith, and Nicholson, Norman, *Selected Poems*, London: Bale, 1943

Hamilton, G. Rostrevor, *Selected Poems and Epigrams*, London: Heinemann, 1945

267

H[arvey], J[ohn] G. R[ussell] and T[homas], C[harles], *Allies in Wilhelmsland*, Bristol: Ford, 1915

Henderson, Hamish, *Elegies for the Dead in Cyrenaica*, Edinburgh: EUSPB, [1977?] (originally London: Lehmann, 1948)

Henri, Adrian, McGough, Roger, and Pattern, Brian, *The Mersey Sound*, Harmondsworth: Penguin, 1967

Herbert, A.P., *Mild and Bitter*, London: Methuen, 1936

Herbert, A.P., *Siren Song*, London: Methuen, 1940

Herbert, A P., *Let Us be Glum*, London: Methuen, 1941

Herbert, A.P., *Bring Back the Bells*, London: Methuen, 1943

Herbert, A.P., *Less Nonsense!*, London: Methuen, 1944

Herbert, A.P., *ATI 'There Is No Need For Alarm'*, London: Ornum, 1944

Herbert, A.P., *Light the Lights*, London: Methuen, 1945

Herbert, A.P., *Full Enjoyment*, London: Methuen, 1952

Herzog, Rudolf, *Ritter, Tod und Teufel. Kriegsgedichte*, Leipzig: Quelle und Meyer, 1915

Hochhuth, Rolf, *Die Berliner Antigone*, Reinbek bei Hamburg: Rowohlt, 1975

Hodgson, William Noel, *Verse and Prose in Peace and War*, London: Murray, 3rd edn, 1917

Hopwood, Ronald A., *The Old Way*, London: Murray, 1917

Horsnell, Horace, *The Horoscope*, London: Hamish Hamilton, 1934

Jacob, Violet, *More Songs of Angus*, London: Country Life, 1918

Jandl, Ernst, *Laut und Luise*, Stuttgart: Reclam, 1976

Kain. Zeitschrift für Menschlichkeit 5 (1918/9), repr. Vaduz: Topos, 1978

Kästner, Erich, *Wer nicht hören will, muss lesen*, Frankfurt/M.: Fischer, 1971

Kennedy, R.A., *The New Benedicite, or Songs of Nations: the True Answer to the 'Hymn of Hate'*, London: Knight [1915]

Kennedy, [Geoffrey Anketell] Studdert [Woodbine Willie], *Rhymes*, London: Hodder & Stoughton, 1929 (and many reprints)

Keyes, Sidney, *Collected Poems*, ed. Michael Meyer, London: Routledge, 1945

Kipling, Rudyard, *Barrack-Room Ballads*, London: Methuen, 19th edn, 1902

Kipling, Rudyard, *Rudyard Kipling's Verse. Inclusive Edition, 1883–1926*, London: Hodder & Stoughton, 1927

Kipling, Rudyard, *Poèmes*, trans. Jules Castier, Paris: Laffont, 1949

Kipling, Rudyard, *Kipling's English History*, ed. Marghanita Laski, London: BBC, 1974

Kolbenheyer, Erwin Guido, *Deutsches Bekenntnis/ Unser Leben. Dichtungen fur Sprechchöre*, Munich: Langen and Müller,1933

Leadbelly [Huddie Ledbetter], *Leadbelly*, ed. John A. and Alan Lomax, New York: Folkways, 1959

Lee, Joseph, *Ballads of Battle*, London: Murray, 1916

Lehrer, Tom, *The Tom Lehrer Songbook*, London: Elek, 1954

Leip, Hans, see: Jessen, Joachim (*Secondary literature*)

Lersch, Heinrich, *Gedichte*, ed. Johannes Klein, Dusseldorf and Cologne: Diederichs, 1965

Leslie, Shane, *Jutland. A Fragment of Epic*, London: Benn, 1930

Lewis, C.S., *Poems*, ed. Walter Hooper, London: Bles, 1964

Liptsin, Sam, *Krig un zig*, New York: Amalgamated Branch 82 Internatsionaler Arbeiter-ordn, 1942

Mann, Hamish [A.J. Mann], *A Subaltern's Musings*, London: Long, 1918

Masefield, John, *Poems*, London: Heinemann, 1946

Mason, John, *The Valley of Dreams*, London: Erskine Macdonald, 1918

Mason, Steve, *Johnny's Song*, Toronto: Bantam, 1987

Mathew, Frank, *A Book of Songs*, London: Elkin Mathews, 1925

Mickel, Karl, *Odysseus in Ithaka*, Leipzig: Reclam, 1976

Miller, Alice Duer, *The White Cliffs*, London: Methuen, 1941

Mills, Angus, *The Gamble of War*, Forfar: Forfar Herald, [1929]

Morgan, Charles, *Ode to France*, London: Macmillan [1942]

Muir, Edwin, *One Foot in Eden*, London: Faber, 1956

Nash, Ogden, *I'm a Stranger Here Myself*, New York: Universal Library, 1962

Newbolt, Henry, *Collected Poems*, London: Nelson [1908]

Newbolt, Henry, *St George's Day and Other Poems*, London: Murray, 1918

Newgass, Edgar, *England in Peace and War*, London: privately published, 1968

Noyes, Alfred, *A Salute from the Fleet*, London: Methuen, 1915

Noyes, Alfred, *If Judgement Come*, New York: Stokes, 1941

Noyes, Alfred, *Shadows on the Down*, London: Hutchinson, [1945]

Orient, 1942/3, ed. Wolfgang Yourgran and Arnold Zweig, repr. with introduction by Hans-Albert Walter, Hildesheim: Gerstenberg, 1982

Owen, Wilfred, *War Poems and Others*, ed. Dominic Hibberd, London: Chatto & Windus, 1973

Oxenham, John [William Arthur Dunkerly], *The King's High Way*, London: Methuen, 1916

Oxenham, John, *The Vision Splendid*, London: Methuen, 1917

Oxenham, John, *Wide Horizons*, London: Methuen, 1940

Poetry of Today. Poetry Review Supplement 2, 1947 (No. 76)

Preradovic, Paula von, *Ritter, Tod und Teufel*, Innsbruck: Oesterreichische Verlagsanstalt, 1946

Prévert, Jacques, *Paroles*, Paris: NRF, 1949

Prévert, Jacques, *Selections from 'Paroles'*, trans. Lawrence Ferlinghetti, Harmondsworth: Penguin, 1965

Pudney, John, *Dispersal Point*, London: Bodley Head, 1942

Pudney, John, *Selected Poems*, London: Bodley Head, 1947 (Guild Books edition; same title also 1946)

Pudney, John, *For Johnny*, London: Shepheard & Walwyn, 1976

Richey, Margaret F. *Herzeloyde in Paradise*, Oxford: Blackwell, 1953

Rippon-Seymour, H., *Songs from the Somme*, London: Long, 1918

Roberts, Cecil, *A Man Arose*, London: Hodder & Stoughton, 1941, 2nd edn, 1952

'Rochan', *Verses of Section 2*, London and Leicester: Adams & Shardlow, 1919

Rutter, Owen, *The Song of Tiadatha*, London: Fisher Unwin, 1920 (originally Salonika, 1919)

Saggitarius [Olga Katzin, Mrs Hugh Miller], *Saggitarius Rising*, London: Cape, 1940

Saggitarius, *London Watches*, London: Cape, 1941

Saggitarius, *Targets*, London: Cape, 1943

Salmond, J.B., *The Old Stalker*, Edinburgh and London: Moray, 1936

Sassoon, Siegfried, *The War Poems*, ed. Rupert Hart-Davies, London: Faber, 1983

Scarfe, Francis, *Forty Poems and Ballads*, London: Fortune [1941]

Scott, Tom, *At The Shrine O The Unkent Sodger*, Preston: Akros, 1968

Seaman, Owen, *War-Time*, London: Constable, 2nd edn, 1916

Service, Robert W., *The Rhymes of a Red Cross Man*, London: Fisher Unwin, 1916

Simmons, James, *Judy Garland and the Cold War*, Belfast: Blackstaff, 1976

Sorley, Charles Hamilton, *Marlborough and Other Poems*, Cambridge: University Press, 4th edn, 1919

Smith, Iain Crichton, *Hamlet in Autumn*, Edinburgh: McDonald, 1972

Smith, Iain Crichton, *Love Poems and Elegies*, London: Gollancz, 1972

Spender, Richard, *The Collected Poems*, London: Sidgwick & Jackson, 1944

Squire, John, *Selected Poems*, London: Moxon, 1948

Stallworthy, Jon, *Root and Branch*, London: Chatto & Windus, 1969

Sterling, Robert W., *The Poems*, London: Oxford University Press, 1916

Steuart, Douglas S. Spens, *The World of Tomorrow and Other Anti-War Poems*, Glasgow, Maclellan, 1948

Streets, J.W. *The Undying Splendour*, London: Erskine Macdonald, 1917

Sullivan, Nancy, *Telling It*, Boston: Godwine, 1975

Sutzkever, Abraham, *Poetishe verk*, Tel Aviv: Yuvelkomitet, 1963

Tennant, Edward Wyndham: Pamela Glenconner, *Edward Wyndham Tennant*, London: Bodley Head, 1919

Wain, John, *A Word Carved on a Sill*, London: Routledge & Kegan Paul, 1956

Wain, John, *Weep Before God*, London: Macmillan, 1961

Watt, Frederick B., *Who Dare to Live*, London: Macmillan, 1943

von Winterfeld, Achim, *So oder so ist das Leben. Heitere Verse*, Leipzig: Boreas, 1943

Wöhrle, Oskar, *Kamrad im grauen Heer. Ein Soldatenbrevier*, Munich: Beck, 1940

Wyatt, Horace, *Malice in Kulturland*, London: The Car Illustrated, 1914

Young, Francis Brett, *The Island*, London: Heinemann, 1944

Zuckermann, Hugo, *Gedichte*, ed. Otto Abeles, Vienna: Lowit, 1915 (and many later editions)

II Prose sources and secondary literature

Adcock, A. St John, *For Remembrance. Soldier Poets Who Have Fallen in the War*, London: Hodder & Stoughton, 1918

Aichinger, Peter, *The American Soldier in Fiction 1880–1963*, Ames: Iowa State UP, 1975

Alderson, Frederick, 'John and "Johnny". John Pudney, 1909–1977', *The London Magazine*, 21/ 9–10 (December/January 1981/2), pp.79–87

Aldington, Richard, *Death of a Hero*, London: Chatto & Windus, 1929

Andersen, Lale, *Leben mit einem Lied*, Munich: dtv, 1972 (originally 1972 as *Der Himmel hat viele Farben*)

Appignanesi, Lisa, *Cabaret*, London: Methuen, 1984

Arnold, H.L., *Text und Kritik 9/9a: Politische Lyrik*, Munich: Text und Kritik, 3rd edn, 1984

Ayme, Denise V., 'Poètes Français d'aujourd'hui', *La France libre*, 3 (17) (16 April, 1942), pp.423–8

Bairnsfather, Bruce, *Fragments from France*, London: The Bystander, 1916–19 and reprints.

Bairnsfather, Bruce, *The Best of Fragments from France*, ed. Tonie and Valmai Hunt, Cheltenham: Phin, 1978

Bairnsfather, Bruce, *Bullets and Billets*, London: Grant Richards, n.d.

Balfour, Michael, *The Kaiser and His Times* Harmondsworth: Penguin, 1975

Barker, Ernest, *The Character of England*, Oxford: Clarendon, 1947

Barker, Francis, *1936: The Sociology of Literature II*, [Colchester]: University of Essex, 1979

Barnett, Anthony, *Iron Britannica*, London and New York: Allison & Busby, 1982

Baxter, Richard, *Hitler's Darkest Secret*, London: Quality, 1941

BBC Music Library, *Song Catalogue*, London: BBC, 1966

BBC-2, *War Poets of '39* (booklet of broadcast on 22 July 1987)

Becker, Jean-Jacques, *The Great War and the French People*, Leamington Spa: Berg, 1985

Bergonzi, Bernard, *Heroes' Twilight. A Study of the Literature of the Great War*, London: Macmillan, 2nd edn, 1980

Berteaut, Simone, *Piaf*, trans. Ghislaine Boulanger, Harmondsworth: Penguin, 1973

Bessel, Richard, *Life in the Third Reich*, Oxford: University Press, 1987

Bevan, Ian, *Top of the Bill. The Story of the London Palladium*, London: Muller, 1952

Biba, Otto, *Gott erhalte! Joseph Haydns Kaiserhymne*, Vienna and Munich: Doblinger, 1982

Bishop, James, *Social History of the First World War*, London: Robertson, 1982

Blunden, Edmund, *Undertones of War*, Harmondsworth: Penguin, 1982 (originally 1928)

Blunden, Edmund, *War Poets 1914–1918*, London: Longmans Green, rev. edn, 1969

Boll, Heinrich, *Hierzulande*, Munich: dtv, 1963

Bradley, A.C., *The Uses of Poetry*, London: English Association, 1912

Bramsted, Ernest K., *Goebbels and National Socialist Propaganda 1925–1945*, Michigan: Cresset, 1965

Brandreth, Giles, *I Scream for Ice Cream. Pearls from the Pantomime*, London: Eyre Methuen, 1974

Bridgwater, Patrick, 'German Poetry and the First World War', *European Studies Review*, 1 (1971), pp.147–186

Bridgwater, Patrick, *The German Poets of the First World War*, London: Croom Helm, 1985

Briggs, Susan, *Keep Smiling Through*, London: Weidenfeld & Nicolson, 1975

British Way and Purpose, collected leaflets from the Directorate of Army Education, 1944

Brown, J.A.C., *Techniques of Persuasion from Propaganda to Brainwashing*, Harmondsworth: Penguin, 1963

Brown, W.J., *Where's it Going to End?*, London: Hutchinson, n.d.

Bryant, Arthur and Shanks, Edward, *The Summer of Dunkirk* and *The Great Miracle*, London: Daily Graphic, 1948 [orig. 1943]

Bryant, Arthur and Shanks, Edward, *Trafalgar and Alamein*, London: Daily Graphic, 1948

Bullock, Alan, *Hitler. A Study in Tyranny*, Harmondsworth: Penguin, 1962

Bullough, Geoffrey, 'The War-Poetry of Two Wars', in: *Cairo Studies in English*, ed. Magdi Wahba, Cairo: University of Cairo Department of English, 1959, pp.43–58

Bundestag, *Fragen an die deutsche Geschichte*, exhibition catalogue, 12th edn, Bonn: Bundestag, 1987

Burgess, Muriel and Keen, Tommy, *Gracie Fields*, London: Allen, 1980

Cadogan, Mary and Craig, Patricia, *Women and Children First*, London: Gollancz, 1978

Caine, Hall, *The Drama of 365 Days*, London: Heinemann, 1915

Calder, Angus, *The People's War*, London: Granada, 1971, repr. 1982

Castle, Charles, *Noel*, London: Allen, 1972

Charters, Samuel, *The Poetry of the Blues*, New York: Oak, 1963

Charters, Samuel, *The Legacy of the Blues*, London: Calder & Boyars, 1975

Churchill, Winston S., *The World Crisis 1911–1918*, abr. and rev. edn, London: Thornton & Butterworth, 1931

Churchill, Winston S., *The Second World War*, Harmondsworth: Penguin, 1960 (originally 1948–54)

Cohen, J.M. *Poetry of this Age, 1908–1965*, London: Hutchinson, 1960, rev. edn, 1966

Cointet-Labrousse, Michele, *Vichy et le Fascisme*, Brussels: Editions Complexe, 1987

Corbett-Smith, A., *The Marne – and After*, London: Cassell, 1917

Costello, John, *Love, Sex and War*, London: Pan, 1986

Craig, David and Egan, Michael, *Extreme Situations. Literature and Crisis from the Great War to the Atom Bomb*, London: Macmillan, 1979

Crewe, Marquess of [Robert Offley Ashburton], *War and English Poetry*, Oxford: English Association, 1917

Cross, Robin, *VE Day. Victory in Europe 1945*, London: Sidgwick & Jackson/Imperial War Museum, 1985

Currey, R.N., *Poets of the 1939–1945 War*, London: British Council/ Longmans, rev. edn, 1967

Daiches, David, *Poetry and the Modern World. A Study of Poetry in England between 1900 and 1939*, Chicago: University of Chicago Press, 1940

Davidson, Mildred, *The Poetry is in the Pity*, London: Chatto & Windus, 1972

Dawson, Coningsby, *The Glory of the Trenches*, London: Bodley Head, 1918

Deutsch, Babette, *Poetry in Our Time*, New York: Columbia University Press, 1956

Dixon, W. Macneile, *An Apology for the Arts*, London: Arnold, 1944

Dunhill, Thomas F., *Sir Edward Elgar*, London and Glasgow: Blackie, 1938

Eckhardt, Karl and Lüllwitz, Adolf, *Fröhlicher Anfang. Ein erstes Lesebuch*, Frankfurt/M.: Diesterweg, 1940, 4th. edn, 1941

Ellis, John, *Eye-Deep in Hell*, London: Croom Helm, 1976

Engelmann, Bernt, *In Hitler's Germany*, trans. Krishna Winston, London: Methuen, 1987

Ewart, Gavin, 'Both Sides of the Trenches', *The Observer*, 12 August 1979, p.37

Falling Leaf, The Aerial Dropped Propaganda 1914–1968, Oxford: Museum of Modern Art, 1978 [Exhibition catalogue]

Ferguson, John, *The Arts in Britain in World War I*, London: Stainer & Bell, 1980

Fichera, Filippo, *Il Duce e il Fascismo nei canti dialettali d'Italia*, Milan: Convivio Letterario, 1937

Focke, Harald, and Reimer, Uwe, *Alltag unterm Hakenkreuz*, Reinbek bei Hamburg: Rowohlt, 1979

Ford, Hugh D., *A Poet's War. British Poets and the Spanish Civil War*, Philadelphia: University of Pennsylvania Press, 1965

Forster, L.W, *German Poetry 1944–1948*, Cambridge: Bowes & Bowes, 2nd edn, 1950

France Libre, La, London: Hamish Hamilton, 1940–47

Freedland, Michael, *Irving Berlin*, London and New York: W.H. Allen, 1974

Fussell, Paul, *The Great War and Modern Memory*, London: Oxford University Press, 1975

Ganzl, Kurt, *The British Musical Theatre*, London: Macmillan, 1986

Garratt G.T., *Mussolini's Roman Empire*, Harmondsworth: Penguin, 1938

Gaucheron, Jacques, *La poèsie, la résistance, du Front Populaire à la liberation*, Paris: Français Réunis, 1979

Gerard, James W., *My Four Years in Germany*, London: Hodder & Stoughton, 1917

Gibbons, S.R. and Morican, P. *World War One*, London: Longmans, 1965

Girscher-Wöldt, Ingrid, *Theorie der modernen politischen Lyrik*, Berlin: Spiess, 1971

Gollancz, Victor, *What Buchenwald Really Means*, London: Gollancz, 1945 [pamphlet, 24 April 1945]

Gorbell, Cyril F., *Reading in War-Time*, London: English Association, 1945

Gorell, Lord, *One Man . . . Many Parts*, London: Odhams, 1956

Grainger, J.H., *Patriotisms. Britain 1900–39*, London: Routledge & Kegan Paul, 1986

Graves, Robert, *Goodbye to All That*, Harmondsworth: Penguin, 1960 (originally 1929)

Graves, Robert and Hodges, Alan, *The Long Weekend. A Social History of Great Britain 1918–1939*, London: Hutchinson, 1940, repr. 1985

Green, Roger Lancelyn, *Kipling. The Critical Heritage*, London: Routledge & Kegan Paul, 1971

Gregory, Kenneth, *The Second Cuckoo*, London: Unwin, 1983

Grew, Joseph C., *Report from Tokyo*, London: Hammond & Hammond, 1943

Griffiths, Richard, *Marshal Pétain*, London: Constable, 1970

Grimm, Reinhold, 'Ein Menschenalter danach: über das zweistrophige Gedicht "Hiroshima" von Marie Luise Kaschnitz', *Monatshefte*, 71 (1979)

Grunberger, Richard, *A Social History of the Third Reich*, Harmondsworth: Penguin, 1974

Guedalla, Philip, *The Two Marshals*, London: Hodder & Stoughton, 1943

Gurney, Ivor, *War Letters*, ed. R.K.R. Thornton, London: Hogarth, 1984

Halls, W.D., *The Youth of Vichy France*, Oxford: Clarendon, 1981

Hamburger, Michael, 'No Hatred and No Flag', *Encounter*, 85 (15/4, October 1960), pp.53–8

Hamburger, Michael, *The Truth of Poetry*, Harmondsworth: Penguin, 1972

Hamilton, Sir Ian and Remarque, Erich Maria: 'The End of War', *Life and Letters*, 3 (1929), pp.399–411

Hamilton, Ian, *The Modern Poet*, London: Macdonald, 1968

Hamilton, Ian, *A Poetry Chronicle*, London: Faber, 1973

Hamm, Charles, *Yesterdays. Popular Song in America*, New York and London: Norton, 1979

Hart, [Basil Henry] Liddell, *A History of the World War, 1914–1918*, London: Faber, 2nd edn, 1938 (and later editions)

Hartung, Günther, *Literatur und Ästhetik des deutschen Fascismus*, Berlin (GDR): Akademie, 1984

Haste, Cate, *Keep the Home Fires Burning. Propaganda and the First World War*, London: Allen Lane, 1977

Heaps, Willard A. and Heaps, Porter W., *The Singing Sixties*, Norman: University of Oklahoma Press, 1960

Herbert, Alan, *APH His Life and Times*, London: Heinemann, 1970

Hersey, John, *Hiroshima*, Harmondsworth: Penguin, 1946

Hester, Gustav, *Als Mariner im Krieg*, ed. Joachim Ringelnatz, Berlin: Rowohlt, 1929

Hewison, Robert, *Under Siege. Literary Life in London 1939–1945*, London: Quartet, 1979

Hewison, Robert, *Footlights*, London: Methuen, 1983

Hibberd, Dominic, *Poetry of the First World War. A Casebook*, London: Macmillan, 1981

Hieble, Jacob, 'Lily Marlene. A Study of a Modern Song', *Modern Language Journal*, 31 (1947), pp.30–4

Hinderer, Walter, *Geschichte der politischen Lyrik in Deutschland*, Stuttgart: Reclam, 1978

HMSO, *The Battle of Britain. 8th August – 31st October, 1940*, London: HMSO, 1941

Hodgson, Pat, *Talking About War*, Hove: Wayland, 1979

Holmes, Richard, *Firing Line*, Harmondsworth: Penguin, 1987

Honri, Peter, *Working the Halls*, London: Futura, 1974

Huie, William Bradford, *The Hiroshima Pilot*, London: Heinemann, 1964 and World, 1966

Hyams, Jay, *War Movies*, New York: Smith, 1984

Ibuse, Masuji, *The Black Rain*, trans. John Bester, London: Secker & Warburg, 1971

Inter Nationes, *Der Nationalsozialismus. Eine Dokumentation über die zwölf dunkle Jahre deutscher Geschichte*, Bonn: Inter Nationes, 4th edn, 1984 [book and cassettes]

Jarrell, Randall, *Poetry and the Age* London: Faber, 1955

Jenkins, Alan, *The Thirties*, London: Heinemann, 1976

Jessen, Joachim and Lerch, Detlef, *Das Hans-Leip-Buch*, Frankfurt/M.: Ullstein, 1985

Jowett, Garth S. and O'Donnell, Victoria, *Propaganda and Persuasion*, Newbury Park, Beverly Hills: Sage, 1986

Jungk, Robert, *Brighter Than a Thousand Suns*, trans. James Cleugh, Harmondsworth: Penguin, 1960 [*Heller als tausend Sonnen*, 1956]

Jungrichter, Cornelia, *Ideologie und Tradition. Studien zur nationalsozialistischen Sonettdichtung*, Bonn: Bouvier, 1979

Kedward, H.R., *Occupied France: Collaboration and Resistance 1940–1944*, Oxford: Blackwell, 1985

Kernahan, Coulson, *Nothing Quite Like Kipling Had Happened Before*, intro. Leslie F. Church, London: Epworth, 1944

Kershaw, Ian, *The 'Hitler Myth': Image and Reality in the Third Reich*, Oxford: Clarendon, 1987

King and Country. Selections from British War Speeches 1939–1940, London: Chatto & Windus, 1940

Kinne, Michael, *Nationalsozialismus und deutsche Sprache*, Frankfurt/M.: Diesterweg [1981]

Kipling, Rudyard, *France at War*, London: Macmillan, 1915

Klein, H.M. 'Tambimuttu's *Poetry in Wartime'*, *Forum for Modern Language Studies*, 21 (1985), pp.1–18

Knebel, Fletcher and Bailey, Charles, *No High Ground*, London: Weidenfeld & Nicolson, 1960

Kocka, Jurgen, *Facing Total War. German Society 1914–1918*, trans. Barbara Weinberger, Leamington Spa: Berg, 1984

Köppen, Edlef, *Heeresbericht*, ed. Michael Gollbach, Reinbek bei Hamburg: Rowohlt, 1979 (originally 1930: trans. as *Higher Command*, London: Faber, 1931)

Kriegs-Almanach 1915, Leipzig: Insel, 1915

Lagerfeuer, Am, Paderborn, 1914–16

Lancaster, Osbert, *Signs of the Times*, London: Murray, 1961

Landy, Marcia, *Fascism in Film. The Italian Commercial Cinema, 1931–1943*, Princeton: UP, 1986

Langer, Lawrence L., *The Holocaust and the Literary Imagination*, New Haven: Yale UP, 1975

Langer, Lawrence L., *Versions of Survival. The Holocaust and the Human Spirit*, Albany: SUNY Press, 1982

Lauder, Sir Harry, *A Minstrel in France*, London: Melrose, 1918

Lauder, Sir Harry, *Roamin' in the Gloamin'*, London: Hutchinson [1928]

Lehmann, John, *Rupert Brooke. His Life and Legend*, London: Quartet, 1980

Leip, Hans: see Jessen, Joachim

Levine, Eugen, *Stimmen der Völker zum Krieg*, Berlin: Malik, 1925

Lewis, Peter, *The Fifties*, London: Heinemann, 1978

Liddle, Peter, *Testimony of War*, Wilton: Russell, 1979

Liddle, Peter, *Voices of War. Front Line and Home Front*, London: Leo Cooper, 1988

Liptzin, Sol, *The Maturing of Yiddish Literature*, New York: David, 1970

Lucas, Robert [Ehrenzweig], *Teure Amalia, vielgeliebtes Weib!*, Frankfurt/M.: Fischer, 1984 (originally 1945)

Lynn, Vera, *Vocal Refrain*, London: Wyndham, 1976

MacGill, Patrick, *The Diggers*, London: Herbert Jenkins, 1919

MacKenzie, John M., *Propaganda and Empire*, Manchester: University Press, 1984

MacKenzie, John M., *Imperialism and Popular Culture*, Manchester: UP, 1986

Malone, Bill, *Country Music USA*, Austin and London: University of Texas Press/American Folklore Society, 1968

Mander, John, *Our German Cousins*, London: Murray, 1974

Mellers, Wilfred, *A Darker Shade of Pale. A Backdrop to Bob Dylan*, London: Faber, 1984

Meurer, Renate and Meurer, Reinhard, *Texte des Nationalsozialismus*, Munich: Oldenbourg, 1982

Monk, James R. and Lawson, Cedric, *Words that Won the War. The Story of the Committee on Public Information 1917–1919*, Princeton: University Press, 1939

Montague, C.E. with drawings by Muirhead Bone, *The Front Line*, London: Hodder & Stoughton, 1917

Moonraker, The (Magazine of the Wiltshire Regiment), Salonika, 1917

Morley, Sheridan, *Marlene Dietrich*, London: Sphere, 1978

Mottram, R.H., *The Spanish Farm Trilogy*, Harmondsworth: Penguin, 1979 (originally 1927)

Mottram, R.H., *Ten Years Ago*, London: Chatto & Windus, 1928

Mowrer, Edgar, *Germany Puts the Clock Back*, Harmondsworth: Penguin, rev. edn, 1938

Muggeridge, Malcolm, *Tread Softly, For You Tread On My Jokes*, London: Fontana, 1968

Mühsam, Erich, *Kain*, 5 (1918/9) No. 1

Murdoch, Brian, 'Transformations of the Holocaust', *Comparative Literature Studies*, 11 (1974), pp.123–50

Murdoch, Brian and Read, Malcolm, 'An Approach to the Poetry of Ernst Jandl', *New German Studies* 5, (1977) pp.125–55

National Yiddish Book Centre, *Mel and Shifra Gold Yiddish Music Project/Catalog of Yiddish and Hebrew Sheet Music*, New York: NYBC, January 1987

New York Times, Film Reviews, Collected Vol. 1939–48

Nolte, Ernst, *Der Faschismus in seiner Epoche*, Munich: Piper, 7, ed. 1986

Noyes, Alfred, *The Edge of the Abyss*, London: Murray, 1944

Orłowski, Hubert, *Literatura w III Rzeszy*, Poznan: Wydawnictwo Poznanskie, 1979 [with German summary]

Ory, Pascal, *Le petit Nazi illustré: 'Le Téméraire' (1943–1944)*, Paris: Albatros, 1979

Os'makov, Nikolai Vasilyevich, *Russkaya proletarskaya poeziya 1890–1917*, Moscow: Akademiya Nauka SSSR, 1968.

Oxenham, John, *High Altars. The Battle-Fields of France and Flanders as I Saw Them*, London: Methuen, 1918

Palmer, Tony, *All You Need is Love. The Story of Popular Music*, London: Futura, 1977

Panichas, George, *Promise of Greatness. The War of 1914–1918*, London: Cassell, 1968

Petley, Julian, *Capital and Culture. German Cinema, 1933–1945*, London: British Film Institute, 1979

Peukert, Detlev J.K., *Inside Nazi Germany*, trans. Richard Deveson, London: Batsford, 1987

Pli[e]vier, Theodor, *Des Kaisers Kulis*, Munich: dtv, 1984 (originally 1929; trans. W. F. Clarke, *The Kaiser's Coolies*, London: Faber, 1932)

Press, John, *Poets of World War I*, Windsor: Profile, 1983

Pritt, D., *The USSR Our Ally*, London: Muller, 1941

Punch's History of the Great War, Mr, London: Cassell, 1919

BIBLIOGRAPHY

Reilly, Catherine W., *English Poetry of the First World War. A Bibliography*, London: Prior, 1978

Reilly, Catherine W., *English Poetry of the Second World War. A Biobibliography*, London: Mansell, 1986

Remarque, Erich Maria, *Im Westen nichts Neues*, ed. Brian Murdoch, London: Methuen, 1984 (originally 1929, trans. A. W. Wheen, *All Quiet on the Western Front*, London: Putnam, 1929 and many later editions)

Remarque, Erich Maria, *Der Weg zurück*, Berlin: Ullstein, 1931 (trans. A. W. Wheen, *The Road Back*, London: Putnam, 1936)

Renaudot, Francoise, *Le Français et l'occupation*, Paris: Laffont, 1975

'Resource Guide to Yiddish Music, A', *The Book Peddler: Newsletter of the National Yiddish Book Center*, Winter 1988, Nos 9/10, pp.58f.

Richards, I.A., *Science and Poetry*, London: Kegan Paul, 1926

Ritchie, J.M., *German Literature Under National Socialism*, London: Croom Helm, 1983

Robbins, Keith, *The First World War*, Oxford: University Press, 1984

Rogers, Timothy, *Georgian Poetry 1911-1922. The Critical Heritage*, London: Routledge & Kegan Paul, 1977

Roosevelt, Franklin D., *Addresses and Messages*, London: HMSO, 1943

Rose, Norman, *Vansittart. Study of a Diplomat*, London: Heinemann, 1978

Rosenfeld, Alvin H., *A Double Dying. Reflections on Holocaust Literature*, Bloomington and London: Indiana UP, 1980

Ross, Robert H., *The Georgian Revolt*, London: Faber, 1967

Rothe, Wolfgang, *Die deutsche Literatur in der Weimarer Republik*, Stuttgart: Reclam, 1974

Rubin, Ruth, *Voices of a People*, New York: Yoseloff, 1963

Rutherford, Andrew, *The Literature of War*, London: Macmillan, 1978

Ryan, Brendan, 'Songsmith to George Formby', *Call Boy*, 24/ii (Summer, 1987), p.13

Sarfatti, Margherita G., *The Life of Benito Mussolini*, trans. Frederic Whyte, London: Thornton & Butterworth, 1925

Sayers, Dorothy L., *Those Mysterious English*, London: Macmillan, 1941

Scannell, Vernon, *Not Without Glory. Poets of the Second World War*, London: Woburn, 1976

Schaub, Gerhard, 'Totentanz 1916. Hugo Balls literarische Opposition gegen den Krieg', *Trierer Beiträge*, 15 (October 1985), pp.29-52

Schnell, Rolf, *Kunst und Kultur im deutschen Faschismus*, Stuttgart: Metzler, 1978

Scholes, Percy, *'God Save the King.' Its History and its Romance*, London: OUP, 1942

Schöne, Albrecht, *Über politische Lyrik im 20. Jahrhundert*, Göttingen: Vandenhoek und Ruprecht, 3rd edn, 1972

Schwarz, Wilhelm J., *War and the Mind of Germany, I*, Berne and Frankfurt/M.: Lang, 1975

Seghers, Pierre, *La résistance et ses poètes*, Paris: Seghers, 13. edn, 1974

Shanks, Edward, *Rudyard Kipling. A Study in Literature and Political Ideas*, New York: Doubleday, 1940

Shaw, Arnold, *The Rock Revolution*, London: Collier-Macmillan, 1969

Shires, Linda M., *British Poetry of the Second World War*, London: Macmillan, 1985

Silkin, Jon, *Out of Battle. The Poetry of the Great War*, London: Oxford University Press, 1972

Sillars, Stuart, *Art and Survival in First World War Britain*, London: Macmillan, 1987

Smith, Denis Mack, *Mussolini's Roman Empire*, London: Longman, 1976

Smith, Denis Mack, *Mussolini*, London: Weidenfeld & Nicolson, 1981

Sola Pinto, Vivian de, *Crisis in English Poetry, 1880–1940*, London: Hutchinson, 1951

Spear, Hilda D., *Remembering, We Forget. A Background Study of the Poetry of the First World War*, London: David-Poynter, 1979

Spurgeon, C.F. *Poetry in the Light of War*, Oxford: English Association, 1917

Stand 21, No. 2 (1980), 'The First World War'.

Stanford, Derek, 'The poetic achievement of Alfred Noyes', *English* 12 (1958), pp.6–8

Strothmann, Dietrich, *Nationalsozialistische Literaturpolitik*, Bonn: Bouvier, 1968

Struss, Dieter, *Das war 1914*, Munich: Heyne, 1982

Struss, Dieter, *Das war 1943*, Munich: Heyne, 1983

Taganov, Leonid, *Dolgoye ekho voyni. Literaturno-kriticheskiye stat'yi*, Yarolslavl: Verkhnye-volorskoye knizhnoye izdatel'stvo, 1983

Tannenbaum, Edward R., *The Fascist Experience. Italian Society and Culture 1922–1945*, New York and London: Basic, 1972

Taylor, A.J.P., *Rumours of War*, London: Hamish Hamilton, 1952

Taylor, A.J.P., *The Origins of the Second World War*, Harmondsworth: Penguin, 1964

Taylor, A.J.P., *The First World War. An Illustrated History*, Harmondsworth: Penguin, 1966

Taylor, A.J.P., *The War Lords*, Harmondsworth: Penguin, 1978

Taylor, Richard, *Film Propaganda. Soviet Russia and Nazi Germany*, London: Croom Helm, 1979

Taylor, Ronald, *Literature and Society in Germany, 1918–1945*, Brighton/Sussex: Harvester, 1980

Thompson, Denys, *The Uses of Poetry*, Cambridge: University Press, 1978

Thorpe, Michael, *Siegfried Sassoon*, London: Oxford University Press, 1966

Thünecke, Jorg, *Leid der Worte. Panorama des literarischen Nationalsozialismus*, Bonn: Bouvier, 1987

Valencia, Heather, 'The Poetry of Abraham Sutzkever', *Lines Review*, 102, September 1987, pp.4–22

Vansittart, Lord [Robert Gilbert] *Black Record. Germans Past and Present*, London: Hamish Hamilton, 1941

Vansittart, Lord, *Lessons of My Life*, London: Hutchinson [1943]

Vernillat, France, 'La chanson politique et la vie des Français, II', *Vie et langage*, 262 (January 1974), pp.79–93

Viereck, George Sylvester, *Spreading Germs of Hate*, London: Duckworth, 1931

Vondung, Klaus, *Volkisch-nationale und nationalsozialistische Literaturtheorie*, Munich: List, 1973

Walshe, William, *D.J. Enright. Poet of Humanism*, Cambridge: University Press, 1974

Warstat, Willi, *Das Erlebnis unserer jungen Kriegsfreiwilligen*, Gotha: Perthes, 1916

Wavell, Earl [A.P. Wavell], *Soldiers and Soldiering*, London: Cape, 1953

Welch, David, *Propaganda and the German Cinema, 1933–1945*, Oxford; Clarendon, 1983

Welland, D.S.R., *Wilfred Owen*, London: Chatto & Windus, 1960

Whitcomb, Ian, *After the Ball*, London: Allen Lane, 1972

Wilder, Alec, *American Popular Song (1900–50)*, New York: Oxford University Press, 1972

Williams, John, *The Home Fronts. Britain, France and Germany 1914–1918*, London: Constable, 1972

Williamson, Henry, *The Patriot's Progress*, London: Bles, 1930

Wilson, Edmund, *The Wound and the Bow*, London: Methuen, rev. edn, 1961

Wilson, Edmund, *Patriotic Gore. Studies in the Literature of the American Civil War*, London: Deutsch, 1962

Wilson, Jean Moorcroft, *C.H. Sorley*, London: Cecil Woolf, 1985

Winstanley, Jack, 'With a Little Ukelele in His Hand', *The Guardian*, 8 March 1986, p.11

Winter, J.M., *The Great War and the British People*, London: Macmillan, 1985

Wipers Times, The, ed. Patrick Beaver, London: Peter Davies, 1973 (originally 1916–18)

Witkop, Philipp, *Kriegsbriefe gefallener Studenten*, Munich: Müller, 5th edn, 1928 (trans. as *German Students' War Diaries*, London: Methuen, 1929)

Wohl, Robert, *The Generation of 1914*, London: Weidenfeld & Nicolson, 1980

Wulf, Joseph, *Literatur und Dichtung im Dritten Reich*, Gutersloh: Mohn, 1963 and Reinbek bei Hamburg: Rowohlt, 1966

Wulf, Joseph, *Musik im Dritten Reich*, Gutersloh: Mohn, 1963 and Reinbek bei Hamburg: Rowohlt, 1966

Wulf, Joseph, *Theater und Film im Dritten Reich*, Gutersloh: Mohn, 1964 and Reinbek bei Hamburg: Rowohlt, 1966

Wyk Smith, M. van, *Drummer Hodge. The Poetry of the Anglo-Boer War (1899–1902)*, Oxford: Clarendon, 1978

Zürcher, Gustav, *'Trummerlyrik'. Politische Lyrik 1945–1950*, Kronberg/T.: Scriptor, 1977

INDEX OF NAMES

This index includes personal names and the titles of films, recordings, collections and anonymous works, but not the titles of collections or individual poems by named authors.

Political and military figures are listed only when they have made a literary contribution, and critics only when mentioned in the body of the text. Individual songs mentioned without their composers are included.